W9-BQK-481

THREE RENAISSANCE PASTORALS

PASTORALS

Tasso ❖ Guarini ❖ Daniel

MEDIEVAL & RENAISSANCE
TEXTS & STUDIES

VOLUME 102

THREE RENAISSANCE PASTORALS

Tasso ✣ Guarini ✣ Daniel

Edited and Annotated by

Elizabeth Story Donno

Medieval & Renaissance texts & studies
Binghamton, New York
1993

Library of Congress Cataloging-in-Publication Data

Three Renaissance pastorals : Tasso—Guarini—Daniel / edited and annotated by
    Elizabeth Story Donno.
        p. cm. — (Medieval & Renaissance texts & studies ; v. 102)
    Includes bibliographical references.
    Contents: Aminta / Torquato Tasso—Pastor Fido / Battista Guarini—Queenes
Arcadia / Samuel Daniel.
    ISBN 0-86698-118-7
    1. Daniel, Samuel, 1562–1619. Queenes Arcadia. 2. Drama—15th and 16th
centuries—History and criticism.   3. Pastoral drama—History and criticism.
4. Tasso, Torquato, 1544–1595. Aminta. 5. Guarini, Battista, 1538–1612. Pastor
Fido. 6. Daniel, Samuel, 1562–1619. Queenes Arcadia. I. Donno, Elizabeth
Story, 1921–   . II. Tasso, Torquato, 1544–1595. Aminta. English. 1992. III.
Guarini, Battista, 1538–1612. Pastor Fido. English. 1992. IV. Daniel, Samuel,
1562–1619. Queenes Arcadia. 1992. V. Series.
PN1801.T48 1992
852'.4080321734—dc20   92- 16043
                                                                                      CIP

Table of Contents

TORQVATO TASSOS
AMINTA
Englisht
By Bold

To this is added ARIADNE's Com-
plaint in imitation of ANGVILLARA;
Written by the Tranſlater of TASSO's
AMINTA.

*Meglio è il poco terreno ben coltuiare, che'l molto laſciar per
mal gouerno miſeramente imboſchire.   Sannaż°.*

LONDON,
Printed by AVG: MATHEWES for WILLIAM LEE,
and are to bee ſold at the Signe of the *Turkes*
Head in *Fleetſtreet.* 1628.

Title page from Torquato Tasso's *Aminta* (1628). Reproduced by permission
of *The Huntington Library, San Marino, California.*

Preface

Given the appeal of the various Italian genres in the English Renaissance and given the appeal of the pastoral *mode* which was introduced into a variety of non-dramatic forms—the lyric, the romance, and the epic—it seems surprising that there was no English pastoral drama *per se* until the seventeenth century. When Samuel Daniel avers in the dedication of the *Queene's Arcadia* (1606) that he is the first to essay the form, he is, it appears, altogether correct. It is true that pastoral elements appear in the earlier plays of Lyly and Peele, but as these were designed for a courtly audience, they tended to present mythological figures (like those in Peele's *Arraignment of Paris*, c. 1580) rather than characters in an Arcadian landscape. Similarly, though this time intended for a popular audience, Shakespeare's *As You Like It* (which Daniel himself may have seen in 1599 or 1600) presents its characters in brief sojourn from the courtly world.

When undertaking to write this "first" pastoral drama, Daniel accordingly, and not surprisingly, availed himself of the two most popular Italian exemplars, the *Aminta* and the *Pastor Fido*. They were closely linked: Guarini following—with enlarged steps—Tasso's thematic and lyrical example but adding a social and even, in some eyes, a philosophical dimension; more importantly, Guarini stressed the tragicomic element, only slenderly represented in *his* prototype, and so introduced a new "mixed" form. Recognizing this progression, Daniel, in turn, took a further step by adding a more pronounced satirical element to his "pastoral Trage-comedie," as he carefully labels it. The three works included here, taken together, are thus both linked and incremental.

The Italian texts in their English dress have been little known to students of the drama, while Daniel's contribution has been available since the seventeenth century only in the limited edition of the *Works* edited by A. B. Grosart; and he was unaware of Daniel's revisions for the second edition.

Introduction

John Wolfe and Italian Pastoral

In 1591 John Wolfe, a printer-publisher only lately elevated to professional respectability in the Stationers' Company, issued the Italian texts of Battista Guarini's *Pastor Fido* and Torquato Tasso's *Aminta* in one duodecimo volume. Since this was only a year after the first of these works was published in Venice, the event was indicative of its international appeal and its sponsor's, as well as its publisher's, acumen in responding to it. But before the appearance of this volume, Wolfe had already exhibited considerable business acumen in recognizing the appeal of other Italian authors, particularly those of some notoriety like Aretino and Machiavelli, both of whom he had printed in the 1580s under fictitious imprints. The two parts of Aretino's *Ragionamenti*, for example, appeared in 1584 with the printer's name given as "Il Barbagrigia" (The Graybeard) in the preface and the place of publication as "Bengodi" (Pleasaunce) in the colophon. The two authors were on the *Index Librorum Prohibitorum* (1559, rev. 1564) and so, of course, could not be published in Italy, which left a ready market for their works in England; the reason for the use of fictitious imprints in these cases, it is said, was the poor reputation that English printers had for handling foreign languages. Thus in 1584 and 1585 when the London printer John Charlewood issued the texts of Giordano Bruno, he gave the places of publication as Venezia and Parigi.[1]

---

[1] The sketch of Wolfe's professional activities here and elsewhere derives from the following informative articles: Denis B. Woodfield, *Surreptitious Printing in England, 1550–1640*, Bibliographical Society of America (1973); K. T. Butler, "Giacomo Castelvetro," *Italian Studies* 5 (1950): 1–42; Harry R. Hoppe, "John Wolfe, Printer and Publisher, 1579–1601," *The Library*, 4th ser., 14 (1933–34): 241–48; Eleanor Rosenberg, "Giacopo Castelvetro: Italian Publisher in Elizabethan London and His Patrons," *Huntington Quarterly* 6 (1942–43): 119–48; Sheila E. Dimsay, "Giacopo Castelvetro," *Modern Language Review* 23 (1928): 424–31; Harry Sellers, "Italian Books Printed in England Before 1640," *The Library*, 4th ser., 5 (1924–25): 105–28; and A.

Wolfe displayed entrepreneurial shrewdness again during this same period when he, along with other underprivileged printers, took on stationers holding lucrative patents, among them the queen's printer, Christopher Barker, who held the sole right to print the Bible and the *Book of Common Prayer*. He and the others did so by the simple expedient of printing and marketing their own copies of these privileged works. Despite being called before the Privy Council, despite a raid of his premises which revealed he had five presses while other established printers, except Barker, had only three or four or fewer, and despite more than one imprisonment, Wolfe, along with his cohorts, won the day by being given the right to print certain patented texts. He then did a right-about-face, becoming a reputable member of the Stationers' Company and in 1587 its beadle; in that capacity he hunted down his former cronies for *their* infringements.

Wolfe's expertise in printing Italian texts had been acquired during a sojourn in Italy, apparently in Florence since two short religious poems were printed there in 1576 "ad instanzia di Giovanni Vuolfo Inglese"; he had interrupted his apprenticeship to the printer John Day in order to gain this experience, serving only seven of the usual ten years. On his return, probably in 1579 since the tentative date assigned to his first book is 1580, he brought with him a font of italic type which he used in printing first the *Pastor Fido* and then the *Aminta*, the order indicating their respective popularity.

These two works were published "a spese di [at the expense of] Giacopo Castelvetri," a refugee apparently well acquainted with a number of courtiers and literati, the latter including the queen, to whom he had dedicated an edition of the first two cantos in Latin of Tasso's *Gerusalemme Liberata* which Wolfe published in 1584. For the dedicatee of the two pastorals he chose Charles Blount, later Lord Mountjoy. The dedication is signed "Servitore affetionatissimo, Giacopo Castelvetri," language which suggests that he was on familiar terms with Blount, perhaps having tutored him in Italian as he later tutored King James and Queen Anne. Blount was twenty-eight at the time. Accord-

---

Gerber, "All of the Five Fictitious Italian Editions of Writings of Machiavelli and Three of Those of Pietro Aretino Printed by John Wolfe of London (1584–89)," *Modern Language Notes* 22 (1907): 129–35. Castelvetro's name is sometimes spelled with a final -*i*; his first name variously given as Giacomo or Giacopo, abbreviated Giac°.

To these references must now be added the only book-length study of Wolfe, Clifford Chalmers Huffman's *Elizabethan Impressions: John Wolfe and His Press* (AMS, 1988) and the article by Joseph Lowenstein, "For a History of Literary Property: John Wolfe's Reformation," *English Literary Renaissance* 18.3 (1988): 389–412.

ing to the inveterate traveller Fynes Moryson, he had left Oxford
when he was young and not well grounded in learning so that he then
spent his vacant hours in London reading French and Italian histories
and, above all, works of divinity.[2] The matter of selecting a receptive
patron was not one to be slighted, and a number of writers, including
Daniel, were later to seek Blount's encouragement and aid. Early on
Wolfe himself had shown due astuteness when he described himself in
his first published book (1580?) as "Servitore dell' Illustrissimo Cava-
liere Felippo Sidnei."[3]

Between 1584 and 1592 Castelvetro edited eight volumes of Italian
texts, all published by Wolfe, including the two pastorals issued together in one volume (Butler, 9); in the latter case Castelvetro's os-
tensible reason for subventing their publication was his inability to
supply friends and clients with copies of the *Pastor Fido*, the longer
and more popular of the two. In view of Wolfe's current propriety in
the Stationers' Company, it is perhaps surprising that the volume was
not entered in the Register, a procedure that in theory was obligatory
but in practice was frequently ignored.[4] The popularity of Italian letters doubtless guaranteed its financial success: during the period between 1550 when William Thomas published the first Italian grammar
and 1640 when Giovanni Torriano published the first English-Italian
dictionary, there were translations of over 400 separate titles representing some 225 authors.[5] It is perhaps somewhat surprising, then,
that the *Pastor Fido* did not join this list until almost the end of the
queen's reign, in 1602 according to the date on the title page, and
that the *Aminta* had to wait until the end of the second decade of
James's reign, 1628. Courtiers to whom these *raffiné* texts appealed
could of course cope with the originals.

Though the second to be translated, the *Aminta* soon became a
paradigm of pastoral drama and was translated early on into French,
Spanish, German, and English. Its mixed mode combining tragic and

---

[2] Moryson, *An Itinerary*, 4 vols. (Glasgow: J. MacLehose, 1907–8), 2:265.

[3] This was *Una essortatione al timor di Dio* (*STC* 92), attributed to Jacobus Acon-
tius (Giacomo Aconcio), a protestant refugee living in London. It was printed for
Wolfe by John Charlewood, who was also a vigorous opponent of the privileged
publishers. Woodfield, *Surreptitious Printing* (16 n. 14), however, doubts that the
book was published in London; to account for the dedication he suggests that Wolfe
may have met Sidney in Frankfurt during the Book Fair in 1573 since Sidney was
there at that time and Wolfe later was to become a regular vendor.

[4] According to W. W. Greg, only about one-third of the copies actually printed
were entered (*Some Aspects and Problems of London Publishing Between 1550 and 1650*
[Clarendon Press, 1956], 68).

[5] J. R. Hale, *England and the Italian Renaissance* (Faber and Faber, 1954), 18.

comic elements is dressed in luxuriant verse though the action of the drama is simplicity itself. Its thematic focus is on the different aspects of love, ranging from natural innocence and open sensuality to worldly-wise maturity, with the opening chorus hymning an age before the dreaded notion of Chastity—*Onor*—contravened all that was natural and free. The drama was first performed by the famed travelling troupe the Gelosi, directed by the poet himself in the sylvan setting of the Belvedere del Po outside of Ferrara; the text, however, was not to be published until 1581 (by Aldo Manuzio), at a time when Tasso was incarcerated as a madman in the hospital of Santa Anna.[6]

The *Aminta*

seals
Which nature, injur'd by late law, sets free
Donne

The English translator of the *Aminta* was Henry Reynolds, identified not on the title page but by an entry in the Stationers' Register under the date 7 November 1627.[7] His name is perhaps best known to students of the period from Michael Drayton's having addressed a critical epistle to him as his dearly loved friend (pub. 1627); but precise biographical information has long been scant since there were others having the same name.[8] A critical essay entitled *Mythomystes*, in prose in contrast to Drayton's verse epistle, was entered in the Stationers' Register in 1632;[9] it too was published with no date or author given but with the dedication carrying the initials H. R. Since the time of John

---

[6] The first Aldine edition included the choruses to Acts i and v; the second (also 1581) included that to Act ii, while those to Acts iii and iv were not included until the Aldine 1590 edition; the only early edition to include the Epilogue by Venus, which with the Prologue by Cupid frames the drama, was published in 1581 by Vittorio Baldini. See C. P. Brand, *Torquato Tasso* (Cambridge Univ. Press, 1965), 311, citing B. T. Sozzi's textual studies.

[7] E. Arber, *A Transcript of the Registers of the Company of Stationers of London, 1554–1640*, 5 vols. (1875–94), 4:188.

[8] Now, however, see Mary Hobbes, "Drayton's Most Dearely-Loved Friend Henery Reynolds Esq.," *Review of English Studies*, n.s., 24, no. 96 (1973): 414–28. Her investigations indicate that Reynolds was a minor court employee in 1606 and then acted as secretary to the lord chamberlain, the earl of Suffolk, from 1608 to 1611. See also Jean R. Brink, "Bathusa Reginald Makin: Most Learned Matron," *Huntington Library Quarterly* 54.4 (1991): 313–26.

[9] Arber, 4:282. *Mythomystes* is available in a facsimile edition, published by the Scolar Press (1972), and in *Critical Essays of the Seventeenth Century*, edited by J. E. Spingarn, vol. 1 (1908).

Payne Collier its author has been identified as Drayton's friend. From the allusions in it as well as from comments by contemporaries, one may conclude that Reynolds was a member of a literary circle which included not only Drayton but also George Chapman and Ben Jonson, with whom he shared similar metrical concerns (see note 13 below).

In the *Mythomystes* Reynolds presents a survey of the "nature and value of true poesy," and, like Drayton, he, too, offers evaluations of contemporary authors. In terms recalling Drayton's estimate of Daniel in his *Civil Wars* as "too much *Historian* in verse," he considers it "though otherwise a commendable worke, yet somewhat more than a true Chronicle history in rime," adding, however, that "in other lesse laboured things" he wrote more happily and "always clearly and smoothly" (B4–C1). He also refers to Chapman as his "old good friend" and the best of our Greek translators, identifying him not by name but by the allusions to Musaeus, Homer, and Hesiod, each of whom he had translated (H2). This friendship is evidenced, in turn, by Chapman's warm dedication to him in a copy of his *Crowne of All Homers Works* (c. 1626):

> In love and honor of ye Righte Virtuous / And worthie
> Gent: Mr Henry Reynolds / And to crowne all his deservings /
> wth eternall Memorie / Geo: Chapman joines this Crowne &
> Conclusion / of All the Homericall Meritts wth his / Accomplisht
> Improvements.[10]

Lastly, in his capacity as secretary to the lord chamberlain for three years, Reynolds was involved in entertainments given at court, including the one at Shrovetide in 1608/1609 when Jonson's most splendid example, the *Masque of Queens*, was performed.[11] Given the small literary world of London, one expects in any case that writers and translators were known to each other.

When listing those who should be commended "in these our moderne times," Reynolds mentions a number, including Guarini but singling out three especially—Tasso, Ariosto, and Marino. The first of these he terms "the grave and learned Tasso," specifying his *Sette Giorni*—a divine work— and his *Gerusalemme Liberata*, commending it "so farre as an excellent pile of meerely [that is, only] Moral Philosophy may deserve" (B4); this, no doubt, reflects the theoretical position he is adumbrating, which is con-

---

[10] From a copy now in the Houghton Library, Harvard, cited by Hobbes (419), and in Allardyce Nicoll's *Chapman's Homer*, Routledge & Kegan Paul, 2d ed. (1967), 1:503.

[11] Hobbes, 415.

cerned with the cabalistic and arcane mysteries of "true poesy." As a consequence (or perhaps out of modesty), he makes no mention of the *Aminta*, which only four years before he presumably had "Englisht."[12]

The translation is an altogether satisfactory one, with Reynolds rendering the hendecasyllables of the dialogue into iambic pentameter and adopting the shorter rhymed lines of the lyrical passages (*settenari*). To accommodate the English to the more flexible Italian line, he relies on elision, but his printer's application of it, like that of many others, was erratic; during this period printers frequently omitted the apostrophe or, equally frequently, they included it, variously placed, along with the vowel to be elided (to 'imbrace; thou' Aminta).[13]

In addition to demonstrating metrical skill in the handling of the text, Reynolds adroitly renders the near-proverbial aspect of the dialogue; this perhaps reflects the period's delight in "wise saws" and "modern instances." Though not to be found in a dictionary of proverbs, his examples have the proper ring:

> Too late repentance is a double woe ...
> Somewhat more worth than rime to bear away ...
> Who hopes to find that never means to seek ...
> but he
> That thinks too much does little commonly ...

Finally one may note the idiomatic phrasing, which gives a naturalistic turn to the preciosity of the plot:

> Fine spirits no doubt and sure a goodly life ...
> Let her a good yeere weepe, and sigh, and rayle ...
> I ... tooke me to my heeles ...

From a historical perspective, one may well wonder what it was in Tasso's drama that proved so quickly appealing to so many non-Italian readers. The readiest explanation, it seems to me, is his having introduced into the brief pat plot with its blending of tragicomic elements

---

[12] A further example of how easily Renaissance writers could shift from a theoretical stance to poetic practice is shown by Reynolds's many pastoral lyrics, nine of which are attributed to him in Henry Lawes's *Ayres and Dialogues* (1653-58). Hobbes prints additional instances from manuscripts in the British Library (420–28).

[13] The "learneder sort," Jonson observes in his *English Grammar* (2.1), use the apostrophe to indicate elision, though he notes that it is often omitted through the "negligence" of the printer, a situation he experienced with the quarto version of *Sejanus* (1605). For Daniel's text, printed the following year by Simon Waterson, elision is carefully observed. See *Ben Jonson*, edited by C. H. Herford and P. and E. Simpson (Oxford: Clarendon Press), 8:528.

a number of literary motifs that were to surface many times over, not only in other pastoral dramas but also in other genres. Like the pastoral ambiance itself, many of these derive from classical sources.

At the outset of Act I, the worldly-wise Daphne, herself a redeemed-Diana-figure, tries to persuade the reluctant shepherdess to respond to love by invoking the Platonic thesis that children offer a form of immortality (a thesis that of course becomes the thematic basis of Shakespeare's first seventeen sonnets). Next she adapts the *beatus ille* motif of Horace (Epode 2) and argues that only the life of a lover can provide contentment. Then, invoking the argument from nature, she demonstrates that all *natural* things are impelled to love—birds, savage beasts, even trees. To this the reluctant Silvia responds,

> When I heare trees sighe (as belike they do)
> I'le be content to bee a lover too.

The last argument of her *suasoria*, which occupies all of scene 1, projects a harsh view of old age, which, even though it comes to all, is worse for cruel and ungrateful women: their fate, as earlier projected by Ariosto in the *Orlando Furioso*, will be to endure an eternal hell, lamenting their situation in vain (34.11ff.).

The famed chorus that concludes the first act by extolling an age when the golden laws of nature were sovereign is countered by the scene immediately following. Here the Satyr, representing primitive sexuality, delivers a monologue setting forth his intent to ravish the shepherdess who so resolutely spurns his prayers and his gifts. Included in it are motifs that were to become familiar: the catalogue of female beauties, common to sonnets and erotic narrative; the Polyphemus-motif, with the Satyr, like the gross Cyclops, vaunting his manly prowess, which corresponds to the invitational element on the part of either the male or female in many epyllia; and, finally, satiric reference to the current use of gold since now gold alone prevails. This, too, becomes a stock motif in different dramatic kinds and in satires.

Other motifs run through the remaining acts—the emphasis on feminine wiles which are declared to be natural in women as well as nurtured in them (by other women); the courtly love emphasis on pity as the precursor of love, like the lightning before the thunderclap; and, lastly, the characterizing of the distraught lover's leap from the precipice as a "fortunate and happy fall," since it is this action that prompts the reluctant shepherdess to respond. Such christianizing touches are more evident in the English than in Italian, as, for example, in the chorus to Act IV where "Love" is termed "Great Prince of happy peace," while the Italian simply has "*Signor*."

In addition to these literary motifs, one may note the romance element: the sensational instance of the attempted ravishment of the shepherdess, which is foiled by the timely rescue by her lover. Serving to moderate this happy resolution, however, is the expression of the last chorus: the singers question here whether the happiness of a lover is indeed more pleasing because of the pain he has endured; if this is so, they would leave such happiness to others and settle instead for a "little lesse adooe."

A NOTE ON THE TEXT OF THE *AMINTA*

The text of the translation was printed by Augustine Mathewes (active in the period from 1619 to 1653) for the bookseller William Lee, two of whose shops were located in Fleet Street during the period 1627 to 1665. That the translator himself read proof is suggested by the nine press variants introduced into one or another of the four copies I have collated. There is, in addition, a note to the reader ("in favour of Tasso, the great author of this small Poeme") giving a list of faults that had escaped in the printing. This appears on the bottom half of sig. A3^v, which concludes the Prologue, a clear sign of the economics of production. A few errors did escape notice, and these are silently corrected here.

Following the chorus of Act V is the statement (note the elision) "Th' end of Tasso's *Aminta*"; then comes "Venuses Search for Cupid," a kind of Epilogue paralleling the Prologue though so far as early printings this text appeared only in the 1581 edition by Vittorio Baldini (see n. 6). It does not appear in Wolfe's 1591 edition and so Reynolds made use of an Italian one. The text-page K^4 is completed by an eight-line madrigal, clearly to fill it out; after this comes Reynolds's translation of "Ariadnes Complaint in Imitation of Anguillara" (L1–M3), omitted from this edition. The full collation of the volume is 4°: A–M$^{4-1}$, last leaf presumed blank; 48 leaves unnumbered. Some signatures are cropped in Huntington copies 69597 and K–D 182, the latter with text inlaid.

This Edition: As indicated earlier, Reynolds was concerned about metrical niceties, particularly elisions; like others of the period he, too, used a variable stress either for the sake of rhyme or of meter. This is perhaps most conspicuous in his handling of proper names (e.g., O Sil'via, Silvia, thou dost not feele). He has also carefully marked with apostrophes final *-eds* that are not sounded.

The original text is in italic with roman for the Prologue, the dramatis personae, the deities, and personifications (like that "vaine and idle name" Honour). This printing practice has been reversed in this edition: the text in roman, deities and personifications in italic. (The other two texts treated in this edition—the Guarini and the Daniel—accord with modern practice.) Other accidentals (e.g., *Scen:*, *Scena*, and tildes) have been regularized in conformity with modern practice, with printing errors silently corrected.

Like that of many writers of the period, Reynolds's punctuation is heavy, particularly to indicate caesuras; this has been lightened where it would prove distracting. An exclamation here replaces the question mark which was frequently substituted for it in the period; the printing convention of the use of *i/j*, *u/v* according to position has been rendered in accord with modern typographic practice; and abbreviations have been expanded. One nicety of the manuscript which the seventeenth-century printer adopted irregularly was the running together of two elided words (on't, th'hast); this is also rendered according to modern practice, that is, with a space introduced between the words, though, admittedly, in terms of the metrics the seventeenth-century printed text would have been clearer to readers. The text presented here is intended as a reading, not a critical edition.

Il Pastor Fido

For wit in us is over-rul'd by fate
Marlowe

Clearly taking his point of departure from Tasso's *Aminta*, Battista Guarini undertook (c. 1580) "to overgo" his model, spending nearly a decade in the process. He did this by expanding the pastoral theme with a subplot focusing on the hunter Silvio, beloved of Dorinda, who is as utterly devoted to him as he is disdainful of her. Reminiscent of the story of Cephalus and Procris, this subplot is finely engineered into the main plot, which centers on the faithful love of Mirtillo, the eponymous hero, for his disdainful shepherdess. The two plots are set in a distressed Arcadian society, the result of an earlier feminine figure who, having spurned her lover, has brought a curse on the country; according to an oracle, the only means of mollifying their outraged patron-deity is through the marriage of two offspring of divine origin. In the view of the Arcadians the two are the disdainful huntsman and the faithful shepherd's beloved, Amarillis.

To these paradigmatic characters with their differing responses to love Guarini adds two figures who determine the outcome of the plot by acting in accord with their natures: the Satyr, as to be expected, representing primitive sexuality, and the former urbanite Corisca, representing a sexually liberated, if somewhat jaded, female. The two not only manipulate the plot but also comment realistically on aspects of a Renaissance social world that is scarcely Arcadian. Comment, rather than action, provides Guarini the means of working out the complexities of his plot, with the result that the thematic focus emerges from a succession of poetic recitations on the part of his several characters. These multiple views thus add up to a survey of a kind of metaphysics of love, wherein its sovereignty in nature—"Soule knit to soule by th' earthly knot of love"—is ultimately seen to coalesce with the ineluctable dictates of Fate.[14]

The curse of the goddess, the oracular pronouncement which is misinterpreted until the blind priest Tirenio reveals its true meaning, and the apparent conflict between the operational force of nature and that of fate all show the dramatist responding to elements of classical tragedy but ultimately bringing them to a happy conclusion. The result exemplifies Guarini's theory of a mixed genre of drama which he set forth some years later in a *Compendium of Tragicomic Poetry* (1601). He was prompted to set forth this justification because the *Pastor Fido* had come under attack both before it was published and later—Cardinal Bellarmino informing the dramatist in 1605 that he had done as much harm to morals as Luther and Calvin had done to religion.[15]

The reading public, however, was not to be deterred by charges of the work's moral inadequacy, its violation of Aristotelian canons, or its "gallant sensualism." Its reading public extended far beyond the borders of Italy and far beyond its own era; with translations into French, Spanish, English, German, Greek, Swedish, Dutch, and Polish, the *Pastor Fido* had an enormous vogue during the seventeenth century and was to remain a predominant favorite among secular writings for nearly two centuries.

---

[14] For an account of extrapolated philosophic issues, see Nicolas J. Perella, "Fate, Blindness and Illusion in the *Pastor Fido*," in the *Romanic Review* 49 (1958): 252–68; and for a "moral rehabilitation" of the work, see Louise George Clubb's remarks in "The Moralist in Arcadia: England and Italy," *Romance Philology* 19 (1965): 340–52.

[15] W. W. Greg, *Pastoral Poetry and Pastoral Drama* (A. H. Bullen, 1906), gives an account of this and other contemporary charges, while Vittorio Rossi, *Battista Guarini ed Il Pastor Fido* (Turin, 1886), devoted chapter 5 to them with a concluding account of the work's *fortuna*. Guarini's text is available in the *Opere*, edited by Marziano Guglielminetti, *UTET* (1971), and in a partial English translation in *Literary Criticism, Plato to Dryden*, edited by Allan H. Gilbert (American Book Company, 1940).

Following the appearance of the French and Spanish versions, the translation into English was next in line, this within a dozen years of the initial publication of the play in 1590. Although the Italian text had already aroused sufficient interest for John Wolfe to publish an edition of it along with the *Aminta* in 1591, the genre of Italian pastoral had yet to be acclimated in England; thus the translator was clearly someone who had been exposed to its exemplars either directly or through his connections with those who had. To determine his identity with certainty is perhaps not possible, but by putting the circumstantial evidence together it is possible to come up with a likely candidate.

What is certain is the translator's connection to the long-established Dymoke family of Lincolnshire, a family distinguished by its hereditary office of performing as "Champion" to the sovereign at his coronation. Connection with the office dates back to the time of Richard II, when on 18 July 1377, Sir John Dymoke served as Champion, *jure uxoris*. His duty was to ride his horse into Westminster Hall at the beginning of the coronation banquet and offer a challenge three times to anyone who disputed the sovereign's title; when no one accepted, the sovereign drank to him from a golden cup, handed it to the Champion whe drank in turn to him and then accepted it as a gift, along with other perquisites of office—an elaborate suit of armor, a well-caparisoned horse, and twenty yards of crimson satin. The essential requirements for holding this office were that the holder be a Dymoke who owned the Manor of Scrivelsby in the county of Lincolnshire.[16]

At the coronation of Queen Elizabeth the office was performed by Sir Edward Dymoke, who married Anne, daughter of Sir George Tailboys and co-heir of her brother, the first Baron Tailboys of Kyme (whose family name, it may be noted, was given to a grandson who was, in all likelihood, the future translator of the *Pastor Fido*). Their son Sir Robert was, in turn, to form an important connection in the county by his marriage to the daughter and co-heir of Edward Fiennes de Clinton, first earl of Lincoln, though it was a connection that proved to be exceedingly troublesome to his children, particularly to the eldest son and heir, also an Edward, and to a younger son, the aforementioned Tailboys. Like others of the county, these two Dymokes were to be continually at odds with their uncle, the second earl, whose

---

[16] See the Rev. Samuel Lodge, *Scrivelsby, the Home of the Champions*, 2d ed. (1894), *passim* and the *DNB*, *sub* Sir John Dymoke.

many quarrels with his own family, his servants, and his neighbors seemed to be the result of a "tincture of insanity," or so it has been termed, though as a peer of the realm he seems not to have suffered any diminution of social status.[17]

As the inheritor of the Manor of Scrivelsby, Edward became a figure of some importance in the county. Having entered Gray's Inn in 1577, he was knighted by the queen in 1584 and attended the parliament of that year as knight of the shire; in the following year he was named sheriff of Lincolnshire and deputy lieutenant. But he was also of some importance in terms of his literary interests and literary connections. Such interests seem to have been a family tradition, Thomas Wilson having noted in the dedication of his *Art of Rhetoric* (1553), that it had been written the previous summer in Lincolnshire during a "quiet time of vacation" at the home of the "right worshipfull Sir Edward Dimmoke,"[18] the grandfather of Sir Edward and Tailboys.

Of Sir Edward's own literary connections, the most important was with Samuel Daniel, who as a young man of twenty-two or -three had dedicated his first fruits—the translation of Paolo Jovio's *Dialogo dell' Imprese*—to him (1585), thus establishing a relationship that was to last for many years and that included a trip the two made together to Italy in 1590–1591. It was during this sojourn (discussed below) that they met Battista Guarini, newly famous as the author of the *Pastor Fido*.[19] While in Italy the two travellers also met Robert Tofte, who was later to dedicate a translation of Benedetto Varchi's *Blazon of Jealousy* to Sir Edward (1615), and William Fowler, the uncle of Drummond of Hawthornden, who exchanged Latin verses with him in Padua.[20] After his return from Italy, Sir Edward received a dedication from Thomas Churchyard, ever ready to solicit patronage through multiple approaches, this time in the *Challenge* (1593): "doubting," i.e., thinking, "that verse delights you not, and Tragicall discourse breeds but a heavie conceit in a pleasant disposition" (sigs. I1ᵛ–K2ᵛ), he sets forth

---

[17] See Norreys J. O'Conor, *Godes Peace and the Queenes* (Cambridge Univ. Press, 1934), passim, and for the Dymokes, pages 108–25. According to Sir William Dugdale, the earl of Lincoln's single memorable act was to have served as one of the commissioners for the trial of Mary, Queen of Scots (cited in the *Progresses of Queen Elizabeth*, edited by John Nichols, 3 vols. [1788, 1805], 2:635).

[18] *Arte of Rhetorique*, edited by G. H. Maier (Clarendon Press, 1909), Aiij.

[19] For an account of the date of the trip to Italy, see Mark Eccles, "Samuel Daniel in France and Italy," *Studies in Philology* 34 (1937): 148–67.

[20] One of Dymoke's poems begins "Virtutes (Fowlere) tuas ego semper amabo" (*The Works of William Fowler*, edited by H. W. Meikle, 3 vols. [1914–40], 1:398).

a "Discourse of True Manhood" in prose. This seems a curious statement in view of Sir Edward's literary tastes. In 1612 he received a second multiple dedication, this of the *Second Booke of Ayres* by William Corkine, who addresses him as "valerous and Truely Magnanimous Knight," the King's Champion, thus recalling that Sir Edward had served in that office at the coronation of King James.

But the dedications to him that are of most interest to readers of this edition are those included in the *Pastor Fido*. Here we find a sonnet by the translator dedicated to him as "kinsman," a sonnet to him by Daniel "concerning this translation," and a prose dedication by its publisher, Simon Waterson, in which he remarks on Sir Edward's awareness of the "great worth of the Italian author" and his "nearnesse of kinne" to the "deceased" translator.[21] This is dated the "last of December 1601," a date that becomes problematic in view of later sources.

Of Sir Edward's four (or perhaps five) brothers included in the genealogy provided by the Rev. Lodge, all were alive in 1610/11 except for Tailboys, and what little we know about his personal life lends credence to his having been the translator of the *Pastor Fido*. In May 1584 Tailboys entered Lincoln's Inn.[22] Like others of his social station he may then have travelled abroad, but in the 1590s he seems to have been living with his elder brother on one or another of his Lincolnshire estates. During this period, the friction between the Dymokes and the earl of Lincoln became intense, with the charges and countercharges, suits and countersuits not finally resolved until 1610. From the earl's charges we learn that Tailboys, termed a "common contriver and publisher of infamous pamphlets and libells," was the author of a long poem called "Faunus his four Poetical Fancies" and the maker of a May-day play in which he impersonated his uncle before an audience of three or four hundred persons.[23]

In addition to these reported local efforts, Tailboys is now credited with having written a fanciful topical allegory in verse, *Caltha Poetarum*

---

[21] For "nearnesse of kinne," the *OED* gives examples for "closely related" and "most closely related; (IVb and IVc). Daniel's use of "thy kind Countrey-man" in his dedicatory sonnet may well be intended to specify one from the same county; see the example for 1575–76, *OED*, sub. 2.

[22] *Records of the Society of Lincoln's Inn, Admissions, 1420–1799* (1896), 1:100.

[23] Huntington Library, Ellesmere MSS. 2733 and 2774, which date from 1610 when a severe sentence was meted out to Sir Edward and to some of his retainers. See also O'Conor, *Godes Peace*, and Leslie Hotson, "Marigold of the Poets," *Essays by Divers Hands, Transactions of the Royal Society of Literature of the United Kingdom*, n.s., 17 (1938): 47–68.

or the Bumble Bee. Entered in the Stationers' Register on 17 April 1599 as *Caltha poetarum or Chrysanthemon,* it was published that same year with the author's name given as T. Cutwode. Thanks to the detective efforts of Leslie Hotson (as cited in n. 23), the pseudonymous author is now recognized in *STC²* as Tailboys Dymoke (from *Taille-bois*). On 1 June 1599, Archbishop Whitgift ordered the poem burned together with satirical and erotic works by Marston, Hall, and John Davies, but, inexplicably, the order for *Caltha Poetarum* was then "stayed" (*S.R.* 3:677–78).

On the basis of this evidence, Tailboys Dymoke may, I think, be accepted as the probable translator of the *Pastor Fido,* but as mentioned earlier, there remains the problem of reconciling the date of his death given in the printed text with the several dates given in later sources. The work was entered in the Stationers' Register on 16 September 1601 (*S.R.* 3:192), and its publisher but *not* its printer (who is not identified) dates his dedication, it may be recalled, on the "last day of December 1601." Both of these dates would concur well enough with a publication date of 1602 as given on the title page. In his genealogy of the Dymoke family, the Rev. Lodge gives the date for the burial of Tailboys at Horncastle (one of the locales associated with the Dymokes) as 13 October 1602, which seems questionable in light of other sources. But it also raises the possibility of the *printer's* having misread the date of the publisher's letter (with its reference to the "deceased" translator) as 1601 instead of 1602, an easy graphic error in a manuscript written in secretary hand.

In tracing the legal proceedings that the earl of Lincoln brought against the Dymokes in 1602, Norreys J. O'Conor states that Tailboys testified on 7 December 1602 and that the following year he was referred to (by a Dymoke retainer) as now "decesed," though he gives no precise sources for these two dates. *Burke's ... Landed Gentry* says that Tailboys died c. January 1602/1603 and was possibly the translator of the *Pastor Fido.*[24]

The conclusions to be deduced from these several and variable dates are that Tailboys Dymoke in all probability was the translator of the *Pastor Fido* and that the letter of the publisher should read the "last of December 1602" (not 1601), at which time Tailboys was deceased. The burial date of 13 October 1602, given by Lodge, remains a discrepancy in view of Tailboys's having testified on 7 December 1602, as given by O'Conor.[25]

---

[24] For O'Conor, see 124–25, and for *Burke,* see the 18th ed., edited by Peter Townsend (1965), 1:220–21.

[25] The same burial date is given in *Lincolnshire Pedigrees* (4 vols., Publications of

The translation is a most interesting one on several counts. Though some portions of the nearly 7,000 lines of the original are omitted, the translator knows the Italian well and renders it closely, exhibiting, moreover, a wide range of English diction, including words that have now become archaic or obsolete, a practice consistent with Guarini's own mixed level of diction. Scant attention has been paid to it.

At the beginning of this century, W. W. Greg in *Pastoral Poetry and Pastoral Drama* was harshly critical of the translation; acknowledging that it keeps "pretty faithfully" to the original, he found that it does no more than "emphasize" its "tedious artificiality." In his view, Fanshawe's version in 1647 is the only one "worthy of Guarini's masterpiece," particularly because of that translator's "constant reminiscences" of Shakespeare with whole lines being introduced—an aspect that to most readers would be anything but a commendation, as in Greg's example:

> Poor soul! Concealment like a worm i' th' bud,
> Lies in her Damask cheek sucking the blood.[26]

A comparison of the noted choral passage from Act II in which Guarini extols the Renaissance concept of the "soul kiss" points up—to my mind—the rather coarse reading of 1647 in contrast to the attractive rendering in 1602:

> It is a pretie thing to kisse
> The delicate vermilion Rose
> Of some faire cheeke; they that have prov'd that blisse
> (Right happie Lovers) so will say. Yet those
> Will say againe, kisses are dead and vaine
> Where beautie kist restores it not againe.
> The strokes of two inamour'd lips are those
> Where mouth on mouth loves sweetest vengeance showes;

---

the Harleian Society [1902–6], 4:1206), but as noted in 1:319, the date is based on Lodge.

It may also be noted that the entry in *STC*[2] queries the translator as *John* Dymoke, while for the second edition of the translation, published in 1633, Arber (4:305) gives the translator as *Charles*. It is true that Sir Edward had a brother named John, but he was not deceased until after 1610; and another brother named Charles for whom Lodge supplies only the name; nothing connects either of these two brothers with literary matters (not even the infamous May-Day play).

[26] Greg, *Pastoral Poetry*, 243–45. Greg's response to Renaissance pastoral here (and again with Daniel's play) was at odds with that of contemporary and near-contemporary judgment; in 1691 Langbaine termed this the "first Version of the Famous Guarini," "Excellent for those Times" (*An Account of the English Dramatic Poets*, 544).

Those are true kisses where with equall wills
We ever give and take againe our fills.
Kisse but a curious* mouth, a daintie hand,
A breast, a brow, or what you can demand,
You will confesse no part in woman is,
Save for sweet mouth that doth deserve a kisse,
By which two soules with lively spirits meet,
Making live rubies kindly entergreet;
So mongst themselves those sowly sprightfull kisses
Do enter-speake, and in a little sown
Great things bewray, and sweetest secret blisses
To others hidden, to themselves well knowne.

*delicate   Act II, Chorus (1602)

Well may that kisse be sweet that's giv'n t' a sleek
And fragrant rose of a vermilion cheek;
And understanding tasters (as are true
And happy Lovers) will commend that too.
'Tis a dead kisse, say I, and must be poor,
Which the place kist hath no means to restore.
But the sweet ecchoing, and the Dove-like billing
Of two encountring Mouthes, when both are willing;
And when at once both Loves advance their bows,
Their shafts drawn home, at once sound at the loose
(How sweet is such Revenge!) This is true kissing,
Where there is one for t'other without missing
A minute of the time, or taking more
Then that which in the taking they restore.
Where by an interchange of amorous blisses
At the same time they sow and gather kisses.
Kisse a red swelling lip, then kisse a wrist,
A breast, a forehead, or what else thou list,
No part of a fair Nymph so just will be,
Except the lip, to pay this kisse to thee.
Thither your souls come sallying forth, and they
Kisse too, and by the wandring pow'rs convey
Life into smacking Rubies, and transfuse
Into the live and sprightly kisse their use
Of reason; so that yee discourse together
In kisses, which with little noyse deliver

Much matter; and sweet secrets, which hee spels
Who is a Lover, Gibbrish to all else.

Richard Fanshawe, 1647

A NOTE ON THE TEXT OF THE *PASTOR FIDO*

The translation went through two editions within thirty years, after
which it appears to have been generally ignored though it was certainly known at the end of the century (see n. 26 above). Fanshawe's
version subsequently became the accepted one.

The text of the translation was entered in the Stationers' Register by
Simon Waterson on 16 September 1601, and was printed for him by
Thomas Creede, who is identified by his device, number 299 in R. B.
McKerrow's *Printers and Publishers Devices*, 1913. The collation of the
1602 edition is 4^0: A^2, B–Q^4, 62 unnumbered leaves. It is to be noted
that from Daniel's earliest publication, in 1585, Simon Waterson was
his long-time publisher and "loving friend" (as the poet calls him in
his will); this suggests Daniel's close involvement in the publication of
the Dymoke translation.

John Waterson, the son of the original publisher, dedicated the second edition to Charles Dymoke, son of the former and now the current Champion, as "Heire of what ever else was his Fathers; as well as
of his Vertues." It was printed by Augustine Matthewes for William
Sheares and collates 12^0: A^6, B–H^{12}. Huntington copies 59040 and
12514 lack A1, H11 and 12 (presumed blank), 90 unnumbered leaves.

Minor changes have been made in the text in accord with the principles set forth for the *Aminta* (xvi above).

The Queenes Arcadia: The "First" English Pastoral

Sometime during 1590 and, it seems, for most of 1591, Samuel
Daniel visited Italy in the company of Sir Edward Dymoke, the
Queen's Champion and the earliest of the poet's many patrons, Daniel
having dedicated to him the "first fruites" of his varied and produc-
tive career. This was the translation of Paolo Giovio's *Imprese*, which
had been published in 1585 and undertaken at Sir Edward's request,
his "offered courtesies" having prompted the translator to the "tillage
of so hard a soyle." Five years later Sir Edward, an enthusiast of Italian letters, provided the further stimulus of taking the twenty-eight-

year-old Daniel to Italy, and the near contemporaries—Sir Edward himself was thirty-three—took the occasion to meet with the playwright and critic Battista Guarini, who was at this date spending his time in Venice and Padua and in the Polesine at his Villa San Bellino.[27]

In meeting with Guarini at this time, whether in 1590 or 1591, the two Englishmen must have felt as if they were the literary vanguard for their countrymen; some dozen years later Daniel recalled the occasion to Sir Edward in a sonnet addressed to him that prefaced the 1602 translation of the *Pastor Fido*. Calling the author here Sir Edward's "deare esteem'd Guarini," he also recalls the Italian's arrogant comments on the poetic inadequacy of the English language:

> Though I remember he hath oft imbas'd
> Unto us both, the vertues of the North,
> Saying, our costes were with no measures grac'd,
> Nor barbarous tongues could any verse bring forth.
>
> lines 9–14

And he adds, "I would he sawe his owne," that is, the translator's rendering of the play, "or knew our store."

In fact, as early as 1594, he had answered Guarini in kind in the dedication of his neo-classical drama *Cleopatra*, where he says,

> O that the Ocean did not bound our stile,
> Within these strict and narrow limmites so:
> But that the melodie of our sweete Ile
> Might now be heard to Tyber, Arne, and Po,
> That they might know how far Thames doth out-go
> The Musick of Declynéd Italie.... lines 73–78

Again in 1599 in his eloquent defense of learning, *Musophilus*, he asks rhetorically:

> Or should we carelesse come behind the rest
> In powre of wordes, that go before in worth,
> When as our accents equall to the best
> Is able greater wonders to bring forth:

---

[27] Rossi, *Battista Guarini*, 98. Mark Eccles has carefully correlated dates and references to the Daniel-Dymoke journey in "Samuel Daniel in France and Italy" (cited in n. 19). He points out that there is no trace of Dymoke in England between March 1589/1590 when he signed a letter as one of the three deputy lieutenants of Lincolnshire and November 1591 when legal records indicate he was again in England (165).

When all that ever hotter spirits exprest
Comes bettered by the patience of the North?[28]

lines 951–56

Nonetheless, he invoked his Italian journey in the captions to two of the sonnets: number 47 in the 1594 edition of *Delia*, which is labelled "At the Authors going into Italie" and in number 48, which is labelled, "This Sonnet was made at the Authors beeing in Italie."

After a dozen years of experimenting with many genres and after almost as many worthy patrons, Daniel gained one of the worthiest of all in Queen Anne, becoming "licenser of the Children of the Queen's Revels" in 1604. The following year he wrote his first pastoral play, avowed to be the earliest attempt in English; this was performed at Christ Church, Oxford, during a royal visit and published the next year as the *Queenes Arcadia* with a dedication to "The Queenes most excellent Majestie."[29] Given the closeness of date to the 1602 translation of the *Pastor Fido* and given the similarity of certain episodes in the two, it may well be that the appearance of this translation by a Dymoke prompted Daniel to try his hand at a new form.[30] As a thorough professional he had already tried his hand at many—sonnet, complaint poem, classical tragedy, versified history, verse epistle, literary criticism, philosophic poem, panegyric, and court masque. Why not pastoral drama too? Indicating its novelty for an English audience is Daniel's ending his dedication with *Chi non fa, non falla.*

Rather scant attention has been paid to this pastoral play, readers having been put off perhaps by the hostile comments on the piece by W. W. Greg, who, while acknowledging the general influence of both Tasso and Guarini during the first half of the seventeeth century, charges that the *Queenes Arcadia* and Daniel's second pastoral, *Hymens*

---

[28] In a useful study of the poet's life and works, *Samuel Daniel* (Twayne Series, 1967), Cecil Seronsky remarks that the imputation of the inferiority of English haunted Daniel throughout his career, and he notes instances (17–18).

[29] In claiming to have written the first English pastoral, Daniel clearly has in mind Italian examples of the genre versus the earlier largely mythological plays of Lyly and Peele which do include some pastoral elements. Its original title seems to have been *Arcadia Reformed* (E. K. Chambers, *The Elizabethan Stage*, 4 vols. [Oxford Univ. Press, 1923], 3:276).

[30] One unnamed person at the Oxford festivities who did not attend the performance but who reported the *Queenes Arcadia* as having been "well acted and greatly applauded" asserted that it was drawn out of a Latin version (*Pastor Fidus*) "sometimes acted" by King's College students (cited by W. W. Greg, *Pastoral Poetry*, 252n). An edition of that play is said to be forthcoming in the series Renaissance Latin Drama in England, edited by Marvin Spevak *et al.* (George Olms Verlag: Hildersheim, Germany), cited in *Records of Early English Drama*, 2 vols. (1989), 2:914–15, where it is dated c. 1604.

Triumph (1615), are the only two examples to which the term "imitation" can with full justification be applied. The first of these, he finds, shows the greater dependence and the less intrinsic merit.[31] Before considering this charge of "imitation," I should point out that Greg's evaluation of the two pieces is at odds with a seventeeth-century estimate of them, this by an inveterate attendant at court festivities. Of the *Queenes Arcadia*, John Chamberlain commented that while the other three plays presented were dull, Daniel's made amends for all; "being indeed very excelent, and some parts exactly acted"; of *Hymens Triumph* he commented that it was "solemn & dull," adding (what would perhaps explain its greater merit for Greg), "but perhaps better to be read than represented."[32]

Some twenty years after Greg, V. M. Jeffrey extended the charge by adding a third Italian author to the roster of Daniel's sources. This was Luigi Groto, known as "Cieco d'Adria," whose pastoral play *Il Pentimento Amoroso* was performed in 1575, two years after Tasso's *Aminta*. He seems to have been well known to an English audience, as she points out, since Lady Politick Would-be in *Volpone* queries, "Which of your Poets? Petrarch or Tasso or Dante? / Querrini? Ariosto? Aretine? / Cieco di Hadria? I have read them all" (III.4). Jeffrey points out that the scene in the *Queenes Arcadia* where two shepherds wrangle over which of them is entitled to say he is beloved is something more than imitation, that it is, in fact, a "word for word" translation from Groto's play, and she cites the two passages.[33] The situation is indeed the same in both. However, Daniel has slightly elaborated the exchanges between the two rivals (I.2) and particularized the imagery so that his rendering creates a subtly different effect from what one expects from a word for word translation.[34] She also points out (439–40) that a suicide attempt by one disconsolate lover in the *Queenes Arcadia* looks back to a similar attempt in Tasso's *Aminta* (this by a leap off a precipice); but again Daniel has elaborated with *two* intended suicides, the first by a leap off a "craggie Rock," the second by poison, and additional touches derive from one or other of the three Italian playwrights. What the replication of these fairly obvious devices

---

[31] Greg, 252–53. Like others, he seems to have been unaware of Daniel's revisions in the second edition of the play.

[32] Cited in Chambers, 3:276–77.

[33] "Italian and English Pastoral Drama of the Renaissance," *Modern Language Review* 19 (1924): 435–44.

[34] Jeffrey acknowledges this difference, as it were, by observing that Daniel's "flowing and musical lines seem even more graceful when placed side by side with the harshness and stiff monotony of Groto's 'endecasillabi sdruccioli' " (438).

suggests to me is that Daniel was conscious of a developing dramatic form.

It should be acknowledged that the configuration of specific motifs, incidents, character types, and even names in a given exemplar can set a pattern which, reappearing in other exemplars, become the characteristics that determine a genre. A tendency toward generic patterning, buttressed by the humanistic tradition of imitating the classics (and for many English this included the Italians), accounts to a large degree, I think, for the charge of "imitation" frequently used in reference to such genres as the epyllion, the pastoral, and a lyrical form like the sonnet.[35]

That Tasso's *Aminta* had served as an exemplar for Guarini is also acknowledged, but in the *Pastor Fido* he, too, has elaborated by complicating the plot and introducing a more complex thematic element with the result that his pastoral is three times as long as its prototype. Since Guarini also borrowed from Groto, there is an affiliation among the three Italian playwrights which Daniel seems to have recognized, just as others recognized an affiliation in the pastoral poetry of Theocritus, Bion, and Moschus and borrowed indiscriminately from each.

In Daniel's pastoral the Arcadian locale ("this little angle of the world") is disordered as the result of an intruding city wench, Techne, and a corrupted traveller, Colax, who manipulate the affairs of *four* sets of lovers, with a pettifogger and a quacksalver contributing to the disorder. Such stock satirical figures provide topical relevance which includes an anti-tobacco diatribe intended for a royal auditor (though here delivered by the quack doctor). The city wench parallels Corisca in the *Pastor Fido* and, like Corisca, she, too, makes use of the device of an assignation in a cave to smirch the character of a shepherdess, a device, as Jeffrey points out (439), that Groto had used earlier. The plight of Dorinda, whose beloved disdains her for the joys of hunting, parallels a situation in the *Pastor Fido*, and she, too, seeks to woo him while she plays with his dog (V.1), an episode that Jeffrey again points out (440) is reminiscent of Groto.

But Daniel has also introduced his modifications. In place of a satyr to voice the stock denunciation of women, as in the *Aminta* and the *Pastor Fido*, he uses a disenchanted lover (II.3); he drops the tribute-motif of the *Pastor Fido* altogether, adds the incident of a wayward shepherdess seeking a remedy for her waywardness from the quack

---

[35] Even so, one (or more) of Daniel's contemporaries alluded to his too generous use of "others' wit" in his "sugred sonetting" (*Return from Parnassus*, edited by J. B. Leishman [Nicholson and Watson, 1949], Pt. 2.1.2, 235–40).

doctor, and multiplies the action with his four sets of lovers; in place of choral commentary he uses two voyeuristic elders of Arcadia to comment on the action, sort out the wrongs, and expel the intruders. Into this literary, and therefore artificial, ambiance he has introduced, most particularly, local coloring by means of comic and satiric elements having topical appeal. This topical appeal would both amuse and flatter a university and courtly audience responsive to the inflated diction—as well as candor—of the two would-be professionals: doctor and lawyer admittedly overwhelming their patients and clients by means of the "hideous termes" and abstruse language which their special arts afford—and which their humanistic author knows well. In thus providing the novelty of a "first" Italianate pastoral but seasoning it with native English elements, Daniel has deftly shaped his royal entertainment for an audience that he deemed would indeed acknowledge the "vertues of the North."

A NOTE ON THE TEXT OF THE *QUEENES ARCADIA*

Labelled a "Pastoral Tragi-comedie," Daniel's *Queenes Arcadia* went through four editions in the seventeenth century, the fourth and last of them appearing in the collection of his works that his brother arranged to have published and dedicated to Prince Charles four years after Daniel's death in 1619. After the first edition dedicated to the queen in 1606, it appeared a second time (without the dedication) in the 1607 edition of *Certaine Small Workes*, which was "corrected and augmented" by the author, now a groom of the queen's Privy Chamber, and printed by John Windet for Simon Waterson. Rather carelessly printed, it is textually correct and shows some authorial revision, particularly from V.3.70 to the end of the scene; here Daniel has deleted a passage introducing a religious imposter named Pistophoenax though he appears in the following and final scene. The text appeared for a third time (with the dedication) in the 1611 edition of *Certaine Small Workes*, also said to be "corrected and augmented" by the author and printed by John Legatt, again for Waterson. Set from the first, this third edition of the *Queenes Arcadia* thus ignores the revisions of the 1607 edition, and it is even more carelessly printed in respect to both text and typography. (Some copies of *Certaine Small Workes* include an errata listing—e.g., the British Library copy—along with a note to the effect that letters "turned, changed, or wanting in the words" have been ignored).[36] The text in the 1623 collection of

---

[36] Since the *Queenes Arcadia* lacks pagination and the errata listing offers its own

his works, which was printed by Nicholas Okes, again for Waterson, derives from this faulty edition, so it, too, lacks the revisions and reproduces many of its errors; it is the one A. B. Grosart used in the *Collected Works* (5 vols., 1885–1896) and his is the only post-seventeenth-century edition of the play.

The first edition, well printed in 1606 by Nicholas Okes for Waterson, is the copy-text used here, supplemented by the 1607 edition for the corrections and revisions.[37]

The Queenes Arcadia was entered in the *Stationers' Register* by Samuel Waterson on 26 November 1605 (Arber, 3:305). It was printed in 1606 by G. Eld for Waterson and collates 4^0: $A^{2(-1)}$, B-K^4, $L^{2(-1)}$, 38 leaves.

It was printed again in 1607 by J[ohn] W[indet] for Simon Waterson in a collection called *Certaine Small Workes*, with the Epistle to the queen omitted; 8^0, it occupies sigs. P2–V1, [68]-106^r; 40 leaves with some irregular numbering.

The same collection under the same title was printed again in 1611 by J[ohn] L[egatt] again for Waterson, with the Epistle to the queen included: 12^0: K9–O1^v, 40 unnumbered leaves.

This was re-issued in the same year to correct a misimposition.

The final edition appeared in the posthumous *Whole Works*, dedicated to Prince Charles by Daniel's brother John; it was printed by Nicholas Okes for Simon Waterson in 1623: 4^0 (in eights), sigs. 2K1–207^v, pp. 325–402.

For additional bibliographical information to that set forth here, see W. W. Greg, *A Bibliography of the English Printed Drama to the Restoration*, vols. 1 and 2 (1939, 1951) and H. Sellers, "A Bibliography of the Works of Samuel Daniel," *Oxford Bibliographical Society, Proceedings and Papers II* (1930), 29–45.

Minor changes in the text accord with the principles set forth for the *Aminta* (xvi above).

---

errors, the seventeenth-century buyer was scarcely well served by its inclusion. More informative of authorial attitude is Daniel's ignoring in this reprint his revisions of four years earlier.

[37] It should be noted that commentators on the "first" English pastoral (as shown by their quotations) have had recourse to the faulty 1623 posthumous edition and so have failed to reckon with its author's revisions.

Tasso's *Aminta*

Tasso's *Aminta*

THE SPEAKERS ARE

Cupid, in shepherds weedes.
Daphne, companion of Silvia.
Silvia, beloved of Aminta.
Aminta, lover of Silvia.
Thirsis, companion of Aminta.

Satyr, in love with Silvia.
Nerina, Nymphe.
Ergastus, Shepherd.
Elpine, Shepherd.
Chorus, of Shepherds.

THE PROLOGUE.

CUPID, *in habit of a Shepheard.*

Who would beleeve that in this human forme,
And under these meane Shepherds weedes were hid
A godhead? Nor yet of the lower ranke,
But the most mighty 'mong the gods, whose powre
Makes oft the bloudy Sword of angry *Mars*   5
Fall from his hand; sterne *Neptune* hurle away
His powerfull trident; and great *Jove* lay by
His thunderbolt; and thus attyr'de, I hope
My mother *Venus* shall have much adoe
To find her *Cupid.* For the troth to tell,   10
Sh' has made me play the run-away with her;
Because (forsooth) shee will sole mistresse bee,
And to her pleasure binde my shafts and mee;
And (vaine ambitious woman as shee is)
Would tye me to live stil 'mongst Crownes, and Scepters   15
And to high Courts confine my power and me;
And to my under-followers graunts to live
Here in these woods; and to advance their powres,
Ore silly Shepherds brests; but I that am

No childe (though childish be my gate and lookes),   20
Will for this once doe as shall please me best.
For not to her, but me allotted were
The ever awfull brande, and goulden bowe:
Therefore I purpose to conceale my selfe,
And runne from her entreates; (for other powre   25
Then to intreate, shee shall not have ore me:)
I heare shee haunts these groves, and promiseth
Unto the Nymphes and Shepherds, which of them
Will bring me to her, kisses for their paines,
And more then kisses too; and cannot I   30
To them shall hide me from her liberall be
Of kisses, and more too, as well as she?
The Nymphes I know will like my kisses best,
When I shall woe them that am god of love:
Therefore my mother doth but looze her paine,   35
Here's none will bring her home her sonne againe.
But to be surer that she may not know
Or finde me out by the usd'e markes I beare,
I've layd my quiver, bowe, and wings from me;
Yet come I not hither unarm'de; this rodd   40
I carry is my brand transforméd thus,
And breathes out unseene flame at ev'ry pore;
And this dart (though it have no goulden head)
Of hev'nly temper is; and where it lytes
Inforceth love; and ev'ne this day shall make   45
A deepe and cureless wound in the hard brest
Of the most cruell Nymph, that ever yet
Hath bin a follower of *Dianas* traine;
Nor will I pitty Silvia more, (for so
Th' obdurate stony-brested Nymph is call'd)   50
Then erst I did the gentle-hearted Swaine
Aminta, many winters since, when he
(Poore wretch) then young, follow'd her younger stepps
From wood to wood in ev'ry game and sport:
And for more sure effecting my intent,   55
I'le pause a while till some remorse and pitty
Of the poore Shepherds sufferings have a little
Thawde the hard yce congeal'd about her brest
With mayden peevishnesse; and when I finde
She growes more plyant, will I launch her brest: 60
And this to doe with better ease and arte,

Amongst the feasting troopes of the crown'd Shepherds
That hither come to sport o' hollydayes,
I'le put my selfe; and heere, even in this place
I'le give the speeding blow unseene, unknowne.   65
To day these Woods shall heare another voyce
Of love then ere before, and more refin'de;
My godhead heere shall in it selfe appeare
Present no longer in my Ministers:
I'le breath soft thoughts into their courser brests,   70
And make their tungs in smoothest numbers move;
For wheresoere I am, still am I *Love;*
No lesse in Shepherds then in greatest Peeres;
And inequallity in people, I
Can temper as I please, such is my power.   75
The Rurall sound of homely Shepherds reede
I can make equall with the learned'st lyre,
And if my mother (which disdaines forsooth
To see me heere) be ignorant of this,
Shee's blinde, not I   80
Whom the blind world reputes blinde wrongfully.

ACTUS PRIMUS Scena Prima

DAPHNE. SILVIA.

[*Da:*] Is't possible (Silvia) thou canst resolve
To spend the faire houres of thy flowring youth
With such contempt of *Venus,* and her Sonne;
And hast no more desire to be a mother,
And leave a part of thee (when thou art dead)   5
Living behinde thee? Change (young fondling) change
Thy minde; and do not leade a life so strange.
Sil. Daphne, let others pleasure take in love,
(If in such thraledome any pleasure bee;)
The life I leade contents me well enough: 10
To chase the flying Deere over the lawne
With Hounde, or well-aym'de Flight, and while I finde
Shafts in my quiver, and beasts for my pray,
I'le want no sport to passe the time away.
Da: Fine sports no doubt, and sure a goodly life   15
For silly mindes that never tasted other,
And for that cause alone it pleases thee:
So duller ages heretofore could thinke

Acornes and water the best meate and drinke,
Before the use of corne, and wine was founde,   20
But now th'are onely eate and drunke by beastes
And hadst thou but once proov'd the thousand part
Of the deare joyes those happy lovers feele,
That truely love, and are belov'd againe,
Thou wouldst with sighes repent thy time mispent,   25
And onely call a lovers life Content.
And say, O my past springtyde, how in vaine
Spent I thy widowy nights? How many dayes
In fruitlesse lonenesse, which I now bewaile?
Why knew I not loves sweetes have this condition   30
To bring new joyes with ev'ry repetition?
Change, change thy minde (young silly one) and knowe
Too late repentance is a double woe.
Sil. When I repent the thoughts I carry now,
Or say such words as these thou fayning framest   35
To sport thy selfe withall, the Flouds shall runne
Backe to their Springs, the Wolfe shall fearing flye
The silly Lambe, and the young Levrett shall
Pursue the speedy Grayhound ore the playne,
The Beare shall in the toyling Ocean breede,   40
And finny Dolphine on the mountaines feede.
Da. I so, just such another peevish thing
Like thee was I, when I was of thy yeares;
So look'd, so pac'de, so goulden trest', so ruddy
My 'tysing lipp, so in my rising cheeke   45
The damaske rose was blowne; and I remember
Just such as thine is now my minde was then,
And ev'ne such silly pastimes as thine be
I likewise usd'e; as with lim'de twigges to catch
Unwares the fethred singers in the wood,   50
Track the Deeres footing, till I had intrapt them
And such like; when a gentle lover woode me,
With such a peevish grace hang downe the head
And blush for scorne I would, as oft thou doe'st;
And that unseemely forme me thought became mee,   55
Nay ev'ne dislik'd what others lik'de in me,
So much I counted it a fault, and shame
To be desir'de or lov'de of any one;
But what cannot time bring to passe? And what
Cannot a true and faithfull lover do   60

With importunity, desert and love?
And I confesse plainely the troth to thee
So was I vanquisht; nor with other armes
Then humble suff'rance, sighes, and pitty craving:
But then I soone found in one short nights shade,   65
What the broade light of many hundred dayes
Could never teach me; then I could recall
My selfe, shake off my blinde simplicitie,
And sighing say, here *Cinthia*, take thy bowe,
Quiver, and horne, for I renounce thy life.   70
And I hope yet to see another day
Thy wilde thoughts bridled too, and thy hard brest
Yeeld, and growe softer at Aminta's plaints.
Is he not young and fresh, and lovely too?
Does he not love thee dearely', and thee alone?   75
For though belov'de of many Nymphes, he never
For others love, or thy hate, leaves to love thee.
Nor canst thou thinke him to meane borne for thee;
For (be thou daughter of Cidippe faire,
Whose sire was god of this our noble floud)   80
Yet is Aminta ould Sivanus heire,
Of the high seed of Pan the Shepherds god.
The sleeke-browd' Amarillis (if ere yet
In any fountaines glasse thou saw'st thy selfe)
Is not a whit lesse lovely then thou art;   85
Yet all her sweet alurements he rejects,
And madly dotes on thy despightfull loathings.
Well, but suppose now, (and the heav'ns forbid
It come to more then supposition)
That he falling from thee, his minde remoove,   90
And cleave to her, that so deserves his love;
What will become of thee then? With what eye
Wilt thou behould him in an others armes
Happily twyn'de, and thy selfe laught to scorne?
Sil. Be it to' Aminta and his loves, as best   95
    Shall like himselfe; I'me at a point for one;
    And so he be not mine, be' he whose he list.
    But mine he cannot be against my will,
    Nor yet though he were mine, would I be his.
Da. Fye, whence grows this thy hate?
Sil.   Why from his love.   100
Da. Too soft a syre to breed so rough a Sonne;

But who ere sawe Tygars of milde Lambes bred,
Or the blacke Rav'ne hatcht of a silver Dove?
Thou dost but mocke me, Silvia, dost thou not?
Sil. I hate his love, that doth my honour hate;   105
  And lov'de him, whilst he sought what I could graunt.
Da. Tis thou offend'st thy selfe; he doth but crave
  The same for thee that he desires to have.
Sil. I pre'thee, Daphne, either speake no more,
  Or somwhat else that I may answer to.   110
Da. See, fondling, see
  How ill this peevishnesse of youth becomes thee;
  Tell me but this yet, if some other lov'de thee,
  Is this the welcome thou wouldst give his love?
Sil. Such and worse welcome they deserve, that ar   115
  These theeves of silly maydes virginities,
  Which you call lovers, and I enimies.
Da. Is the ramme then to th' ewe an enimy,
  The bull to th' hayfer, is the turtle too
  An enemy to' his mate that loves him so?   120
  And is the Spring the season of debate
  That (sweetly smiling) leades to coupling bands
  The beast, the fish, the fowle, women and men?
  And see'st thou not that e'vry thing that is,
  Breathes now a soveraign ayre of love, and sweetnesse, 125
  Pleasure, and health? Behold that Turtle there
  With what a wooing murmur he sighes love
  To his belov'de; harke of yon Nitingall
  That hops from bough to bough,
  Singing, I love, I love; nay, more then these,   130
  The speckled Serpent layes his venim by,
  And greedy runnes to' imbrace his lovéd one;
  The Tygar loves, and the proud Lion too;
  Thou onely savadge more then savadge beasts
  Barr'st against love thy more-then-yron brest.   135
  But what speake I of Lions, Tygars, Snakes,
  That sensible ar? Why all these trees doe love;
  See with what amorous and redoubled twinings
  The loving Vine her husband faire intangles;
  The Beech tree loves the Beech, the Pine the Pine,   140
  The Elme the Elme loves, and the Willows too
  A mutuall languish for each other feele.
  That Oake that seemes so rough and so impenitrable,

Doth no lesse feele the force of amorous flame;
And hadst thou but the spirit and sence of love,   145
His hidden language thou wouldst understand.
Wilt thou be lesse and worse then trees and plants,
In being thus an enimy to Love?
Fye, silli' one, fie; these idle thoughts remove.
Sil. When I heare trees sighe (as belike they do)   150
  I'le be content to bee a lover too.
Da. Well, mock my words, laugh my advice to scorne,
  (Deaffe to Loves sound, and simple as thou art)
  But goe thy wayes; be sure the time will come
  When thou shalt flye from the now-lovéd fount   155
  Where thou behold'st and so admyr'st thy selfe,
  Fearing to view thy selfe so wrinkled fowle
  As age will make thee; but I note not this
  To thee above the rest, for though age be
  Evill, 'tis so to all as well as thee.   160
  Heard'st thou what Elpine spake this other day,
  The rev'rend Elpine to the Faire Licoris,
  (Licoris whose eyes wrought upon him that
  Which his songs should have wrought upon her heart,
  If Love could learne but to give each his due).   165
  He tould it (Batto' and Thirsis being by,
  Those two learn'd lovers) in Auroras denne,
  Over whose doore is writt—*hence yee prophane,*
  Hye yee farre hence which words he writt (sayd he)
  That in that high pitch sang of loves and armes,   170
  And when he dyed bequeath'd his pipe to him;
  There was (he said) lowe in th' infernal lake
  A dungeon darke, aye fill'd with noysom fumes
  Breath'd from the furnaces of *Acaron,*
  And there all cruell and ingratefull women   175
  Live in eternal horror, and ar fedd
  With onely their owne bootelesse plaints and cryes.
  Looke to 't betimes, or I am sore afraide
  There must a roome be taken up for you,
  To quite this cruelty to others usd'e.   180
  And 'twere but justice, that those fumes should drawe
  A sea of sorrow from those eyes of thine,
  That pitty could ne're make to shed a teare:
  Well, runne on thine owne course, and marke the ende.
Sil. But what did then Licoris (pre'thee tell me)   185

What reply did shee make to Elpine's words?
Da. How curious th' art in other folkes affaires,
   And carelesse quite in what concernes thy selfe?
   Why, with her eyes Licoris answer'd him.
Sil. How, could she answer only with her eyes? 190
Da. Yes; her faire eyes wrapt in a sunny smile,
   Tould Elpine this: her heart and we are thine;
   More cannot she give, nor must thou desire.
   This were alone enough to satisfie
   And serve for full reward to a chast lover, 195
   That held her eyes as true as they were faire,
   And put entire and harty trust in them.
Sil. But wherfore does not he then trust her eyes?
Da. I'le tell thee; know'st thou not what Thirsis writ
   When harried so with love, and loves disdaine 200
   He wont to wander all about the woods,
   In such a sort, as pitty mov'de, and laughter
   Mong'st the young Swaines and Nymphes that gaz'de on him?
   Yet writ he nought that laughter did deserve,
   Though many things he did deserv'd no lesse, 205
   He writ it on the barkes of sundry trees,
   And as the trees, so grew his verse. 'Twas this—
   Deluding eyes, false mirhors of the heart,
   Full well I finde how well yee can deceive:
   But what availes, if love inforce my will 210
   To' imbrace your harmes, and dote upon you still?
Sil. Well thus we wast the time in ydle chatt,
   And I had halfe forgot, that 'tis to day
   We did appoint to meet in th' Oaken grove,
   To hunt an houre; I pre'thee if thou wilt, 215
   Stay for me till I have in yon fresh fount
   Layd off the sweat and dust that yesterday
   I soyld me with, in chase of a swift Doe,
   That at the length I overtooke, and kill'de.
Da. I'le stay for thee, and perhaps wash me too, 220
   But first I'le home a while, and come againe,
   For the daye's younger then it seemes to be.
   Goe then, and stay there for me till I come;
   And in the meane time, thinke on my advice,
   That more imports thee then the chase or fount; 225
   And if thou dost not thinke so, thou must know
   Thou little know'st; and ought'st thy judgement bowe

To their direction that know more then thou.

ACTUS PRIMUS Scena Secunda

AMINTA. THIRSIS.

[Am.] At my laments I've heard the rocks, the waters
    For pitty answer; and at my complaint
    The leav'd boughes murmur, as they griev'd for me;
    But never saw, nor ever hope to see
    Pitty in the faire and cruell (shall I say   5
    Woman or) tygar? For a woman shee
    Denyes to be, in thus denying me
    The pitty this my miserable state
    Drawes from things senceless, and inanimate.
Thir. Lambes on the grasse, the Wolfe feedes on the Lambe;   10
    Love (cruellest of things) with teares is fedd.
    And though he ever feedes is never full.
Am. Alas, alas, love hath bin with my teares
    Long since full fedd, and now thirsts onely for
    My bloud; and long it shall not be, ere he   15
    And the faire Cruell drinke it with their eyes.
Thir. Ay me, what say'st thou', Aminta? Fye, no more
    Of this strange dotage; be of comfort, man,
    And seeke some other; others thou mayest finde
    As true, as this is cruell, and unkinde.   20
Am. Alas, how weary' a worke were it for me
    Other to seeke, that cannot finde my selfe;
    And having lost my selfe what can I gaine
    With busie'st search that shall requite the paine?
Thir. Dispaire not yet, unhappy though thou bee,   25
    Shee may in time relent, and pitty thee:
    Time makes the Tygar and the Lion tame.
Am. O but so long to hope and be delaid,
    Is worse then death to one in miserie.
Thir. Perhaps thy suffrance shall not long endure;   30
    For mayds so' inconstant ar of disposition,
    That as th'ar soone at odds, th'ar as soone wonne;
    Uncertaine as the leafe blowne with each winde,
    And flexible as is the bladed grasse.
    But, gentle Shepherd, let me crave to know   35
    More throughly thy loves hard condition;
    For though I've often heard thee say thou lov'st,

Thou never tould'st me yet, who' twas thou lov'st;
And well it fitts the nearenesse of our lives,
And frendship, that such counsayls should be none   40
Betweene us two, but free to both, as one.

Am. Thirsis, I am content to ope to thee
What the woods, hills, and flouds ar privy to,
But no man knowes: so neere, alas, I finde
Th' approaching period of this loathéd breath,   45
That reason 'tis I leave some one behinde,
That may relate th' occasion of my death,
And leave it written on some Beech-tree barke,
Necre where my bloudlesse carkasse shall be lay'd;
That as the cruell Faire shall passe along,   50
She may at pleasure spurne with her proud foote
The unhappy bones,
And smiling say, loe here, loe where he lyes,
The triumph and the trophey of mine eyes;
And (to encrease her fame) rejoyce to see   55
In my sad ende her beauties victory
Knowne to the Nimphes, and Shepherds farr and neere,
Whom the report may thither guide; perhaps
(Ah, hopes too high) shee may bestow a sigh,
And though too late, with some compassion rue   60
The losse of him dead, whom shee living slue,
And wish he liv'd againe. But I digresse.

Thir. On with thy story, for I long to heare 't;
Perhaps to better ende then thou supposest.

Am. Being but a Lad, so young as yet scarse able   65
To reach the fruit from the low-hanging boughes
Of new growne trees, inward I grew to bee
With a young mayde, fullest of love and sweetnesse,
That ere display'd pure gold tresse to the winde;
Thou know'st her mother hight Cidippe, no?   70
Montano the rich Goteheard is her father.
Silvia, faire Silvia, 'tis I meane, the glory
Of all these woods, and flame of every heart;
'Tis shee, 'tis she I speake of; long, alas,
Liv'd I so neare her, and then lov'de of her,   75
As like two turtles each in other joy'de;
Neere our abodes, and neerer were our hearts;
Well did our yeares agree, better our thoughts;
Together wove we netts t' intrapp the fish

In flouds and sedgy fleetes; together sett   80
Pitfalls for birds; together the pye'd Buck
And flying Doe over the plaines we chac'de;
And in the quarry', as in the pleasure shar'de;
But as I made the beasts my pray, I found
My heart was lost, and made a pray to other.   85
By little' and little in my breast beganne
To spring, I know not from what hidden roote
(Like th' herbe that of it selfe is seene to growe)
A strange desire, and love still to be neere
And hourely drinke from the faire Silvias eyes   90
A sweetnesse past all thought, but it had still
(Me thought) a bitter farewell; oft I sigh'd,
Yet knew no cause I had to sigh; and so
Became betimes a lover, ere I knewe
What love meant; but, alas, I knewe too soone;   95
And in what sort, marke, and I'le tell thee.
Thir.   Onn.
Am. All in the shade of a broad Beech-tree sitting,
   Silvia, Phillis, and my selfe together;
   A Bee, that all about the flowry mede
   Had hunny gathred, flew to Phillis cheeke;   100
   The rosie cheeke mistaking for a rose,
   And there (belike) his little needle left.
   Phillis cryes out, impatient of the paine
   Of her sharp sting, but th' ever-lovely Silvia
   Bad her be patient; Phillis (said shee) peace,   105
   And with a word or two I'le heale thy hurt
   And take the sting, and soothe the griefe away;
   This secret erst the grave Aretia taught mee,
   And her I gave (in recompence) the horne
   Of Ivory tipt with gould I wont to were;   110
   This said, the lips of her faire sweetest mouth
   Upon th' offended cheeke she laid; and straite,
   (O strange effect) whether with the sound it were
   Of her soft murmur'd verse of Magick powre,
   Or rather (as I rather doe beleeve)   115
   The vertue of her mouth,
   That what it toucheth cures, Phillis was cur'de,
   And with the paine soone was the swelling gone.
   I, that till then ne're dream't of more delight,
   Then on the shine of her bright eyes to gaze,   120

And joy to heare her speake, (musique more sweete,
Then makes the murmur of a slow pac'de brooke,
When tis with thousand little pebbles crost;
Or the winde prattling 'mongst the wanton leaves)
Gan then, ev'n then to feele a new desire   125
Possesse me, of touching those deare lips with mine;
And growne more suttle then I was before,
(So love perhaps th' imagination whets,)
I found this new deceipt, whereby to' aspire
With greater ease to th' end of my desire;   130
I faynde my selfe stung on the nether lip
In like sort with a Bee as Phillis was;
And in such manner gan to moane my selfe,
As th' helpe my tongue crav'd not, my lookes implored;
The harmlesse Silvia, pittying strait my case,   135
Offred her ready cure to my fayn'd hurt;
But th' unfayn'd wound I bleede of, deeper made,
And farre more deadly, when those corall twinnes
On mine shee layd. Nor do the greedy Bees
Gather from any flowre honey so sweete,   140
As I did from those freshest roses gather;
Though bashfull shame, and feare had taught to barre
Hot kisses from desire to presse too farre,
T' imbathe themselves; and did their heate withholde
And kill, or made them slower and lesse bolde.   145
But while downe to my heart that sweetnesse glided,
Mixt with a secret poyson, such delight
I inly felt, that faigning still the griefe
Of the sting had not left me yet; so dealt,
That shee the charme repeated sundry times.   150
Since when till now, still more and more I finde,
For all her charme, she' has left the sting behinde.
Whose paine ere since hath so increas'd upon me,
As my love-labouring breast could hold no longer,
But that upon a time, when divers Nymphes   155
And Shepherds of us in a ring were sitting,
Whilst the play was, each one should softly whisper
Some word in th' eare of her that next him sat;
Silvia (quoth I soft in her eare) for thee
I pine, and dye, unlesse thou pitty mee.   160
No sooner heard she this, but downe she hangs
The faire looke, whence I might perceive to breake

A suddaine and unwonted ruddinesse,
That seem'd to breathe forth anger mixt with shame;
Now would shee' in other language answer mee,   165
Then such a troubled silence, as appear'd
Threatning and deadly; nor since then would ever
Willingly see, or heare me. Thrise the Sunne
His yearly course hath runne, thrise the greene fields
Hath the nak'd Sythman barb'd; and three times hath   170
The Winter rob'd the trees of their greene Lockes,
That I have tryde all meanes I could, t' appease her,
And nought remaines, but that I dye to please her;
And gladly would I dye, were I but sure
'Twould either please, or but drawe pitty from her;   175
Each were a blessing to mee, though no doubt
Her pitty were of both the greater meede.
And worthyer recompense for all my love,
And for my death; yet I were loth to wish
Ought that too rudely might those eyes molest,   180
Or do the least offence to that deare brest.
Thir. Did she but heare thus much from thee, bcleev'st thou
It would not make her love, or pitty thee?
Am. I neither knowe, nor can I hope so much.
She flyes my speech, as th' Adder doth the charme.   185
Thir. Well, be of comfort; my minde gives mee yet
Wee'll finde a mcane that she shall heare thee speak.
Am. 'Twill come to nought; to begg such grace were vaine,
For mee to speake, where speech no grace will gaine.
Thir. For shame dispaire not thus.
Am.   Alas, just cause   190
Bids mee dispaire; my cruell destinie
Was read by the grave Mopso long agon,
Mopso that knowes the hid language of birds,
And understands the force of herbs and founts.
Thir. What Mopso's this thou speak'st on? Is't not he   195
That carryes honey in his supple tongue,
And friendly smiles for all he lookes upon,
But in his heart deceipt, and hidden beares
Under his coate a rasor? Shame befall him;
The vilde unlucky doomes he lewdly sells   200
To silly fooles with that grave looke, and grace,
Ar farr from trueth; take 't of my word, and triall.
I'le rather hope (and sure my hope will thrive)

That from this fellowes ydle auguryes
Much happyer fate will to thy love arise.   205
Am. If ought by proofe thou know'st of him, good swayne
   Hyde it not from me.
Thir.   Ile tell thee willingly.
   When first my hap led mee to know these woods,
   I knew this fellow, and esteeméd him
   As thou do'st. So it fortun'd once, I had   210
   Desire and bus'nesse to go see the great
   Wonder of Citties, at whose ancient feete
   The broad-fam'd river runnes; and him I made
   Acquainted with my purpose; he replyes,
   And thus began to preach. My sonne, beware   215
   Now thou art going to that seate of fame,
   Where those deceiptfully crafty Cittizens,
   And evill minded Courtiers live, and wont
   To scoffe at us, and hould in such a scorne
   Our plaine distrustlesse homely carriage;   220
   Be well adviz'd (my sonne) and presse not there
   Where the fresh colour'd robes with gould ar wrought,
   Gay plumes, and dayly-varied dressings shine;
   But above all, beware accurséd Fate,
   Or thy youths jollity conduct thee not   225
   Unto that magazine of restlesse chatt,
   But flye that curséd and inchaunted place.
   What place is that (quoth I)? 'Tis there (said he)
   Where dwell th' inchantresses that have the powre
   And arte to make men, and their minds transparent;   230
   And what so Diamonds seeme, and finest gold,
   But glasse and copper ar; those silver chestes
   That seeme full of rich treasor ar no more
   Then kennells full of filth, and cozen men;
   The walles ar built too with that wondrous arte,   235
   That they will speake, and answer them that speake;
   Nor in halfe words, and such imperfect sounds,
   As wont the Eccos that heere haunt our grounds,
   But ev'ry word whole, and entyre repeating.
   Nay, more then this, the tables, chaires, and stooles,   240
   Hangings, and all that to each roome belongs,
   Have toung and voice, and never silent ar;
   False-lyes there, formde into the shape of babes,
   Ar hopping all about; and be he dumbe

That enters there, findes straite a tongue to prate   245
And lye with; but there is yet worse then this
May happen thee; thou mayst perhaps be turn'd
Into a beast, a tree, a floud, a flame,
Into a floud of teares, a fire of sighes.
All this he tould mee; and I forward went   250
To see the Cittie with this false beliefe;
And (as good happ would have it) chaunc'd to passe
Along the place where stands that blessed dwelling,
Whence I might heare breath out such melody,
By Swans, and Nimphes, and heav'nly Syrens made,   255
With voyce so shrill, so sweet and full of pleasure,
That all amaz'd, I stay'd to gaze, and listen.
Before the doore there stood (mee seem'd) as guard
Of the faire showes within, a man in showe
And of proportion stout, and knightly hue;   260
Such as (for what he seem'd me) made me doubt
Whether for Armes he were, or counsaile fitter.
With a benigne, and milde, though grave aspéct,
He highly-faire bespake, and led me in;
He great in place, mee poore and homely man.   265
But then, what did I see? What did I heare?
Celestiall goddesses, and lovely Nimphes,
New lights, new *Orpheuses;* and others too
Unvayl'd, unclouded, as the virgin-morne
When silver dewes her golden rayes adorne.   270
There *Phœbus* shone, inlightning all about,
With all his sister Muses; among whom
Satt Elpine; at which sight, all in a trice
I felt my selfe growe greater then my selfe,
Full of new powre, full of new deity!   275
And sang of warres, and Knightly deedes in Armes,
Scorning the rurall Songs I wont to make;
And though I after did (for others pleasure)
Turne to these woods againe, yet I retaynde
Part of that Spirit; nor yet sounds my pipe   280
So lowly as before, but shriller farr.
And through the woods rings with a trumpets voyce.
Afterward Mopso heard me'; and with so vilde,
And sowre a count'nance greeted mee, that I
Became straighte hoarce, and was a long time mute;   285
When all the Shepherds said, sure I had bin

Scar'd with the Wolfe; but Mopso was the Wolfe.
This I have tould thee, that thou mayst beleeve
How little this mans words deserve beliefe;
And out of doubt, th' hast the more cause to hope,   290
For that this fellow bids thee not to hope.
Am. I'me glad to heare this troth of him; but now
I leave my life, and my lives care to you.
Thir. Feare not, 'tis all my care to cure thy paine:
Within this houre see thou be here againe.   295

CHORUS.

O Happy Age of Gould, happy' houres;
Not for with milke the rivers ranne,
And hunny dropt from ev'ry tree;
Nor that the Earth bore fruits and flowres,
Without the toyle or care of Man,   5
And Serpents were from poyson free;
    Nor for th' Ayre (ever calme to see)
Had quite exil'de the lowring Night;
Whilst clad in an eternall Spring
(Now fiery hott, or else freezing)   10
The cheekes of heav'n smil'de with cleare light;
Nor that the wandring Pine of yore
Brought neither warres, nor wares from forraine shore;
    But therefore only happy Dayes,
Because that vaine and ydle name,   15
That couz'ning Idoll of unrest,
(Whom the madd vulgar first did raize,
And call'd it *Honour*, whence it came
To tyrannize or'e ev'ry brest,)
    Was not then suffred to molest   20
Poore lovers hearts with new debate;
More happy they, by these his hard
And cruell lawes, were not debar'd
Their innate freedome; happy state;
The goulden lawes of Nature, they   25
Found in their brests; and then they did obey.
    Amidd the silver streams and floures,
The winged Genii then would daunce,
Without their bowe, without their brande;

The Nymphes sate by their Paramours,   30
Whispring love-sports, and dalliance,
And joyning lips, and hand to hand;
   The fairest Virgin in the land,
Nor scorn'de, nor glor'yed to displaye
Her cheeks fresh roses to the eye,   35
Or ope her faire brests to the day,
(Which now adayes so vailéd lye,)
But men and maydens spent free houres
In running Rivers, Lakes, or shady Bowres.
   Thou, *Honour*, thou didst first devize   40
To make the face of Pleasure thus;
Barr water to the thirst of Love,
And lewdly didst instruct faire eyes
They should be nyce, and scrupulous,
And from the gazing world remoove   45
   Their beauties; thy hands new netts wove
T' intrap the wilde curles, faire dispred
To th' open ayre; thou mad'st the sweet
Delights of Love seeme thus unmeete;
And (teaching how to looke, speake, tread,)   50
By thy ill lawes this ill hast left,
That what was first Loves gift is now our theft.
   Nor ought thy mighty working brings
But more annoyes, and woe to us;
But thou (of Nature and of Love   55
The Lord, and scourge of mighty Kings,)
Why do'st thou shrowde thy greatnesse thus
In our poore cells? Hence, and remoove
Thy powre; and it display above,
   Disturbing great ones in their sleepe;   60
And let us meaner men alone
T' injoye againe (when thou art gone),
And lawes of our Forefathers keepe.
Live we in love, for our lives houres
Hast on to death, that all at length devoures.   65
   Love we while we may; the wayne
Of Heav'n can set, and rise againe;
But we (when once we looze this light)
Must yeeld us to a never ending Night.

ACTUS SECUNDUS Scena Prima

SATYR *solus.*

Small is the Bee, but yet with his small sting
Does greater mischiefe then a greater thing.
But what of all things can be lesse then Love,
That through so narrow passages can pierce,
And in so narrow roome lye hid? Sometime   5
Under the shaddow of an eye-lids fault,
Now in the small curle of a shining tresse,
Now in the little pitts which forme sweet smiles
In an inamo'ring cheeke, yet makes so deepe,
So deadly and immedicable wounds.   10
Ay me, my brest is all one bleeding wound
A thousand arméd darts, alas, are lodg'd
By that fell tyrant Love in Silvia's eyes;
Cruell Love, cruell Silvia, savadger
Then the wilde desarts; O how well thy name   15
Sutes with thy nature (Silvan as thou art):
The woods under their greene roofes hide the Snake,
The Beare, the Lyon, and thou in thy brest
Hydest disdaine, hate, and impietie,
More baleful then the Lion, Beare, or Snake;   20
For they will some way be reclaim'de; thou neither
With prayers or gifts. Alas, when I present thee
Fresh floures, thou frowardly refusest them;
Perhaps because th' hast in thy lovely face
Fairer then those. Alas, when I present thee   25
Faire Apples, thou do'st scornfully reject them;
Perhaps because thy bosome beares a paire
Fairer then those. Ay mee, when I present thee
Sweet honey, thou disdainfully deny'st it,
Perhaps because thy lips breathe sweeter honey   30
Then the Bee makes; but if my poverty
Can give thee nought that thou hast not more faire,
And lovely in thy selfe, my selfe I give thee;
But thou, unjust, scorn'st, and abhorr'st the gift.
Yet I'me not so fowle to be so dispizde,   35
If well I mark'd my selfe when th' other day
I view'd my shadowe in the watry mayne,
When the winde blew not, and the sea lay still.
The manly tincture of my sanguine brow,

These muscled armes, and shoulders large enough;   40
This hairy brest of mine, and hory thyes
Proclaime my able force, and manlyhood.
Make triall of mee if thou doubt'st of it.
What wilt thou do with these same tenderlings,
On whose bare cheeke the young downe scarsely springs?   45
With what an art they place their haire in order!
Women in shew, and women in their strength.
Tell mee, who wilt thou have to follow thee
O're the bald hills, and through the leavy woods,
And fight for thee with Beare, and arméd Bore?   50
No, no, my shape's not it thou hat'st mee for,
But 'tis my poverty thou dost abhorre,
Ah, that poore Cottages will follow still
Great Townes example in what ere is ill.
This may be truely call'd the Golden age,   55
For gould alone prevailes, gould only raynes.
O thou (who ere thou wert) that first didst teach
To sell love thus, accurséd be thy dust;
And thy colde buried bones; nor ever may
Shepherd or Nimphe say to them, rest in peace;   60
But be they washt with raines, and tost with windes,
And may the passers by, and all the rout
Of beasts with fowle feete spurne them all about.
Base mercinary love, thou has deflour'd
Loves noblenesse; and turn'd his happy joyes   65
Into such bitternesse, and sharpe annoyes.
Love to be slave to golde? O miracle
More odious, and abominable farre
Then the large earth produces, or the Mayne.
But why, alas, why do I vexe my selfe   70
Thus all in vaine? No, let each creature use
Those armes that Nature for his ayde hath giv'n him,
The Hart his speede, the Lyon his strong pawe,
The foaming Bore his tuske; the womans armes
And powre lye in her beauty', and gracefull shape;   75
I, since my strength is the best helpe I have,
And am by nature fit for deedes of force,
Will for reward of all my love mispent,
Force this proud cruell to my owne content.
And by so much as I can understand,   80
(As yon Goteherd that hath observ'd her wayes

Hath lately tolde me) she doth oft repaire
To' a water-fount to wash her selfe; the place
He made me knowe, and there I meane to lye
Close in a thickett neere, t' attend her comming,   85
And as occasion fits, I'le make her myne.
What can she do then, what avayle, alas,
Can her hands give her, or her leggs to flye
(Poore wretch) from me so forcible, and swift?
Let her a good yeere weepe, and sigh, and rayle,   90
And put on all the powre her beauty hath;
If once I catch her by the snary curles,
We will not part in hast, till I have bath'd
(For my revenge) my armes in her warme bloud.

ACTUS SECUNDUS Scena Secunda

DAPHNE. THIRSIS.

[Da.] Thirsis (as I have tolde thee) well I knowe
How well Aminta Silvia loves; heav'n knowes
How many friendly offices I have,
And will do for him; and so much the rather
For that thou do'st intreate in his behalfe;   5
But I would sooner take in hand to tame
A Beare, or Tygar then a fond young wench;
The silly thing (simple as faire) sees not
How sharpe and burning be her beauties rayes,
But smiles or cries; yet wounds where ere shee goe   10
And fondly knowes not if shee hurt or no.
Thir. Tush, there's no wench so simple but she knowes
Soone as shee leaves the cradle, how to seeme
Spruce and delightfull; and what armes to use
To hurte, or kill outright, and what to heale   15
A wounded heart, and give it life withall.
Da. What Master is't that shewes 'hem all these arts?
Thir. He that instructs the birds to sing and flye;
The Fish to swimme, the Ramme to butt, the Bull
To use his horne, the Peacocke to display   20
His many-ey'ed-plumes beautie to the day.
Da. How name you this same teacher?
Thir.   H' has a name.
Da. Go, trifler.

Thir.   Why, I pre'thee, art not thou
   Fitt enough to teach twenty girles their lessons?
   I'le warrant thee, I; and yet to speake the troth   25
   They neede no teacher; Nature teacheth them
   Although the nurse and mother have a part.
Da. Come y'ar unhappy; but in earnest now
   I'me not resolv'd Silvia so simple is
   As by her words she seemes; for th' other day   30
   One deede of hers put me in doubt of her.
   I found her in those broad fields neere the towne,
   Where amongst drown'de grounds lies a little Isle,
   And round about, a water cleare and calme;
   There o're she hung her head; and seem'd (me thought)   35
   Full proud to see her self; and tooke advice
   O' th' water, in what order best to lay
   Her locks, and then about her brow display,
   And over them her vaile, and over that
   The flowres shee carried in her lapp; now heere   40
   She hung a Lilly, there shee stuck a Rose;
   Then layd them to her neck, and to her cheeke,
   As to try whethers hew the other past;
   At last (as joyfull of the victory)
   Shee smiling seem'd to say, the day is mine;   45
   Nor do I weare you for my ornament,
   But for your owne disgrace (counterfait floures)
   To shew how much my beauty passeth yours.
   But while shee thus stood decking of her selfe,
   Shee turn'd her eye by chance, and soone had found   50
   That I had noted her, and blusht a mayne,
   Downe fell her flowres; I laught to see her blush;
   And she blusht more, perceiving that I laught;
   But (for of one side of her face, the haire
   Was hung abroad, and th' other not), shee turnes   55
   To th' water once or twice, to mend the fault,
   And gaz'd as 'twere by stealth (fearfull belike
   That I too neerly ey'd her), where she sawe
   Her haire (though orderlesse, yet) hanging so
   As grac'd her well; I saw, and saw her not.   60
Thir. All this I will beleeve; guest I not well?
Da. Thou didst; but yet I will be bolde to say
   That I have seldome seene a Shepherdesse
   Or Nimph whatever of her yeares discreeter;

Nor was I such when I was of her yeares.   65
The world growes olde, and of a troth I thinke
It growes as ill as olde.
Thir.   True; heretofore
Those of the Cittie were not wont so much
To haunt these woods as now adayes they do,
Nor meaner people in the village bredd,   70
To come so much among the cittizens;
Their blouds are now more mingled, and their customes.
But leave we this discourse; and tell me now
Could'st thou not finde a time Aminta might
Either alone, or in thy presence come   75
To speake to Silvia?
Da.   I cannot tell;
Silvia is nyce and strange beyond all measure.
Thir. And he nicely respectfull beyond measure.
Da. He's i' the wrong then; fye on such a lover;
Nice (quoth you?) counsel him to leave that vice,   80
If he will learne to love, he must be bould,
And urge with speeding importunitie;
Let him a little filtch; if that be vaine,
Then ravish; tush, know'st thou what women ar?
They flye but ev'ry step wish to be tane;   85
What they denie, they wish were snatch from them;
They fight, but still wish to be overcome.
I tell thee this, Thirsis, but in thine eare:
Blabb not what I' say to thee'; I cannot speake
In rime (thou know'st) but if I could, I'de say   90
Somewhat more worth then rime to beare away.
Thir. Feare not, I will not speake
Ought from thy lips what ere they ope to me.
But, gentle Daphne, for the deare dayes sake
Of thy past youth, helpe me to helpe Aminte   95
Poore wretch that dyes.
Da.   Ah, what a propper stile
Of conjuration (foole) hast thou deviz'd
To moove me with: bringing my youth to minde,
The pleasures I have lost, and paine I finde.
But what would'st have me doe?   100
Thir. Th' art not to seeke of wit, not yet of powre,
Do but dispose thy will, I'le aske no more.
Da. Well then, I'le tell thee: wee ar going now,

Silvia and I together all alone
Unto Diana's fount, to wash our selves;   105
There where the planetree with his safer shade
Ore-spreds the coole streame, and is wont t' invite
The weary huntresses to rest, and coole them.
There shee'll uncase her so-belovéd limbs.
Thir. And what of that?
Da.   What of that? Th' art silly   110
Or else thou would'st not aske me, what of that.
Thir. Suppose I hit thy meaning, who knowes yet
If he will dare to meete her there or no?
Da. No? Why then truely let him stay till shee
Come to wooe him; and when will that be trow yee?   115
Thir. Do shee or not, he does deserve shee did.
Da. But now let's leave this theame, and talk a word
Or two of thee; say, Thirsis, wilt not thou
Resolve at last to be a lover too?
Th' art not yet olde; fewe more then thirty yeeres   120
Have over-slipt thee, and I well remember
Thy infancie; will thou live joylesse still?
For only' a lovers is the happy life.
Thir. The joyes of Venus he injoyes as well,
That shunning lovers painfull miseries,   125
Tastes of the sweet, and lets the sowre alone.
Da. O but that sweet growes dull, and gluts betime,
That is not seas'ned with a little sowre.
Thir. Better 'tis to be glutted (of the two)
Then pine before one feedes, and after two.   130
Da. But if the foode be pleasing, and possest,
'Tis good before; and in the tasting best.
Thir. No man can so possesse what he desires,
As just t' injoy it then when's hunger craves it.
Da. Who hopes to finde, that never meanes to seeke?   135
Thir. 'Tis dangerous to seeke that which once found,
Pleases a little, but not found, torments
Much more; no, no, I'le go no more a wooing;
Cupid shall triumph over me no more;
I know a little what those sufferings be,   140
Let others proove them if they list for me.
Da. Belike th' hast not injoy'd loves pleasures yet.
Thir. Nor do I wish to buy the plague so deare.
Da. You may perhaps be forc'd against your will;

Thir. Who keepes himselfe farr off, cannot be forc'd.   145
Da. Who can be far from love?
Thir.   Who feares and flies.
Da. But what avayles to flye from him hath wings?
Thir. Love but new borne hath wings but short and small,
  And hardly strong enough to flye withall.
Da. Be'ing young, we know him not; but after, long;   150
  And when we feele him once, he's growne too strong.
Thir. Not if we never felt him grow before.
Da. Well, yee shall hav't; wee'll see how well you will
  Bridle your eye and heart; but I protest
  Since thou canst play both Hound and Hare so well,   155
  If ere I heare thee call and cry for helpe,
  I will not moove a foote, not yet a finger,
  Nor stirr an eye, nor speake a word for thee.
Thir. Would'st have the heart (cruell) to see me dye?
  If thou wouldst have me love, why love thou mee,   160
  And lett's now make a loving bargaine on 't.
Da. Away, you mocke me now; well, well, perhaps
  You do not merit such a love as mine.
  I've seene many a ladd as fine as you
  Deceiv'd with a faire seeming painted face.   165
Thir. I doe not jest nor mock thee; this is but
  A couler now to barr me loving thee,
  As 'tis the custome of you all to do.
  But if you will not love me, I'm content
  To live still as I do.
Da.   I, live so still,   170
  Happyer then twenty others; live in ease;
  Perhaps unwares ease may ingender love.
Thir. O Daphne, a God this ease hath bred mee; he
  That hath appear'd a second god to mee
  By whom so many heards and flocks ar fedd   175
  From th' one to th' other Sea, upon the faire
  And fruitfull Plaines, and on the craggy backs
  Of the steepe *Apenines;* he said to mee,
  When as he made me his; Thirsis (quoth he)
  Let others chase the Wolfe, and Thiefe, and keepe   180
  A watchfull eye over my wallèd sheepe;
  Let others care be to reward, or punish
  My Ministers; let others feede and tende
  My flocks, and keep the accoumpt of milke and wooll;

And take, and pay. Take thou thine ease, and sing.　　　185
Wherefore 'tis reason good, I let goe by
All looser straines, and vainer carrolings;
And sing his Auncesters, and their high praise,
Who is to me *Jove* and *Apollo* both;
Since in his lookes and deeds he both resembles　　　190
Issue of *Saturne* and of *Heav'ne.* Poore Muse
To meane for such a taske; and yet how e're
Horce voic'd, or clere she sings, he not contemns her.
I sing not him, too high for my lowe rimes,
Whom silent adoration only can　　　195
Worthily honour; but still shall his altars
Be sprinckled with my floures, and ne're without
My humble Incense fuming all about.
Which simple (yet devoute) religion in me
When it shall leave my heart, the Harts shall feede　　　200
In th' ayre on ayre; and so the flouds shall change
Their bedd, and course; that *Sone* shall *Persia* greete,
And the large *Tigris* beat the French-*Alpes* feete.
Da. O thou fly'st high; pre'thee descend a little,
And to our purpose.
Thir.　　　　　　　Then heere lyes the poynt;　　　205
That as thou go'st with her unto the fount,
Thou use thy best cunning to make her comming
And heare Aminta speake; meane time my care
Shall be to make Aminta meete you there.
I feare my taske will be the hard'st of both.　　　210
Onn then a' Gods name.
Da.　　　　　　　Yes, I goe; but Thirsis,
We were discoursing of an other matter.
Thir. If mine eye faile me not, yon same should be
Aminta, that comes hitherward; 'tis he.

ACTUS SECUNDUS Scena Tertia

AMINTA. THIRSIS.

[Am.] Now shall I see what Thirsi' has done for me;
And if he have done nothing, ere my woes
Melt me' into nothing, I'le go kill my selfe
Before the proud face of that cruell mayde,
That so delights to see my hearts deepe wound　　　5

Made by her murth'ring eyes, as sure it can
Please her no lesse, to see her sad command
Fulfill'd on my owne brest with my own hand.

Thir. Newes, newes, Aminta, happy newes I bring thee;
Cleare then thy browe, and cast thy griefes away. 10

Am. What is't thou sayst, Thirsis, what bringst thou me,
Life, or death? New joy, or new miserie?

Thir. I bring thee life and joy, if thou but dare
To goe and meet them; but I tell thee true
Thou must not faint but play the man, Aminta. 15

Am. Why against whom should I advance my force?

Thir. Suppose the Nymphe thou lov'st were in a wood
That (walde' about with mountaines of sharpe briars)
Were full of Tygars, and of greedy Lyons,
Wouldst thou go thither?

Am.   Yes, more cheerefully, 20
Then village-lasse to the daunce o' holly dayes.

Thir. Were she ingag'd 'mongst troopes of arméd theeves,
Wouldst thou goe thither?

Am.   Yes, more greedily,
Then runnes the thirstie Hart to the coole streeme.

Thir. O but a harder taske askes greater labour. 25

Am. Why, I would passe through the devouring torrents,
When the dissolv'de snowes downe the mountaines raine,
And headlong runne t' ingulph them in the mayne,
Or through the fire; or indeed downe to hell;
If any place a hell may terméd bee, 30
That shall containe so heav'nly a thing as shee.
But pre' thee, tell me all.

Thir.   Here then.

Am.   Say on.

Thir. Silvia' at a Fount, starnak'd, and all alone
Attends thy comming; dare'st thou now goe thither?

Am. Silvia? And all alone? And staies for me? 35

Thir. Yes, all alone, unlesse haply there bee
Daphne', who thou know'st is all in all for thee.

Am. Naked?

Thir.   I, naked, but—

Am.   But what? Ah, do not
Mangle me thus.

Thir.   Why but she does not knowe
That you should meete her there; though (as I say) 40

Shee'll there attend you, do but hast away.
Am. Bitter conclusion; that infects, and poysons
 What ever sweet thy former speeches promis'd
 Why with such art
 Do'st thou delude me, cruell as thou art?   45
 Is 't not enough
 Think'st thou for me thus full of griefe to be,
 But thou must come to mock my misery?
Thir. Be rul'd by me, Aminta, and be happy;
Am. What should I do?
Thir.   Why not let slip that good   50
 That fortune (much thy friend) presents thee with.
Am. The heav'ns forbid that ever I should do
 Ought to displease her; nor yet ever did I
 The thing that justly merited her frowne,
 Unlesse it were my loving her so much;   55
 Which yet if 'twere a fault, was none of mine;
 It was her beauties; and by heav'n I vowe
 I meane not to begin to' offend her now.
Thir. Why but yet tell me, if 'twere in thy powre
 To leave to love her, wouldst thou do 't to please her?   60
Am. No, sure; love will not let me say, or thinke
 That ere I should desist from loving her,
 Though 'twere in my owne powre.
Thir.   Why an't be so,
 In her dispight whether she will or no,
 Youl'd love her.
Am.   No, no, not in spight of her,   65
 But I would love her.
Thir.   Yet against her will?
Am. Why, yes, against her will.
Thir.   And wherefore then
 Dare you not take of her against her will,
 That which (although 't erkes thee at first to doo)
 In th' end will quite thy paines and please her too.   70
Am. Thirsis, let love that speakes within my brest
 Make answer for me; thou (through thy long use
 Of reas'ning much of love), too suttle art
 For me; love tyes my tongue, who tyed my heart.
Thir. Why then thou wilt not goe?
Am.   Yes, yes, I'le goe;   75
 But not where you would have me.

Thir.   Whether then?
Am. To death, if this be all y' have done for me.
Thir. Is this that I have done then nothing worth?
   And do'st thou thinke Daphne would counsaile thee
   To goe, unlesse shee saw a little more   80
   Into thy Silvias heart, then thou and I?
   Suppose shee has reveal'd her minde to her;
   Thinke you shee would abide that any else
   Should know 't? Or know she knew it ere the more?
   So that to covet an expresse consent   85
   On her part, thinke you not it were to seek
   What in all reason must offend her most?
   Where's this your care then, and desire to please her?
   Perhaps shee would that your delight should bee
   Your owne theft, not her gift; what skil' t I pray.   90
   Whether you have it this, or th' other way?
Am. What certainty' have I that her minde is such?
Thir. See still how sillily you seeke to have
   That certainty which must of force displease her;
   And which 'bove all things else you should not crave.   95
   But who assures you to the contrary
   But that she may meane so as well as not?
   Now if shee did, and that you would not goe;
   (Since both the doubts and dangers equall be)
   Is not a valiant then a base death better?   100
   Th' art mute; th' art overthrowne;
   Confesse it then.
   Nor doubt but this thy overthrow will bee
   Th' occasion of a greater victorie.
   Go' we.
Am.   Stay.
Thir.   Why stay?   105
   Know'st not how swiftly the time runnes away?
Am. Pre'thee lett's thinke first what, and how to doe.
Thir. Wee'll thinke of all things as we goe, but he
   That thinks too much, does little, commonly.

CHORUS.

   O Love, of whom, and where is taught
   This thy so doubtfull Arte, and long

Of loving, that instructs the tounge
At ease to utter ev'ry thought
That the wilde fant'sie doth devize   5
Whilst with thy wings above the heav'n it flyes?
   The learned *Athens* taught it not;
Nor was it to *Liceus* knowne;
Apollo, god of *Helicon*
For all his knowledge knew it not.   10
Faint and colde is what he speakes,
Nor from his voice such a fire breakes
As doth thy greatnesse (Love) befitt.
   Nor can his witt,
Or thoughts unto the height arise   15
Of thy profounder misteries.
Thou readst thy owne lesson best
(Great Love) and onely' art by thy selfe exprest.
Thou of thy grace and bounty daynest
T' instruct th' unlearnedest, and plainest   20
Men of thousands, how to see
And reade these wondrous things that he
Writ with thine owne hand in an others eyes.
   That teachest those thou lovest best,
A purer language then the rest,   25
And with smoth ease to breath their fantasies.
Nay often times, such is thy rare
And most misterious eloquence,
That in a confusd'e broken sence
And halfe words that imperfect are,   30
The heart is best reveal'd and seene;
   And such perhaps moove more by farr
Then many words that better polisht beene.
Yea, ev'ne Loves silences oft doth more expresse
Then words could doe the mindes unhappinesse.   35
   (Love) let others if they please
Turne ore the workes of *Socrates,*
And these great volumes of the wise,
While I but reade what's writ in two faire eyes.
   Perhaps the penn that higher climes,   40
Will but halt after the rimes
That in the rough and uncooth tree
With my rude artlesse hand ingraven bee.

ACTUS TERTIUS Scena Prima

THIRSIS. CHORUS.

[Thir.] O Savadge cruelty'; O th' ungratefull minde
 Of a most most ungratefull Mayde; O Sexe
 Full of ingratitude; and thou lewd Nature,
 Negligent mistresse, and maker of things,
 Wherefore, ah, wherefore mad'st thou womankinde   5
 So faire, and sweet, and milde onely without,
 And didst forget to make their insides good?
 Poore youth, I feare 'has made away himselfe
 Ere this; alas, I cannot finde him out.
 Three houres from place to to place, and wher I left him 10
 Have I bin seeking him; but cannot finde
 Or him, or any print of his strai'd foot:
 Sure, sure hee's dead.
 I will goe aske yon Swaines I see, if they
 Can tell me any tyings of him. Friends,   15
 Did you not see Aminta', or happly heare
 Newes of him lately?
Cho.   Thou dost seeme to me
 Full of distraction; what is 't troubles thee?
 How cam'st thou so' out of breath, and to sweat so?
 What ayl'st thou? Say what is' t thou fear'st or wantest. 20
Thir. I feare Amintas harmes; tell me I pray
 Saw yee him not?
Cho.   Not since he went with you
 Awhile agon; but what d' yee feare in him?
Thir. Alas, I feare
 Lest he have slaine himselfe with his owne hand. 25
Cho. Slaine with his owne hand? How so? What might cause
 Such vengeance on himselfe?
Thir.   Why love, and hate.
Cho. Two powerfull enemies:
 What cannot they doe when they meet together?
 But speake yet clearer.   30
Thir. His too much love, and her too much disdaine
 Whom he lov'd so.
Cho.   Ah, tell thy story out;
 This is a way of passage, and ere long
 Perhaps some one will bring us newes of him,
 Or himselfe come.

Thir.   I'le tell it willingly;   35
   For 'tis not just that such ingratitude
   Should rest without the due deservéd blame.
   Aminta heard (and I had told it him,
   And was his conduct too, the gods forgive mee)
   That Silvia was with Daphne gone to' a Founte   40
   To wash themselves; thither then (not without
   A thousand doubts and feares in him) we went;
   And twenty times we turn'd againe (his heart
   Being all against it), but that I was faine
   Almost against his will to force him onn;   45
   But drawing neere unto the Fount, we heard
   A sadd lamenting voice; and all at once
   Daphne wee spy'de wringing her hands, and straite
   Seeing us comming, Ah runne, runne (she cryes)
   Silvia's deflowr'd. Th' inamoured Aminta   50
   No sooner heard it, but swift as a Pard
   He flung away; and I made after him.
   Nor farre we went, when loe before our eyes
   We saw the young mayde nak'd as at her birth,
   Fast fettred by the faire haire to a tree;   55
   About whose branches in a thousand knotts
   The curles were link'd, and entertwind'de; the girdle
   That wont to decke, and guard her mayden loynes,
   Serv'd as an actor in her ravishment;
   Binding her armes about the trees hard trunke,   60
   The tree it selfe became a helper too,
   For by her feete a branch or two grew out,
   Which (easie bending) both her tender leggs
   Had fastned to the tree; and face to face
   A beastly Satyr stood, who but ev'ne then   65
   Had newly made an ende of binding her,
   All the defence shee could (poore soule) shee made;
   But sure 'twould have but little steeded her,
   Had not we come. Aminta with his dart
   Flue like a Lyon   70
   Upon the Satyr; and I gathered stones,
   Whereat he fledd, and gave Aminta leisure
   To feast his greedy eyes with her faire limbes,
   Which trembling seem'd as tender, white, and soft,
   As unprest curds new from the whey divided.   75
   Full was her face of anger, griefe, and spight;

He gently accosting her with modest lookes,
Spake thus: O lovely Silvia, pardon me;
Pardon my hands for daring to approache
So neere these beauteous limbes of thine; alas   80
It is necessity inforceth them,
Necessitie t' unloose these bands of thine;
And let it (I beseech thee) not displease thee,
That Fate has rais'd them to this happinesse.
Cho. Words that would mollifie a heart of flint;   85
   But what reply made shee?
Thir.   Why, none at all.
   But with a looke full of disdaine, hung downe
   The head, and hidd her faire lapp all shee could;
   He stood unbrayding her intangled tresses,
   And sighing said (the whiles), O how unworthy   90
   Is this rude trunke of so faire knots as these?
   See what advantage have Loves votaries,
   That (like this tree) have with so pretious bands
   Their hearts entwin'd: Cruell plant, couldst thou see
   This haire thus injur'd, that thus honours thee?   95
   Then with his hands her bands he faire unlooz'd,
   In such a sort, as that he seem'd affraide
   To touch them, yet desir'd to touch them still.
   Then stoup'd he downe t' untye her feet; when shee
   Finding her late bound hands at libertie,   100
   Said with a scornefull, and disdayning looke;
   Shepherd, I am *Diana's;* touch me not;
   Leave me, I shall unbinde my feete my selfe.
Cho. Ah, that the soft brest of a mayde should harbor
   Such pride. O Curtesie full ill repayde.   105
Thir. Straite he with reverence withdrew himselfe,
   Not lifting once his eyes to looke on her;
   Barring himselfe of his delight, that shee
   Might lay no blame on his immodestie.
   I that was hid neere hand, and saw all this,   110
   And heard it all, was ev'ne exclaiming on her
   But that I curb'd my selfe; see the strange creature,
   After she was with much adoe got loose,
   Away shee hurryed strait, swift as a Doe,
   Without so much as Thanke yee, or farewell;   115
   And yet knew well, shee had no cause to feare;
   So modest and respectfull was Aminta.

Cho. Why fled she then?

Thir.　　　　　　　Perhaps she thought it shew'd
　　Better; and argued more her modestie.

Cho. Her foule ingratitude; but what did then,　　　　120
　　What said the poore Aminta?

Thir.　　　　　　　I cannot tell.
　　For (angry) after her I ranne amaine
　　To have oretane, and staid her; but in vaine;
　　For soone I lost her; and againe returning
　　Unto the Fountaine where I left Aminta,　　　　125
　　I found him not; and my heart much misgives me
　　Of some selfe ill befalne him; for I knowe
　　He was resolv'd (before this hapned him)
　　To ende his life and miseries together.

Cho. It is the common use and art of Lovers　　　　130
　　To threaten their owne deaths; but rarely shall
　　We see th' effect in any of them all.

Thir. Pray heav'ne he be not of those rare ones then.

Cho. Tush, feare him not.

Thir.　　　　　　　Well, I'le downe to the Cave
　　Of the sage Elpine; thither he perhaps　　　　135
　　Will be retyr'de, if he be yet alive;
　　For there he wont full oft to' allay and ease
　　The rage of his bitter calamities,
　　With the sweet sound of Elpines Reeds, that winn
　　And draw with their alluring voice to heare them,　　　　140
　　The hard stones from the craggy mountaine topps;
　　Make flouds and waterfounts runne with pure milke;
　　And oft the rough bark'd trees against their kindes
　　Distill sweet honny from their bitter rindes.

ACTUS TERTIUS Scena Secunda

AMINTA. DAPHNE. NERINA.

[Am.] Pittilesse (Daphne), was that Pitty of thine,
　　When thou held'st backe the dart, because my death
　　Will but more painefull be, the more delay'de:
　　And now, why doest thou stay me trifling thus,
　　And hold me' in vaine with these thy long discourses?　　　　5
　　If thou beest fearefull of my death, thou fear'st
　　My happinesse.

Da.   Leave, leave, Aminta,
  This thy unjust despaire: I know her well;
  And 'twas her bashfulnesse, not cruelty,
  That made her runne away so fast from thee.   10
Am. Ah, that my onely friend must be Dispaire,
  Seeing that onely Hope hath bredd my ruyne:
  And yet it would be breeding in my brest
  Againe, and bid me live; when, what can bee
  A greater ill to so great misery,   15
  Then still to live, but to be still unhappy?
Da. Why, live yet, live with thy unhappines;
  And beare it for thy greater happines
  When the times comes; think what thou lately saw'st
  In the faire naked one, and let that serve thee   20
  For a reward sufficient for thy hope,
  And make thee in love with life.
Am.   'Twas not enough
  For love, and fortune, that I was before,
  So wretched, as I scarsly could be more;
  But that I must be shew'd (t' augment my ill)   25
  Part of my blisse, yet go without it still.
Ner. Must I be then the Raven, and sinister
  Relater of so bitter newes? O wretched,
  Wretched Montano; ah, what wilt thou do,
  When thou shalt heare the sad, and killing story   30
  Of thy owne only Silvia? Poore olde man,
  Most haplesse father of a hapless childe;
  Ah, now no father.
Da.   I doe heare a sad
  Lamenting voyce.
Am.   I heare the name of Silvia,
  That strikes mine eare, and my heart through at once,   35
  But who is' t names her?
Da.   'Tis I thinke the Nimphe
  Nerina, she whom *Dian* loves so well,
  That hast so lively eyes and lovely hands,
  And so becomming a behaviour.
Ner. Yet he shall know it; and go gather up   40
  Th' unhappy reliques (if yet any be);
  Ah, Silvia, Silvia, O accurséd fate.
Am. Ay mee, what meanes this Nimph? What says shee?
Ner. Daphne?

Da. Nerina? What's the matter that thou nam'st
    Silvia so oft, and sigh'st at ev'ry word?   45
Ner. There's cause enough, Daphne; ah too, too much.
Am. Ay mee, I feele, I feele my brest so full
    Of yce, my breath halfe stopt; lives shee, or no?
Da. Tell us all, tell the worst, Nerina.
Ner. O heav'n.   50
    Must I be then th' unhappy' historian?
    And yet it's fit I tell my sad tale out.
    Silv'ia starnak'd (whereof yee know perhaps
    The cause) came to our house, where being clad,
    Shee afterward desir'd me I would goe   55
    A hunting with her, as it was before
    Appointed, to the Grove of Okes (for so
    The place yee know is call'd); I did agree;
    And onn we went, and found there many Nimphes
    Gath'red together; not farr off, behold   60
    Rusheth a huge Wolfe foorth, whose yawning jawes
    Foam'd with a bloudy froth; Silvia then neare him
    Let flie a shaft at him; and in his head
    The arrow light; he tooke the wood againe,
    And shee at heeles persu'd him with a Dart   65
    Into the wood.
Am.   Ah, sorrowful beginning;
    I feare, I feare a sad conclusion.
Ner. I with an other Dart follow'd their footing:
    But, setting out too late, was cast farr off;
    And having gain'd the wood, I lost the sight   70
    Of them; yet kept their track, and ranne so farr,
    Till I was got into the desertest
    And thickest of the wood; at length I found
    (And tooke up) Silvia's Dart upon the ground;
    And not farr off a white vaile; which (ere while)   75
    I did my selfe binde up her haire withall;
    And whilst I look'd about me', I spide sev'n Wolves
    Licking bloud off the ground, that scatt'red lay
    Above a few bare bones; and 'twas my hap
    To scape unseene, while they so earnestly   80
    Minded their pray.
    I full of feare turn'd back, and came my way.
    And this is al that I can say of Silvia;
    And heere's the vaile.

Am.   Th' hast sayd, th' has sayd enough;
 O bloud, O vayle, O Silvia, dead, dead—   85
Da. Poore youth he dyes; he's dead; ay me, he's dead
 With griefe.
Ner.   He breath's yet, he's but in a traunce;
 Tarry, he comes againt t' himselfe.
Am.   O griefe,
 Why do'st, why do'st thou thus torment me?
 And wilt not end me? Th' art unjust. Perhaps   90
 Thou leav'st the worke to my owne hand: I am,
 I am content it shall be my owne care,
 Since thou wilt not, or canst not doe 't; ay mee,
 Ay mee, if nothing want to make this cleere,
 And nothing want to make my miseries   95
 Now brimfull; why do' I linger? Why do I stay?
 O Daphne, Daphne, was it to this end,
 This bitter, bitter end thou didst reserve me?
 My death had then bin sweet, and pleasing to me,
 When thou and heav'n held back my Dart, and sav'd me; 100
 Heav'n that was lothe (belike) I should prevent
 With death, the woes it has prepar'd for me;
 But now't has done the very worst it can,
 I hope both heav'n, and you may suffer me
 To dye in peace.
Da.   Stay yet, stay, wretch, and learne 105
 The trueth yet better.
Am.   Ah, the trueth is such,
 I've stay'd too long, alas, I've heard too much.
Ner. Ay mee, wretch that I am, why did I speake?
Am. Gentle Nimphe, let me crave that vayle of thee,
 The poor remaynder of her; that it may   110
 Accompanie me for these fewe sad houres
 Of way, and life yet left me; and increase
 That martirdom, that were no martirdom
 Were it not much more then enough to kill me.
Ner. Shall I denie 't, or shall I give it him?   115
 The cause he askes it for bids me retaine it.
Am. Cruell Nimphe, to deny me' a grace so small
 In my extremity, and ev'n I see
 How in each trifle fortune crosseth mee.
 I yeeld, I yeeld; long may it bide with thee: 120
 Long live yee; my way to my death must bee.

Da. Aminta stay, Aminta', a word, Aminta,
    Harke, stay; alas, how swift he flyes away.
Ner. He runnes so fast, t'will be in vaine for us
    To follow him; 'twere best I onward went   125
    Upon my way; and yet perhaps 'twere better
    I stay'd, and held my peace, then my selfe be
    Author of poore Montano's misery.

CHORUS.

    Death, there is no neede of thee:
    Love alone, and Constancie
    Ar enough (without thy Dart)
    To tyre upon an honest heart.
    Yet so hard is not the way   5
    To Loves fame, as many say;
    For Love no price but love regards;
    And with it selfe, it selfe rewards.
    And oft in seeking it, is found
    Glory that lives, when we are under ground.   10

ACTUS QUARTUS Scena Prima

DAPHNE. SILVIA. CHORUS.

[Da.] Now may the winde upon his wings beare hence
    All ill may happen thee; together with
    Th' accurséd newes so lately spread of thee.
    Thou art alive (the gods be thanked for 't)
    And ev'n but now I did beleeve thee dead;   5
    So had Nerina painted to the life
    Thy late hap; but I would shee had bin dumbe,
    Or some that heard her deafe.
Sil.   Indeede I scap'd
    So narrowly, as I beleeve shee might
    Full well suppose me dead.
Da.   Suppose she might   10
    Yet not have tolde it with such certainty.
    But tell me, pre'thee, how thou didst escape
    The danger so.
Sil.   Why, I in following

A Wolfe into the wood, had thickt with him
So farr, till I at length had lost his track;   15
And as I stood thinking to turne againe
Back as I went, I spide him, and I knew him
By' a shaft that stuck in's head neere to his eare
Which I not long before had shot at him:
He was accompany'd with many more,   20
About the body of some beast new slaine;
But what beast 'twas I knew not; the same Wolfe
I thinke knew me so well, that on he made
Towards me with his head besmear'd with bloud.
I bouldly stood, and bent a Dart at him,   25
And when I thought his distance fit for me,
I threw, but (whether it was fortunes fault
Or mine) I mist him, as thou know'st I use
Not oft to do; he fiercer then before
Rusheth upon me; and was come so neere,   30
That I (my shafts now spent), found it too late
To trust my bowe, and tooke me to my heeles:
Away I ranne; he follow'd me as fast.
See now my hap; a vaile that I had ty'de
My haire withall, was halfe undone, and flew   35
At the windes pleasure loosely, that at length
'T had wound it selfe about a bough; I felt
That somewhat stay'd me; but the feare I had,
Redoubled so my strength, that though the bough
Did all it could to hold me, I broke loose;   40
And as I left my vaile behinde, I left
Part of my haire withall; and so had feare
Lent my feete wings, that I out-went the Wolfe,
And came safe from the wood; when turning home
I met thee thus amaz'd, and am no lesse   45
Amaz'd my selfe to see thee so.
Da.   Ay mee,
Thou liv'st, 'tis well; would all were well besides.
Sil. What ayl'st thou? Pre'thee, art thou sory then
That I'm alive?
Da.   No, that thou liv'st I'm glad;
But for an others death I must be sad.   50
Sil. How's this? For whose death?
Da.   Why, Aminta's death.
Sil. Aminta dead? Alas, how may that be?

Da. Nay, how I cannot tell; nor yet am sure
  Of the deede done; but I beleeve it firmly.
Sil. What's this thou tell'st me? Alas, what might be   55
  Th' occasion of Aminta's death?
Da.   Thy death.
Sil. Make mee conceive thee.
Da.   Ev'n the heavy newes
  Of thy death, which he heard, and credited,
  Hath brought him to his end, some-way or other.
Sil. Fye, th' art deceiv'd; and this thy thought will be   60
  As vaine as was the newes thou heardst of me;
  For surely no man will dye willingly.
Da. O Silv'ia, Silvia, thou dost not feele
  Nor know what loves flame can do, in a brest
  That is a brest of flesh, and not of flint   65
  As thine is; for didst thou but know 't, I know
  Thou wouldst have loved him that lov'd thee more
  Then both his eyes; more then his breath and life;
  I do beleeve it, nay I've seene, and know it.
  I saw, I saw him when thou fledst from him   70
  (Unkinde and cruell as thou were) when he,
  Ev'n then when thou shouldst rather have imbrac'd
  Then scorn'd him so, against his brest had bent
  His Dart, with full intent to kill himselfe:
  Nor any whit repented of the deede,   75
  When (stay'd by me from farther wounding him)
  The sharpe steele had his garment and his skinne
  Dyed in his bloud, and had pierc'd through that heart
  That loyall heart of his, that thou before
  Hadst wounded worse, had not I held his hand,   80
  And sav'd him all I could: but O alas
  That slight wound serv'd but as a triall only
  And small proofe of his desp'rate constancie;
  And but to teach the fatall steele, to do
  The black deede it was preappointed to.   85
Sil. Ay mee, what't this thou tell'st me?
Da.   But at last
  When the newes came that thou were dead, I saw him
  Sound at the hearing on' t, and dye away;
  And came no sooner to himselfe againe,
  But furiously he flings away amayne;   90
  And sure I feare, alas, too sure 'twill proove

Has kill'd himselfe;
Such was his too much griefe, and too much love.
Sil. But hold'st thou this for certaine?
Da.   Tis too true.
Sil. Ay me, why didst thou not straite follow him?   95
   And stay him? Ah, let's seeke, let's finde him out;
   Since from my death, his deaths desire is bredd,
   He must live still because I am not dead.
Da. Alas, I follow'd him, but he had soone
   So farre outrunne me; as I now despaire   100
   That we shall finde him having lost his footing.
Sil. We must, alas, we must inquire him out
   Some way or other speedily, least he
   Through our slownesse his owne murdrer be.
Da. Belike then (Cruell) th' art but griev'd he should   105
   Take from thee th' honour of this goodly deede?
   And would'st thy selfe be the brave murderesse?
   Must no hand else but thine an Actor be
   In th' execution of this Tragedy?
   Well, set thy heart at rest; for howsoe're   110
   He dyes, thou art his onely murderer.
Sil. Ah, thou dost wound me; and thy ev'ry word
   Addes to the agony'e of my bleeding brest,
   Strooke through with feare of him; and with the bitter
   Remembrance of the savadge cruelty   115
   In me, which I call'd honesty', and so 'twas,
   But too severe it was, and rigorous,
   I finde it now; alas, I now repent it.
Da. What's this? What do I heare?
   Why, thou art pittifull then, and thy heart   120
   Seemes to have feeling of anothers harmes;
   What doe I see?
   Why thou do'st weepe too; I'm amaz'd at this!
   Whence ar these teares? Is't love that causes them?
Sil. 'Tis pitty, 'tis compassion causes them   125
Da. Compassion is the messenger of love,
   As is the lightning of the thunder clap.
Cho. 'Tis often times the property of love
   When he would creepe unseene into young hearts
   Which austere Chastity hath long time shut   130
   And barr'd against him, to assume the habit
   And semblance of his handmayd Pitty', and so

Deceives them ere they be aware, and gets
Into their brests unknowne and undiscry'de.

Da. These ar love-teares (Silvia) they flow so fast;   135
   Do'st thou not love indeede? Ha? Not a word?
   Yes, 'tis too true, but, alas, 'tis too late.
   Behold the strange wayes of Loves chastisement;
   Wretched Aminta, thou that (like the Bee,
   Which hurting dyes, and in an others wound   140
   Leaves his owne life), hast with thy death, at last
   Pierc'd that hard heart, which living felt thee not.
   But if, O erring Spirit (as I feare
   Thou art, and sever'd from thy empty corse)
   Thou wandrest here abouts; behold her playnts;   145
   Living thou lov'dst her, see, shee loves thee dead.
   And if thy cruell fate would have it so,
   That thy love could not be repay'd till now,
   And that her love was only to be purchas'd
   By thee at this deare price; let it suffice thee   150
   (Where more thou canst not have) that thou hast bought it
   As dearely now, as shee could rate it thee,
   Even with thy death.

Cho. Deare bargaine for the buyer;
   And all unprofitable, and infamous   155
   Unto the cruell seller.

Sil.   O that I
   Could with my love redeeme his life againe,
   Or with my life his life, if he live not.

Da. O pitty, O discretion, too late bredd;
   Little avail they to revive the dead.   160

ACTUS QUARTUS Scena Secunda

NUNTIUS: [ERGASTUS.] CHORUS. SILVIA. DAPHNE.

[Nun.] I am so full of woe, so full of horror
   As all I heare and whatsoere I look on
   Me thinks afflicts, disquiets, and affrights me.

Cho. What strange news brings this man that seemes to me
   So troubled in his lookes, and in his speech?   5

Nun. I bring the sad news of Aminta's death.

Sil. Ay me, what sayes he?

Nun. Aminta, noblest Shepherd of these woods,

That was so comely and so gratious;
So deare unto the Nymphes, and to the Muses;   10
And dead but ev'ne a ladd.
Cho.   Ah, of what death?
Tell us, ah, tell all; that we may in one
Lament with thee his mischiefe, and our owne.
Sil. Ay me, my heart failes me'; I dare not approach
Th' unwelcome newes which I of force must heare.   15
Vilde breast of mine, obdurate heart of mine,
What fear'st thou now? Go hardly, presse upon
The murth'ring knives that are in yon mans tongue;
And there display thy fiercenes! Freind, I come
To beare my part of all the woe thou bringest;   20
Perhaps it does concerne me more by much
Then th' art aware of. It belongs to me;
Grutch me not on 't then.
Nun. Nimphe, I doe beleeve thee;
For ev'ne upon his death, I hear the wretch   25
Call still upon thy name to his last breath.
Da. Now, now beginnes the heavy history.
Nun. I was upon the middes of yon high hill,
Where I had spred abroad some netts of mine
To drie them, when not far off from me, came   30
Aminta by, with a sad clowdy looke
And altred much from what he wont to bee
Both in his face and fashion; which I spying
Ranne after him, and staying him, quoth hee,
Ergastus, thou must doe a curtesie   35
For me of much importance and availe;
'Tis to goe with me but a little hence,
For witnesse of a deede I have to doo;
But first I'le have thee binde thy faith to me
By a strict oath to stand aloofe from mee   40
And not approach to lett or hinder that
That I shall do. I (that could nere have dream't
Of such a furious madnesse in him) yeelded
To 's will; and made desperate invocations
Calling to witness *Pan,* and *Priapus;*   45
Pales, Pomona, 'and nightly *Hecate,*
Which done, he led me higher up the hill,
Where, clambring through wilde rocky passages,
(By wayes nere found, and never trode before)

Wee gayn'd the top, that over-hung a valley,   50
'Twixt which and us was a steepe precipice,
And there we stay'd; I casting downe mine eye,
Began for feare to tremble, and shrunke back.
After a little pause, he smil'de me thought,
And seem'd more cheerefull then he was before;   55
And that made me misdoubt him lesse then ever.
After that (quoth he to me), see thou tell
The Nymphes and Shepherds what thou shalt behold;
Then looking downe, Ah, that I had (sayd he)
So ready at my will, the throat and teeth   60
Of those same greedy Wolves, as these rocks be;
I would not dye of other death then she
Who was my life; nor have my carkass torne
But by those teeth that tore those delicate
And beautious limbs of hers; but since that heav'n   65
Denies so great a blessing to me, I
Must be content some other way to dye;
And though a worse way, yet a speedier.
Silvia, I follow thee, Silvia, I come
To beare thee company,   70
If thou disdaine me not; O I should dye
Much more contentedly, were I but sure
My follow'ing thee would not disquiet thee,
And that thy hate had ending with thy life:
Silvia, I follow thee, I come. Which sayd,   75
Downe from the place he headlong threw himselfe,
And I turn'd yce to see 't.
Da.   Wretched Aminta.
Sil. Ay mee, ay mee.
Cho.   Why didst not hinder him?
   Perhaps the oath thou took'st barr'd thee to doo 't?
Nun. Not so; for setting all such oathes at nought,   80
   (Vaine doubtlesse in such cases) when I saw
   Whither his fond and headdy madnesse tended,
   I reacht at him; and (as ill hap would have it)
   Layd hold but of this thinne scarfe, wherewithall
   He girt himselfe; which (all too weake to beare   85
   His bodies weight, that rested all upon 't)
   Remayn'd broke in my hand.
Cho.   And what became
   Of the unhappy carkass?

Nun.   I know not;
  For I was so dead strucken at the sight,
  As my heart would not suffer me, to looke   90
  And see him dasht to peeces.
Cho.   O strange fate.
Sil. Ay mee, were I not made of stone indeede,
  This newes would kill me. Ah, if the false death
  Of me that car'd no more for him, was cause
  Enough to end his life;   95
  Much more cause is there that the certaine death
  Of him that lov'd me so, should be enough
  To end my life; and it shall end my life;
  And if griefe cannot do 't, the sharpe steele shall,
  Or else this girdle heere, which justly stayes   100
  As loath to follow his sweet Masters ruines,
  Till it have done on me the due revenge
  Of his sad death, and my ingratitude.
  Unhappy girdle (relique of a more
  Unhappy Master), ah, do not disdaine   105
  T' abide a while with one so odious;
  For thou shalt stay but to be th' instrument
  Of his revenge, and of my punishment.
  I might have bin, alas, I should have bin
  Yoke-fellow with Aminta heere on earth;   110
  But since that cannot be, by thy helpe now
  I'le finde him out among th' infernall shades,
  And there goe beare him better company.
Cho. Content thee (thou sad soule) 'tis Fortunes fault,
  And not by thy meane, that this ill is wrought.   115
Sil. Shepherds, why plaine yee? If yee moane my woes,
  I do deserve no pitty, that have bin
  My selfe so pittilesse; if yee wayle the death
  Of the poore Innocent; ah, tis too small;
  Griefe is too poore to pay his deede withall.   120
  And Daphne, thou, I prethee, dry thy teares;
  If for my sake thou weep'st; for my sake cease.
  And for his sake that was a thousand times
  More worth then I; and go along and helpe me
  To find th' unhappy bones; and bury them;   125
  'Tis that alone that keepes me still alive,
  And that I do not ev'n now kill my selfe.
  It is the least and last duty is left

For me to do him, for the love he bore me;
And though this vile hand of mine might perhaps   130
Blemish the piety' of so just a deede;
Yet he I know will like the deede the better,
For being done by it; for I am sure
He loves me still; his death assures it me.

Da. I am content to' assist thee' in seeking him,   135
But talke (for heav'ns sake) of this death no more.
Alas, wee've had too much of that before.

Sil. Till now I've liv'd only unto my selfe,
And my owne wayward humor: for the rest,
I vowe it all to' Aminta; and if to him   140
I may not, I'le live yet to his colde carkass,
Till I have done it the last obsequies:
So long I may; longer I will not live.
But, Shepherd, set me in the way (I pray)
Unto the valley at the high hills foote.   145

Nun. There, o' that hand 'tis, and not far from hence.

Da. I'le goe along and guide thee, for I well
Remember 't.

Sil.   Farwell, Shepherds, Nimphes farwell;
Farwell woods, fields, and flocks; farwell, farwell,

Nun. This mayden speakes me thinkes in such a straine,   150
As if shee went nere to returne againe.

CHORUS.

Love, thou rejoyn'st what Death unbinds
(Thou freind of Peace but shee of Bloud);
Yet thou her Triumphes over raignest;
And in uniting gentle mindes,
Mak'st Earth so heav'nly an abode,   5
As thou to dwell among us daynest:
Thou smooth'st the rugged hearts of men;
And inward rancors driv'st away
(Great prince of happy peace); and when
Milde breasts are troubled, do'st allay   10
Their woes; and by thy working strange,
Framst of things mortall, and eternall change.

ACTUS QUINTUS Scena Prima

ELPINE. CHORUS.

[Elp.] Doubtlesse the lawes wherewith *Love* governeth
   His Empire evermore, are neither hard
   To follow, nor unjust; and those his workes
   Which many men do condemne wrongfully,
   Are full of providence, and mistery.   5
   Lo, with what art,
   And by how many unknowne waies he leades
   His votaries unto their happinesse;
   And placeth them among the highest joyes
   And pleasures of his amorous Paradise,   10
   When oftentimes they feele themselves sunk downe
   Ev'ne to the very bottome of all ills.
   Behold Aminta with his headlong fall,
   Aspires unto the top of all delight;
   O happy' Aminta; and so much the more   15
   Happy now, as unfortunate before.
   This thy example makes me hope no lesse,
   That once at last my lovelesse faire (that covers
   Under those freindly smiles such cruelty)
   Will with true pitty heale wounds, that shee   20
   Hath with her fainéd pittie made in me.
Cho. Yon is the rev'rend Elpine; and me thinkes
   Speakes of Aminta'; as if he were alive,
   Calling him happy, blest, and fortunate,
   Ah, hard condition of unhappy lovers;   25
   He belike counts him fortunate, that dyes
   For love, and is belov'd (when he is dead)
   Of her he lov'de so well; and this he calls
   The paradise of love; O with how light
   And poore rewards the wing'd Love-god contents   30
   His servants. Art thou (Elpine) then indeed
   In such a pittifull estate, as that
   Thou canst terme fortunate, the miserable
   Death of the poore Aminta? and wouldst thou
   So farr thy life to loves subjection bowe.   35
   And undergoe the like fate?
Elp.   Freinds, be merry
   What of his death perhaps ye have heard is false.
Cho. That were a welcome newes.

Did he not throw himselfe downe headlong then
From yon high Mountaines topp?
Elp.   Tis true he did.   40
But 'twas a fortunate and happy fall;
That look'd so like death, and is proov'd to him
Not life alone, but a most joyfull life;
For now he lyes lull'd in the tender lapp
Of his beloved one that seemes much more   45
Fonde of him now, then she was coy before;
Drying each teare he lets fall, with a sighe,
Or with the like, freindly requiting it.
But I am going to finde out Montano
Her Father, and conduct him where they bee;   50
For there wants nothing else but his consent
To both their boundlesse joyes accomplishment.
Cho. Their age, their bloud and birth, their mutuall loves,
And all agree; and the good oulde Montano
Will be glad doubtlesse of posteritie,   55
And to' arme his gray haires with so sweet a guard,
So that his will no doubt shall second theirs.
But thou (good Elpine) tell what god, what fate
In that so dangerous and deadly fall
Preserv'd Aminta.
Elp.   I am well content;   60
Heare then, heare that which with these eyes I saw:
I was before my Caves mouth, which ye knowe
Lyes at the hills foote, on the valleyes brimme;
There Thirsi' and I were reasoning together
Of the faire shee that in the selfe same nett   65
Had first insnar'd him, and me afterward;
When I preferring my love'd servitude
Before his free state, all at once we heard
A shreeke, and saw a man fall from above,
Upon a bushly knowle; for on the side   70
Of the steepe hill, there growes (all of a heape,
And as 'twere wove together) a round masse
Of brambles, thornes, and certaine weedes among;
There first he light before he lower fell;
And though hee made way through them with his weight,   75
And fell downe to the ground before our feete;
Yet so that stop abated the falls force,
As 'twas not mortall; though so dangerous

As that he lay a while devoyd of sense,
And as a dead man without show of motion.   80
We with amazement, and compassion were
Dumbe-strucken at the sudden spectacle:
And knowing him, and knowing soone (with all)
He was not dead, nor perhaps like to die,
Appeaz'd his woe, and eas'd him all we could;   85
Then Thirsis made me throughly' acquainted with
Th' whole passage of his loves, but while we sought
To bring him to himselfe againe, and sent
To fetch Alphesibeo (t'whom *Appollo*
Taught th' art of Phisicke, when he gave his Harp   90
And Lute to me) came Daphne, and Silvia,
Who (as I heard) had bin to seek him out
Whom they suppos'd dead. But when Silvia
Had found and knew him, and beheld his cheekes
And lips so bloudlesse, and discolouréd,   95
As the wanne Violet's hue their palenesse past;
And saw him languish, as if then he had
Bin drawing his last breath, she gave her sorrowes
A liberall passage through her earnest cryes;
And beating her faire brest, falls downe upon him,   100
Laying her face on his, and on his lipps
Her lipps.
Cho.   And did not bashfull shame restraine
Her more, who is so strict, and so severe?
Elp. Bashfulnes oft barrs weak loves of their longings,
But is too weake a curbe for a strong love.   105
But then as if her eyes had bin two fountaines,
She drown'd his colde face with her powring teares,
Whose water was of so great force, and vertue,
That he reviv'd; and op'ning his dimme eyes,
He sighes foorth a hollow' Ay mee, from the bottome   110
Of his sad brest; she caught the heavy sound
Of that same bitter breath, and mingled it
With her sweet breath; and so restor'd, and heal'd him.
Then who can say? Who can imagine what
Both of them thought, and at that instant felt,   115
Each now assur'd of others life? And he
Assur'd of her love, and to finde himselfe
Intangled in so lov'd, and loving armes?
He that loves firmly may imagine it,

Yet hardly too; but no tongue sure can tell it.   120
Cho. Is then Aminta safe belike, and well,
    And so cleare from all danger of his death?
Elp. He's safe, and well; save that he has a little
    Battred his flesh, and somwhat scracht his face,
    But 'twill be nothing; and he wayes it not.   125
    Thrice happy he t' have giv'n so great and high
    A signe, and earnest of his Constancie;
    And now injoyes the fruit of his firme love;
    To which his sad indurings, and paines past,
    Proove pleasing and sweet sawces at the last.   130
    But peace be wi' yee'; I must goe seeke about
    Till I have found the good Montano out.

CHORUS.

I know not whether the much sowre
This (now blest) Lover (serving, burning,
Now dispairing, and still mourning)
Hath felt; may in one happy' houre
Be thoroughly repay'd againe   5
With pleasure equall to his paine.
But if the good more pleasing be,
And come more welcome, after wee
Have felt the ill, I doe not crave
(O Love) this happiness to have.   10
Let others be so blest by thee,
And graunt the Nimph I love may bee
Wonne with a little lesse adoe;
Less pray'rs, less service when I wooe;
And let the sawce to our loves be   15
Not so much paine, and misery:
But sweet disdaines, repulses sweet,
Fall off a little, and straite meete.
That after a short frowne or twayne,
New peace, or truce may knit our hearts againe.   20

    Th' end of Tasso's *Aminta*.

Notes to the *Aminta*

The Prologue

19 *silly*: Innocent, defenseless, deriving from the conventional (poetic) epithet of sheep.

34 *woe*: Woo, variant spelling.

38 *usd'e*: Customary.

40–41 *this rod . . . my brand transformed*: Cupid's torch now changed to a shepherd's crook.

43 *dart . . . no goulden head*: An arrow with a golden tip inspired love, a leaden one disdain.

60 *launch*: Pierce.

I.i.

11 *lawne*: An open area in a woods.

21 *eate*: Past tense.

28 *widowy nights*: The enforced chastity of a bereaved wife.

36–41 *The flouds . . . feede*: A series of impossibilities; a device termed *adynata* in rhetorical manuals.

38 *Levrett*: Immature hare.

45 *'tysing*: Enticing (aphetic).

69 *Cinthia*: Goddess of the moon and the chase; as a triform goddess identified with Diana at III.i.102 and with Hecate at IV.ii.46.

96 *at a point for me*: Prepared, *OED*, *sb*. point Db.

105 *honour*: Chastity, considered as a virtue of the highest consideration, *OED*, *sb*. 3.

126 *Turtle*: Turtle-dove, symbol of faithful love.

161 *Elpine*: A reference to Giovan Battista Pigna, secretary to Duke Alfonso II, at the court of Ferrara where Tasso and Guarini (Thirsis and Batto of line 166) served as court poets. Lines 167–69 of Elpine's speech refer to a specific locale in the ducal palace—an apartment of the Princess Leonora—where a painting of Aurora (line 167) by Dosso Dossi hung. Reynolds (and other contemporary readers of the drama) did not, of course, recognize Tasso's personal allusions ascertained by modern commentators.

168–69 *hence . . . hence*: Virgil, *Aeneid* 6.258.

169 *Which words . . . (sayd he)*: The use here of the relative (which) in place of the demonstrative pronoun *these* is confusing; (sayd he), refers to Elpine.

170 *That . . . sang of loves and armes*: *That* means *who* (a frequent usage in the period); Elpine alludes to the opening lines of Ariosto's romance epic, the *Orlando Furioso*, which went through some two hundred editions in Italy before the end of the sixteenth century. The definitive version appeared in 1532.

171 *And ... bequeath'd ... to him*: Pigna (Elpine) claimed to be Ariosto's heir.

172-83 *There was ... a teare*: This account of what befalls "cruell and ingratefull women" derives from canto 34.11ff. of the *Orlando Furioso*.

174 *Acaron*: River in southern Epirus which breakes into a lake at the entrance of Hades (Acheron).

200 *harried*: This ed.; *Ital.* forsennato; hurryed *28*.

208-11 *Deluding eyes ... still*: Lines adapted from a sonnet of Tasso's to a lady in the court of Ferrara.

I.ii

36 *condition*: Frequently tetrasyllabic.

45 *period*: End.

80 *fleetes*: Creeks, *OED, sb.* 2.1.

81 *Pitfalls*: Traps.

107 *soothe*: This ed.; soone *28*; *Ital.* "perch' io / Con parole d'incanti leverotti / Il dolor de la picciola ferita."

108 *Aretia*: This ed., *Ital. Arezia*; *Wolfe Aresia*. Reynolds's change may have been intended to evoke the Greek personification of Virtue, or it may have been inadvertent.

110 *wont*: Commonly used as an auxiliary, but cf. Shakespeare's *Comedy of Errors* IV.iv.38. Unless otherwise specified, all references are to the *Riverside Shakespeare*, edited by G. Blakemore Evans (Houghton Mifflin Company, 1974).
     were: Spelling variant of *wear*.

112 *straite*: At once.

186 *my mind gives mee yet*: Suggests to me that, *OED, sv.* give VI.22.

192 *Mopso*: An uncertain topical reference to a member of the court.

200 *doomes*: Judgments.
     lewdly: Wickedly, *OED, adv.* 2.

226 *magazine*: Storehouse, *OED, sb.*1.

230 *transparent*: Manifest.

251-73 *To see the Cittie ... Elpine*: Accepted as a reference to the court of Ferrara with an allusion (258ff.) to Tasso's patron Duke Alfonso II.

261 *what he seem'd me*: He seemed to me, a medievalism.

268 *Orpheuses*: Poets, so designated from the Greek musician Orpheus, sometimes identified as the son of Phoebus Apollo.

281 *shriller*: High pitched; *Ital.* più altera e più sonora.

293 *lives*: Life's, spelling variant; again at line 64. See Appendix 1 for Daniel's rendering of this popular text.

Chorus

18 *Honour*: Chastity, as earlier at I.i.105.

25 *goulden lawes of Nature*: Specified in the Italian, "If it pleases, it is lawful" (S'ei piace, ei lice).

28 *Genii*: Tutelary spirits, Reynolds's substitution for Tasso's "Amoretti"—little loves.

43 *lewdly*: Wickedly, as at I.ii.200.

44 *nyce*: Unwilling, *OED, a.* 5b.
     scrupulous: Distrustful.

49 *unmeete*: Improper.

66-67 *wayne of Heaven*: Chariot of the sun.

68-69 *But we ... night*: This couplet echoes the well-known lines of Catullus, 5.56:

"Nobis cum semel occidit brevis lux, / Nox est perpetua una dormienda," translated by Thomas Campion ("My sweetest Lesbia") and Ben Jonson ("Come, my Celia") among others.

II.i

6 *eye-lids fault*: *Ital.* "sotto a l'ombra / De la palébre"—under the shadow of an eyelid. Reynolds's to us rather bizarre translation derives apparently from *ME lest, last,* fault + eye; see *OED, eyelast, eyelist*; the term *eyelash* was not used in English until 1752.

8 *little pits*: Dimples, characterized as "lovely caves ... enchanting pits" in Shakespeare's *Venus and Adonis*, line 247.

15–16 *how well thy name ... Silvan*: Sylvia is the feminine form of Sylvanus, a woodland deity.

24–31 *in thy lovely face ... the Bee makes*: Catalogue of beauties, a frequent motif in erotic poetry.

35–42 *Yet I'me ... manlyhood*: A boasting motif recalling that of the Cyclops Polyphemus in love with the nereid Galatea (Theocritus, Idyl 6).

37 *mayne*: Ocean.

39 *sanguine*: A temperament deriving from one of the four humours (blood), indicating a bold and amorous nature.

40 *enough*: Probably pronounced *enow* since the same graphic form could represent the two pronunciations.

85 *Close*: Hidden.

87 *avayle*: Aid.

90 *good yeere*: Meaningless expletive; the *OED* cites Roper's *Life of More* as the earliest example (c. 1555) and includes this instance from Reynolds; frequent in Shakespeare in colloquial dialogue.

92 *snary*: Ensnaring; cf. Daniel, *Delia* 14, "those snary locks," a 1594 (and ff.) revision of "amber."

II.ii

11 *fondly*: Foolishly (freq.).

36 *tooke advice*: Consulted.

40 *lapp*: Bosom, *OED, sv. sb.* 2.4.

43 *whethers*: Elision for whether his.
    past: Surpassed.

51 *a mayne*: Exceedingly.

55 *abroad*: Dispersed; anticipates the instance cited in the *OED* by a century and a half.

77 *nice*: Reserved, modest, *OED, a.* 5, a different meaning from its use in Chorus I.44 and as used here later in line 80.

78 *nicely*: Scrupulously, *OED, adv.* 4 c. The earliest usage cited is Shakespeare's *King Lear* (1605).

80–87 *Nice ... overcome*: The views of the worldly-wise Daphne accord with the Satyr's intentions expressed in II.i.

83 *filtch*: Take surreptitiously.

85 *tane*: Taken (obs.).

138 *I'le go ... a wooing*: Cf. Campion's refrain "I will go no more a-maying" in his first *Booke of Ayres* (1601), no. 5 in *Works*, edited by W. R. Davis (Doubleday & Company, 1967).

155 *play both Hound and Hare*: Play a double part, *OED, sb.* 2.

167 *couler*: Pretext.

173-74 *a God ... to mee*: Echoing Virgil's first Eclogue, lines 6-7: "... deus nobis haec otia fecit, namque erit ille mihi semper deus."; again a reference to Duke Alfonso as at I.ii.253-72.

186-88 *I ... sing his Auncesters*: This alludes to Tasso's *Jerusalem Delivered* glorifying the house of Este; the first complete, though imperfect, edition was published in 1581 without authorial sanction.

189 *is to me Jove and Apollo both*: As the ruler of Ferrara and as patron of poetry.

191 *Issue of Saturne and of Heav'ne*: Saturn, the god of agriculture, was the son of Coelus and Terra and reigned during the Golden Age on Mt. Ida before the birth of Jove, who supplanted him and became the sovereign of the world.

202 *Sone*: *Ital.* Sona, the Saône, a river near the border of France.

211 *a'*: A "worn-down" version of "in," *OED, prep.* 10 (obs.).

II.iii

32 *Here*: Hear, spelling variant.

33 *starnak'd*: A fourteenth-century form of *stark naked*, now dialectical.

50 *slip*: Free, used of releasing a dog from his leash; cf. Shakespeare's *Julius Caesar* III.i.273.

63 *an't*: If it.

90 *what skil't I pray*: What does it matter to me, *OED, sv.* skill v. 2b.

Chorus

7 *Athens*: *Ital.* Atene; Athena was the patron deity of the city, which perhaps accounts for Reynolds's substitution; *Athene, Wolfe.*

8-9 *Liceus ... Helicon*: *Lycius* means either wolf-god or golden god of light, an epithet applied to Apollo, one of whose sacred sites was Mt. Helicon in Boeotia. Reynolds follows Tasso in distinguishing them as two deities—Non Liceo ... Non Febo; Ne ... Non, *Wolfe.*

39 *reade ... faire eyes*: A *topos*; cf. Shakespeare's *Merchant of Venice* III.ii.67: "[Love] is engend'red in the eyes."

41 *halt*: Limp.

III.i

3 *lewd*: Bungling, *OED, a.* 4, a meaning to be distinguished from its adverbial use in the chorus I.43.

4 *negligent*: Heedless, *OED, a.* 1.b.

12 *Or ... or*: Either ... or.

39 *conduct*: Escort.

51 *Pard*: Leopard or panther.

68 *have ... steeded*: Been of little use.

76 *spight*: Annoyance, *OED, sb.* 3c.

88 *lapp*: Bosom as at II.ii.40.

96 *faire*: Gently.

102 *I am Diana's*: As a devotee; cf. I.i.69.

112 *strange*: Unnatural.

122 *amaine*: Very fast, as again at IV.i.90.

130-32 *It is the common use ... all*: Cf. Rosalind in Shakespeare's *As You Like It*, IV.i.106-7: "men have died from time to time, and worms have eaten them, but not for love."

143 *kindes*: Natures.

III.ii

27-28 *the Raven and sinister . . . Newes*: "The sad-presaging raven," a common motif.
64 *light*: Current form of the past tense.
75 *ere while*: A while before.
88 *Tarry*: Wait, *OED, v.* 3.
101 *prevent*: Forestall, *OED, v.* 2.5; cf. Wisdom 4:7 (Geneva Bible): "Though the righteous be prevented with death."

Chorus

4: *tyre upon*: Figuratively, to prey upon; cf. Thomas Howell, *Devises* (1581): "Your love the grype [vulture] that tyres upon your heart"; *Ital. stringer*, bind together.

IV.i

14-15 *had thickt . . . so far*: Reynolds's coinage is an attempt to render Tasso's imprecise use of the verb *rinselvare* (to revert to woodland, to grow wild again); it might be translated "had so deeply inwooded myself with him."
57 *conceive*: Understand; cf. Shallow in Shakespeare's *Merry Wives of Windsor* I.i.250: "Nay, conceive me, conceive me, sweet coz."
88 *Sound*: Swoon, *OED, sb.* 4.
90 *amayne*: Very fast, as at III.i.122.
144 *corse*: Corpse.
152 *as she could rate*: Assign (a payment).

IV.ii

9 *gratious*: Trisyllabic.
17 *Go hardly*: Go boldly; *Ital.* "vattene"; "hardly" has ambiguous senses in English, signifying both "boldly" and "with difficulty."
23 *Grutch*: Begrudge, *OED, v.* 1.2.
27 *history*: Tale.
45-46 *Pan . . . Hecate*: The deities Aminta calls upon are all appropriate for a shepherd—*Pan*, god of woods and fields; *Priapus*, of goats and sheep and gardens; *Pales*, of pastures and folds; *Pomona*, of fruits and gardens; and *Hecate* (Diana), of woods and the chase.
56 *misdoubt*: Mistrust.
146 *o'*: On.

Chorus

6 *daynest*: Thinks fit (deign'st).
9 *Great prince of happy peace*: Perhaps a conscious Christian overtone; the Italian reads simply "Signor."

V.i

38 *a . . . newes*: Plural in form but construed as singular.
44 *lapp*: Bosom, as at II.ii.40.
74 *light*: Past tense, as at III.ii.64.
89-90 *Appollo . . . Phisicke*: In his capacity as a god of healing.
120 *hardly*: With difficulty.
125 *wayes it not*: Weighs; i.e., attaches no importance.

Chorus

1 *sowre*: Disagreeableness (fig.), *OED*, III.10.B.
18 *straite meete*: At once conjoin.

Guarini's *Pastor Fido*

Guarini's *Pastor Fido*

To the right worthie and learned Knight,
Syr *Edward Dymock*, Champion to her
Majestie, concerning this translation of
Pastor Fido

I do rejoyce, learned and worthy Knight,
That by the hand of thy kind Country-man
(This painfull and industrious Gentleman)
Thy deare esteem'd *Guarini* comes to light:
    Who in thy love I know tooke great delight   5
As thou in his, who now in England can
Speake as good English as Italian,
And here enjoyes the grace of his owne right.
    Though I remember he hath oft imbas'd
Unto us both, the vertues of the North,   10
Saying, our costes were with no measures grac'd,
Nor barbarous tongues could any verse bring forth.
    I would he sawe his owne, or knew our store,
    Whose spirits can yeeld as much, and if not more.

Sam. Daniell

A Sonnet of the Translator, dedicated to that
honourable Knight his kinsman,
Syr *Edward Dymock*

    A silly hand hath fashioned up a sute
Of English clothes unto a traveller,
A noble minde though Shepheards weeds he weare,
That might consort his tunes with *Tassoes* lute,
Learned *Guarinies* first begotten frute,   5
I have assum'd the courage to rebeare,

And him an English Denizen made here,
Presenting him unto the sonnes of Brute.
  If I have faild t' expresse his native looke,
And be in my translation tax'd of blame,   10
I must appeale to that true censures booke
That sayes, t'is harder to reform a frame,
    Then for to build from groundworke of ones wit,
    A new creation of a noble fit.

TO THE RIGHT WORTHY AND LEARNED KNIGHT,
Syr Edward Dymock, Champion to her
Majestie

SYR, this worke was committed to me to publish to the world, and by
reason of the nearenesse of kinne to the deceased Translator, and the
good knowledge of the great worth of the Italian Author, I knew none
fitter to Patronize the same then your worthinesse, to whom I wish all
happinesse, and a prosperous new yeare. London this last of December, 1601.

Your Worships ever to be commaunded.
Simon Waterson

THE PERSONS WHICH SPEAKE IN IT.

Silvio, the sonne of Montanus.

Linco, an old servant of Montanus.

Mirtillo, in love with Amarillis.

Ergasto, his companion.

Corisca, a Nymph in love with
Mirtillo.

Montanus, the high Priest.

Titirus, a Shepheard [father of
Amarillis].

Dametas, an old servant of
Montanus.

Satir, an old Lover of Coriscaes.

Dorinda, enamoured of Silvio.

Lupino, a Goteheard, her servant.

Amarillis, daughter of Titirus.

Nicander, chiefe minister of the
Priest.

Coridon, a Lover of Coriscaes.

Carino, an old man, the puta-
tive father of Mirtillo.

Urania, an old man, his companion.

Nuntio.

Tirenio, a blind Prophet.

Pastor Fido or The Faithful Shepheard
Shepheards. Huntsmen. Chorus of Nymphes. Priests.
The Scene is in *Arcadia*

Act I Scene 1

SILVO. LINCO.

[*Sil.*]   Go you that have enclos'd the dreadfull beast,
  And give the signe that's usuall to our hunting,
  Go swell your eyes and harts with hornes and shoutes,
  If there be any swaine of *Cinthia's* troupe
  In all *Arcadia* delighted in her sports,   5
  Whose generous affects are stung with care,
  Or glory of these woods, let him come forth
  And follow me, where in circle small
  (Though to our valure large) incloséd is
  The ougly Bore, monster of nature and these woods,   10
  That vast and fierce (by many harmes well knowne)
  Inhabitant of Erimanthus, plague to the fields,
  Terror to country clownes. Go then prevent
  Not onely but provoke with hornes shrill sound
  Blushing *Aurora* out. Linco, wee'le goe   15
  And worship first the Gods: for ther t'is best
  We any worke begin.
Lin.   Silvio, I praise
  Thy worshipping the Gods, but yet to trouble them
  That are their ministers I do not praise.
  The keepers of the temple are asleepe,   20
  They cannot see the day break for the mountaines top.
Sil. To thee perhaps that are not yet awake,
  All things do seeme asleepe.
Lin.   O Silvio,
  Did nature on these youthfull yeares of thine
  Bestow such beautie to be cast away?   25
  Had I but such a ruddie cheeke! So fresh!
  Farewell to woods, I'd follow other sports:
  I'd weare my dayes in mirth— all sommer-tide
  In daintie shades, winter by the fire side.
Sil. Thy counsel (Linco) is like unto thy selfe.   30
Lin. At other pleasures would I aime, were I Silvio.

Sil. So would I, were I Linco, but I Silvio am;
   Therefore I Silvioes deeds do like, not Lincoes.
Lin. O foole, that seekst so farre for hurtfull beasts,
   And hast one lodg'd so neare thy dwelling house.   35
Sil. Art thou in earnest? Or dost thou but jest?
Lin. Thou jests, not I.
Sil.   And is he then so neare?
Lin. As neare as t'is to thee.
Sil.   Where? In what wood?
Lin. Silvio, thou art the wood: the ougly beast
   That's harbour'd there is this thy beastlinesse.   40
Sil. Was 't not wel gest of me thou didst but jest?
Lin. A Nymphe so faire, so delicate! But tush,
   Why do I call her Nymphe, a Goddesse rather.
   More fresh, more daintie then the morning rose,
   More soft, more purely white then swanny downe.   45
   (For whom there's not a shepheard mongst us all so brave
   But sighes, and sighes in vaine) for thee alone
   Reserves her selfe, ordaind by heav'n and men;
   And yet thou neither thinkst of sighes or plaints.
   O happie boy (though most unworthily)   50
   Thou that mighst her enjoy, still fliest her, Silvio,
   Still her despisest. Is not then thy heart
   Made of a beast, or of hard Iron rather?
Sil. If to relinquish love be crueltie,
   Then is it vertue, and I not repent   55
   That I have banisht love my hart, but joy
   That thereby I have overcome this love,
   A beast more daungerous than th' other farre.
Lin. How hast thou overcome that which thou never prov'dst?
Sil. Not proving it, I have it overcome.   60
Lin. O if thou hadst but prov'd it, Silvio, once,
   If thou but knewst what a high favour t' were,
   To be belov'd, and loving to possesse
   A loving hart, I'm sure thou then wouldst say,
   Sweet lovely life, why hast thou staid so long?   65
   These woods and beasts leave, foolish child, and love.
Sil. Linco, I sweare a thousand Nymphs I'le give
   For one poore beast that my Melampo kills:
   Let them that have a better taste then I
   In these delights possesse them, I wil none.   70
Lin. Dost thou tast ought, since love thou dost not tast,

The onely cause that the world tasteth all?
Beleeve me, boy, the time wil one day come
Thou wilt it taste. For love once in our life
Will show what force he hath. Beleeve me, childe,   75
No greater paine can any living prove
Then in old limmes the lively sting of love.
Yet if in youth love wound, that love may heale:
But come it once in that same frozen age,
Wherefore oftentimes the disabilitie   80
More then the wound we plaine. O mortall then
And most intollerable are those paines.
If thou seekest pittie, ill if thou findst it not,
But if thou findst it ten times worse, do not
Protract it til thy better time be past,   85
For if love do assaile thy hoary heares,
Thy silly flesh a double torment teares,
Of this which when thou wouldst thou canst not.
These woods and beasts leave, foolish boy, and love.
Sil. As though there were no life but that which nurst   90
These amorous follies and fond extasies.
Lin. Tell me, if in this pleasant time now flowres renew,
And the world waxeth yong againe, thou shouldst
In stead of flowry valleyes, fragrant fields,
And well clad woods see but the oake, the ashe, the pine   95
Without their leavy heares, grasslesse the ground,
The meadowes want their floures, wouldst thou not say
The world doth languish? Nature did decay?
Now the same horror, that same miracle,
That monstrous noveltie thou hast thy selfe.   100
As love in old men is ridiculous:
So youth without love is unnaturall.
Looke but about (Silvio) what the world hath
Worthy to be admir'd. Love onely made
The heavens, the earth; the seas themselve do love.   105
And that same starre that the dayes-break foretells
Tasteth the flames of her thrise puissant sonne,
And at that houre, because perhaps she leaves
The stolne delights and bosome of her love,
She darteth downe abroad her sparkling smiles.   110
Beasts in the woods do love; and in the seas
The speedie Dolphins and the mightie Whales.
The birds that sweetly sings, and wantonly

Doth flie, now from the oake unto the ashe,
Then from the ashe unto the mirtill tree   115
Sayes in her language, I in love do burne.
(Would I might heare my Silvio answere her the same!)
The Bull amid the heard doth loudly lowe,
Yet are these lowes but bidding to loves feasts.
The Lyon in the wood doth bray, and yet   120
Those brayes are not the voice of rage, but love.
Well, to conclude, all things do love but thou,
Thou onely, Silvio, art in heaven, in earth,
In seas, a soule uncapable of love.
Leave, leave these woods, these beasts, and learne to love. 125
Sil. Was then my youth committed to thy charge
    That in these soft effeminate desires
    Of wanton love, thou shouldst it nurse and traine?
    Remembrest not what thou, and what I am?
Lin. I am a man, and humane me esteeme,   130
    With thee a man, or rather shouldst be so.
    I speake of humane things, which if thou skornst,
    Take heed least in dishumaning thy selfe,
    A beast thou prove not sooner then a God.
Sil. Neither so famous nor so valiant   135
    Had bene that monster-tamer, of whose blood
    I do derive my selfe, had he not taméd love.
Linc. See, blind child, how thou err'st: where hadst thou bene
    Had not that famous Hercules first lov'd?
    The greatest cause he monsters tam'd was love.   140
    Knowest thou not that faire *Omphale* to please,
    He did not onely chaunge his Lions skin
    Into a womans gowne, but also turn'd
    His knottie club into a spindell and a rocke.
    So was he wont from trouble and from toyle   145
    To take his ease, and all alone retire
    To her faire lappe, the haven of happie love.
    As rugged Iron with purer mettall mixt
    Is made more fit (refin'd) for noble use,
    So fierce and untam'd strength that in his proper rage 150
    Doth often breake, yet with the sweets of love
    Well temper'd proveth truly generous.
    Then if thou dost desire to imitate
    Great Hercules, and to be worthy of his race,
    Though that thou wilt not leave these savadge woods   155

Doo follow them: but do not leave to love,
A Love so lawfull as your Amarillis.
That you Dorinda flie I you excuse,
For t' were unfit your mind on honour set
Should be made hot in these amourous thefts: 160
A mightie wrong unto your worthy spouse.
Sil. What saist thou, Linco? Shee's not yet my spouse.
Lin. Hast thou not solemnely receiv'd her faith?
Take heed, proud boy, do not provoke the gods.
Sil. The gift of heaven is humane libertie,   165
May we not force repell that force receive?
Lin. Nay, if thou would'st but undertand! The heavens
Hereto do tye thee that have promiséd
So many favours at thy nuptiall feast.
Sil. I'm sure that gods have other things to do   170
Then trouble and molest them with these toyes.
Linco, nor this, nor that love pleaseth me;
I was a huntsman not a lover borne,
Thou that dost folow love thy pleasure take.   *Exit Sil.*
Lin. Thou cruel boy descended of the gods,   175
I scarce beleeve thou wert begot by man,
Which if thou wert, thou sooner was begot
With venome of *Megér* and *Ptisifo,*
Then *Venus* pleasure which men so commend.

Act I Scene 2

MIRTILLO. ERGASTO.

[*Mir.*] Cruell Amarillis, that with thy bitter name
Most bitterly dost teach me to complaine,
Whiter then whitest Lillies and more faire,
But deafer and more fierce then th' adder is.
Since with my words I do so much offend   5
In silence will I die: but yet these plaines,
These mountaines and these woods shal cry for me,
Whom I so oft have learnéd to resound
That lovéd name. For me my plaints shall tell
The plaining fountaines and the murm'ring windes: 10
Pittie and griefe shall speake out of my face,
And in the end though all things else prove dombe,
My verie death shall tell my martirdome.

Er. Love (deare Mirtillo)'s like a fire inclosde,
    Which straightly kept, more fiercely flames at last,   15
    Thou shouldst not have so long conceald from me
    The fire, since it thou couldst not hide.
    How often have I said Mirtillo burnes,
    But in a silent flame and so consumes.
Mir. My selfe I harméd, her not to offend   20
    (Curteous Ergasto) and should yet be dombe,
    But strict necessitie hath made me bold.
    I heare a voice which through my scaréd eares
    Woundeth, alas, my wretched heart with noise
    Of Amarillis nighing nuptiall feast;   25
    Who speakes ought els to me he holds his peace.
    Nor dare I further search, as wel for feare
    To give suspition of my love, as for to finde
    That which I would not. Well I know (Ergasto)
    It fits not with my poore and base estate   30
    To hope at all a Nymphe so rarely qualifide,
    Of bloud and spright truly celestiall,
    Should prove my wife. O no, I know too well,
    The lowlinesse of my poore humble starre,
    My desteny's to burne! Not to delight   35
    Was I brought forth, but since my cruel fates
    Have made me love my death more then my life,
    I am content to die, so that my death
    Might please her that's the cause thereof;
    And that she would but grace my latest gaspe   40
    With her faire eyes, and once before she made
    Another by her marriage fortunate,
    She would but heare me speake. Curteous Ergasto,
    If thou lov'st me, helpe me with this favour,
    Aide me herein, if thou tak'st pittie of my case.   45
Er. A poore desire of love, and light reward
    Of him that dies, but dang'rous enterprise.
    Wretched were she, should but her father know
    She had bow'd downe her eares to her lovers words,
    Or should she be accuséd to the priest,   50
    Her father in lawe; for this perhaps she shunnes
    To speake with you, that els doth love you well,
    Although she it conceales, for women though
    They be more fraile in their desires,
    Yet are they craftier in hiding them;   55

If this be true, how can she show more love
Then thus in shunning you? She heares in vaine,
And shunnes with pittie that can give no helpe.
It is sound counsell soone to cease desiring,
When we cannot attaine to our aspiring.   60
Mir. Oh, were this true, could I but this beleeve,
  Thrise happie paine, thrise fortunate distresse.
  But tell me, sweet Ergasto, tell me true,
  Which is the shepheard whom the starres so friend?
Er. Knowst thou not Silvio, Montane's onely sonne?   65
  Dianaes priest, that rich and famous shepheard,
  That gallant youth? He is the very same.
Mir. Most happie youth, that hast in tender yeares
  Found fate so ripe. I do not envy thee,
  But plaine my selfe.
Er.   Nor need you envy him   70
  That pittie more then envy doth deserve.
Mir. Pittie! And why?
Er.   Because he loves her not.
Mir. And lives he? Hath a hart? And is not blinde?
  Or hath she on my wretched hart spent all her flames?
  And her faire eyes blowne all their loves on mee?   75
  Why should they give a Jemme so precious
  To one that neither knowes it, nor regards it?
Er. For that the heavens the health of Arcady
  Do promise at these nuptialls. Know you not
  How we do stil appease our goddesse wrath   80
  Each yeare with guiltlesse blood of some poore Nymphe,
  A mortall and a miserable tribute?
Mir. T'is newes to mee, that am a new inhabitant,
  As 't pleaseth love and my poore desteny,
  That did before inhabit savadge woods;   85
  But what I pray you was that greevous fault
  That kindled rage in a celestiall brest?
Er. I will report the dolefull tragedy
  From the beginning of our misery,
  That able are pittie and plaints to drawe   90
  From these hard rocks, much more from humane brests.
  In that same golden age when holy priesthood, and
  The temples charge was not prohibited
  To youth, a noble swaine Amintas call'd,
  Priest at that time, lovéd Lucrina bright,   95

A beauteous Nymphe, exceeding faire, but therewithall
Exceeding false, and light. Long time she loved him,
Or at least, she seeméd so, with fained face
Nursing his pure affections with false hopes
Whilst she no other suters had. But see,   100
Th' unconstant wretch! No sooner was she wooed
By a rude shepheard, but at first assault,
At his first sighe, she yeelded up her love
Before Amintas dream't of Jealousie.
At last Amintas was forlorne, despis'd   105
So that the wicked woman would not see, nor heare
Him speake; now if the wretch did sigh,
Be thou the judge that knowst his paine by proofe.
Mir. Aye me, this griefe all other griefs exceeds.
Er. After he had his heart recoveréd   110
From his complaints, he to his goddesse turnes,
And praying sayes; Great *Cinthia*, if I have
At any time kindled with guiltlesse hands
Thy holy flames, revenge thou then for me
This broken faith of my unconstant Nimphe.   115
Diana heares the praiers of her priest,
And straight out-breathing rage she takes her bowe
And shootes shafts of inevitable death
Into the bowels of Arcadia.
People of every sexe, of every age   120
Soone perishéd; no succour could be found;
T' was bootlesse art to search for remedies,
For often on the patient the phisitian died.
One onely remedie did rest, which was
Strait to the nearest Oracle they went,   125
From whom they had an answere verie cleare,
But above measure deadly horrible.
Which was, our *Cinthia* was displeasd, and to
Appease her ire, either Lucrina or some else for her,
Must by Amintas hands be sacrifiz'd.   130
Who when she had long time in vaine complain'd,
And lookt for helpe from her new friend in vaine,
Was to the sacred Altars led with solemne pompe,
A wofull sacrifice. Where at those feete
Which had pursuéd her long time in vaine   135
At her betrayéd Lovers feete she bends
Her trembling knees, attending cruell death.

Amintas stretcheth out the holy sword,
Seeming to breath from his inflaméd lippes
Rage and revenge; turning to her his face,   140
Speakes with a sigh, the messenger of death:
Lucrina for thy further paines, behold
What Lover thou hast left, and what pursude
Judge by this blow. And with that very word
Striketh the blade into his wofull brest,   145
Falling a sacrifice upon the sacrifice.
At such a straunge and cruell spectacle,
The Nymphe amazéd stands twixt life and death,
Scarce yet assur'd whether she wounded were
With griefe, or with sword. At last, assoone   150
As she recovered had her spright, and speech,
She plaining saies: O faithfull valiant love!
O too late knowne! That by thy death hast giv'n
Me life and death at once. If t'were a fault
To leave thee so, behold I'le mend it now,   155
Eternally uniting both our soules.
And therewithall she takes the sword, all warme
With the blood of her too late lovéd friend,
And strikes it through her hart, falling upon
Amintas that was scarcely dead as yet   160
And felt perchance that fall. Such was their ende;
To such a wretched end did too much love,
And too much trechery conduct them both.
Mir. O wretched Shepheard, and yet fortunate,
That hadst so large and famous scope to showe   165
Thy troth, and waken lively pittie of thy death
Within anothers brest. But what did follow?
Was *Cinthia* pleasd? Found they a remedie?
Er. Somewhat it slak't, but yet not quite put out.
For after that a yeare was finishéd,   170
Her rage began a fresh, so that of force
They driven were unto the Oracle
To aske new counsell, but brought back againe
An answere much more wofull then the first,
Which was to sacrifice them: and each after yeare,   175
A maid, or woman, to our angry power,
Ev'n till the third and past the fourth degree:
So should ones blood for many satisfie.
Besides, she did upon th' unhappie sexe

Impose a wretched and a cruell lawe;   180
And (if you marke their nature) inobservable,
A law recorded with vermilian blood:
What ever maid or woman broken had
Their faith in love, and were contaminate,
If they should find none that would die for them   185
They were condemn'd without remission.
To these our greevous great calamities,
The fathers hop'd to finde a happie ende
By this desired marriage day. For afterward
Having demaunded of the Oracle   190
What end the heavens prescribéd had our ill,
Answere was giv'n in such like words as these:
No end there is to that which you offends,
Till two of heavens issue love unite;
And for the auncient fault of that false wight   195
A faithfull Shepheards pittie make amends.
Now is there not in all Arcadia
Other bowes left of that celestiall roote:
Save Amarillis and this Silvio,
Th' one of *Pans* seed, th' other of *Hercules.*   200
Nor to our mischiefe yet hath never hapt
That male and female met at any time
Till now. Therefore good reason Montane hath
To hope, though all things sort not to the Oracle,
Yet here's a good foundation laid: the rest   205
High fates have in their bosomes bred,
And will bring forth at this great marriage day.
Mir. O poor Mirtillo! Wretched man!
So many cruell enemies! Such warres!
To worke my death cannot great Love suffice?   210
But that the Fates their armes will exercise?
Er. This cruell love (Mirtillo) feeds himselfe
With teares, and griefe, but's never satisfide.
I promise thee to set my wits a worke
That the faire Nymphe shall heare thee speake. Lets goe!   215
These burning sighes do not as they do seeme,
Bring any cooling to th' inflaméd hart:
But rather are huge and impetuous windes,
That blow the fire, and make it greater prove,
With swelling whirlwindes of tempestuous love,   220
Which unto wretched lovers alwaies beares

Thick clouds of griefe, and showres of dreary teares.

Act I Scene 3

CORISCA.

[*Cor.*] Who ever sawe or heard a straunger, and
  A fonder passion of this foolish love?
  Both love, and hate, in one selfe hart combin'd
  With such a wondrous mixture: as I know not how,
  Or which of them hath got the deeper roote.   5
  If I Mirtilloes beautie do behold:
  His gracious count'nance, good behaviour,
  Actions, customes, words and manly lookes,
  Love me assailes with such a puissant fire
  That I burne altogither. And it seemes   10
  Other affections are quite vanquishéd with this.
  But when I thinke upon th' obstinate love
  He to another beares; and that for her
  He doth despise (I will be bold to say)
  My famous beautie of a thousand sought,   15
  I hate him so, I so abhorre the man,
  That's impossible me thinkes at all
  Onc sparke of love for him should touch my heart.
  Thus with my selfe sometime I say: Oh if I could
  Enjoy my sweet Mirtillo! Were he mine,   20
  And had not others interest in him,
  Oh more then any other, happie Corisca.
  And then in me upflames such great good will,
  And such a gentle love to him, that I resolve
  Straight to discover all my hart to him,   25
  To follow him, and humbly sue to him:
  Nay more, ev'n to fall downe and worship him.
  On th' other side, I all reclaiméd say,
  A nice proud foole! One that disdaineth me!
  One that can love another and despise my selfe!   30
  One that can looke on me and not adore me?
  One that can so defend him from my looke,
  That he dies not for love. And I that should
  See him (as I have many more ere this)
  An humble suppliant before my feete,   35
  Am humble suppliant at his feete my selfe.

Then such a rage at him possesseth mee,
That I disdain my thoughts should think on him,
Mine eyes should looke on him. His verie name
And all my love, I worse then death do hate.   40
Then would I have him the wofulst wight alive:
And with these hands then could I kill the wretch.
Thus hate, and love, spight, and desire make warre.
I that have bene till now tormenting flame
To thousand harts must languish now my selfe.   45
And in my ill, know others wretchednesse.
I that so many years in cities, streets, courts,
Have bene invincible to worthy friends,
Mocking their many hopes, their great desires,
Now conquered am, with silly rusticke love   50
Of a base shepheards brat. Oh above all
Wretched Corisca now. What shall I do
To mitigate this amorous furious rage?
Whilst other women have a heape of loves,
I have no other but Mirtillo onely.   55
Am I not stoutly furnished? Oh thousand times,
Ill-counsell'd foole! That now reducéd art
Into the povertie of one sole love:
Corisca was ne're such a foole before.
What's faith? What's constancy, but fables fain'd   60
By jealous men, and names of vanitie,
Simple women to deceive. Faith in a womans hart
(If faith in any womans hart there bee)
Can neither vertue nor yet goodnesse bee.
But hard necessitie of love, a wretched law   65
Of beautie weake that pleaseth onely one,
Because she is not gracious in the eyes of more.
A beautious Nymphe, sought too by multitudes
Of worthy lovers, if she be content
With onely one, and all the rest despise,   70
Either she is no woman, or if so she be,
She is a foole. What's beautie worth unseene?
Or seene, unsought? Or sought too but of one?
The more our lovers be the greater men,
The surer pledge have we in this vild world   75
That we are creatures glorious and rare;
The goodly splendor of a beautious Nymphe
Is to have many friends. So in good Townes

Wise men ever doo. It is a fault,
A foolish tricke, all to refuse for one 80
What one cannot, many can well performe:
Some serve, some give, some fit for other use.
So in the Citie lovely Ladies do,
Where I by wit, and by example too,
Of a great Lady learnd the Art of love. 85
Corisca, would she say, Let thy
Lovers and thy garments be alike.
Have many; use, weare but one, and change often.
Too much conversing breedeth noysomenesse,
And noysomenesse despight, which turnes to hate: 90
We cannot worser do then fill our friends;
Let them go hungry rather from thee still.
So did I alwaies, alwaies loving store,
One for my hand, an other for mine eye:
The best I ever for my bosome kept, 95
None for my heart, as neare as ere I could.
And now I know not how Mirtillo comes
Me to torment; now must I sigh, and worse
Sigh for my selfe, deceiving no man else.
Now must I robbe my limmes of their repose, 100
Mine eyes of sleepe, and watch the breake of day:
Now do I wander through these shadow'd woods,
Seeking the footsteps of my hated love.
What must Corisca do? Shall I entreat him?
No: my hate not gives me leave. Ile give him o're, 105
Nor will my love consent. What shall I do?
Prayers and subtilties I will attempt:
I will bewray my love, but not as mine,
If this prevaile not, then Ile make disdaine
Finde out a memorable huge revenge. 110
Mirtillo, if thou canst not like my love,
Then shalt thou trie my hate. And Amarillis,
Thou shalt repent thou ere my rivall wert,
Well, to your costs you both shall quickly prove,
What rage in her can do that thus doth love. 115

Act I Scene 4

TITIRUS. MONTANUS. DAMAETUS.

[*Tit.*] So helpe me Gods, I know I now do speake
  To one that understands more then I do.
  These Oracles are still more doubtfull then
  We take them, for their words are like to knives,
  Which taken by the hafts are fit for use,   5
  But by the edges held, they may do harme.
  That Amarillis, as you argue, is
  By the high heavenly Destenies elected for
  Aracadias universall health: who ought
  More to desire, or to esteeme the same   10
  Then I that am her father? But when I regard
  That which the Oracle foretold, ill do the signes
  Agree with our great hopes: since love should then
  Unite, how falls it out he flies from her?
  How can hate and despight bring forth loves fruite?   15
  Ill could he contradict had heav'ns ordain'd it.
  But since he doth contrary it, t'is cleare,
  Heavens do not will: for if so they would
  That Amarillis should be Silvioes wife,
  A Lover, not a Huntsman, him they would have made.   20
Mon. Do you not see he is a child as yet:
  He hath attain'd scarcly to eighteene yeares,
  All in good time he may yet taste of love.
Tit. Taste of a beast, heele never woman like.
Mon. Many things alter in a yong mans heart.   25
Tit. But alwaies love is naturall to youth.
Mon. It is unnaturall where yeares do want.
Tit. Love alwaies flowres in our green time of age.
Mon. It doth but flowre, t'is quite without all fruit.
Tit. With timely flowres love ever brings forth fruit.   30
  Hither I came not for to jeast (Montane)
  Nor to contend with you. But I the father am
  Of a deare onely child, and (if 't be lawfull so to say)
  A worthy child and, by your leave, of many sought.
Mon. Titirus, if the Destenies have not ordain'd   35
  This marriage, yet the faith they gave on earth,
  Bindes them untoo't, which if they violate,
  They violate their vow to *Cinthia*,
  Who is enrag'd gainst us, how much thou knowst.

But for as much as I discover can   40
The secret counsailes of th' eternall powers:
This knot was knit by th' and of Desteny.
All to good end will sort; be of good cheere.
I'le tell you now a dreame I had last night.
I sawe a thing which makes my auncient hope   45
Revive within my heart, more then before.
Tit. Dreames in the end prove dreames, but what saw you?
Mon. Do you remember that same wofull night,
When swelling Ladon overflowd his bankes,
So that the fishes swam where birds did breed,   50
And in a moment did the ravenous floud,
Take men and beasts by heapes and heards away?
(Oh sad remembrance) in that very night
I lost my child, more deare then was my heart:
Mine onely child, in cradle warmly laid,   55
Living, and dead, dearely belov'd of me.
The Torrent tooke him hence ere we could proove
To give him succour, being buried quite,
In terrour, sleepe, and darknesse of the night:
Nor could we ever find the cradle where he lay.   60
By which I gesse some whirlpit swallowd both.
Tit. Who can gesse otherwise? And I remember now,
You told me of this your mishap before:
A memorable misadventure sure,
And you may say, you have two sonnes begot,   65
One to the woods, the other to the waves.
Mon. Perhaps the pitious heavens will restore
My first sonnes losse in him that liveth yet;
Still must we hope; now listen to my tale.
The time when light and darknesse strove together,   70
This one for night, the other for the day,
Having watcht all the night before, with thought
To bring this marriage to a happie end,
At last, with length of wearinesse, mine eyes
A pleasing slumber closde, when I this vision sawe: 75
Me thought I sat on famous Alfeus banke,
Under a leavy plane tree with a bayted hooke,
Tempting the fishes in the streame, in midst
Whereof there rose me thought an agéd man,
His head and beard dropping downe silver teares,   80
Who gently raught to me with both his hands

A naked childe, saying, Behold thy sonne,
Take heed thou killst him not. And with that word
He divéd downe againe. When straight the skies
Waxt blacke with cloudes, threatning a dismall showre,   85
And I afraid, the child tooke in mine armes,
Crying, ah heavens, and will you in an instant then,
Both give and take away my child againe?
When on the sudden all the skie waxt cleare:
And in the River fell a thousand bowes,   90
And thousand arrowes, broken all to shivers.
The body of the plane tree trembled there,
And out of it there came a subtill voyce
Which said, Arcadia shalbe faire againe.
So is the Image of this gentle dreame   95
Fixt in my heart, that still me thinkes I see 't:
But, above all, the curteous agéd man.
For this when you me met, I comming was
Unto the temple for to sacrifize,
To give my dreames presage prosperous successe.   100
Tit. Our dreames are rather representments vaine
Of idle hopes then any things to come:
Onely daies thoughts made fables for the night.
Mon. The mind doth not sleepe ever with the flesh,
But is more watchful then, because the eyes   105
Do not lead it a wandring where they goe.
Tit. Well, of our children what the heavens disposéd have,
Is quite unknowne to us, but sure it is
Yours gainst the law of nature feeles not love.
And mine hath but the bond of his faith giv'n   110
For her reward. I cannot say she loves,
But well I wot she hath made many love:
And t'is unlike, she tastes not that she makes
So many taste. Methinkes shee's alter'd much
From that she was: for full of sport and mirth,   115
Shee's wont to be. But t'is a grievous thing,
To keepe a woman married and unmarried thus.
For like a Rose that in some garden growes,
How daintie t'is against the Sunne doth rise,
Perfuming with sweete odours round about,   120
Bidding the humming bees to honey feast:
But if you then neglect to gather it,
And suffer *Titan* in his middayes course

To scorch her sides, and burne her daintie seat,
There ere Sun-set, discolouréd she falls,   125
And nothing worth upon the shadow'd hedge,
Even so a maid whom mothers care doth keepe,
Shutting her heart from amorous desires.
But if the piercing lookes of hungry lovers eyes
Come but to view her, if she heare him sigh,   130
Her heart soon ope's, her breast soone takes in love:
Which if for shame she hide or feare containe,
The silent wretch in deepe desire consumes.
So fadeth beautie if that fire endure,
And leesing time, good fortune's lost be sure.   135
Mon. Be of good cheare, let not these humane feares
Confound thy spright, let's put our trust i'th' Gods,
And pray to them (t'is meet) for good successe.
Our children are their off-spring, and be sure
They will not see them lost that others keepe.   140
Go'w, let us to the Temple joyntly goe,
And sacrifize you a hee Goat to *Pan*,
I a young Bull to mightie *Hercules.*
He that the heard makes thrive can therewithall
Make him thrive, that with the profits of his heard   145
Hallowes the Altars. Faithfull Dametas,
Go thou and fetch a young and lovely Bull
As anie's in the heard, and bring it by the mountaines way,
I at the Temple will attend for thee.
Tit. A he Goat bring, Dametas, from my heard.   150

Exeunt Mon. and Tit.

Da. Both one and other I will well performe.
I pray the Gods (Montane) thy dreame do sort
Unto as good an end as thou dost hope.
I know remembrance of thy sonne thou lost
Inspires thee with a happie prophecie.   155

Act I Scene 5

SATIR *alone.*

[*Sa.*] Like frost to grasse, like drought to gentle flowres,
Like lightning unto corne, like wormes to seeds,
Like nets to deere, like lime to silly birds,
So to mankind is love a cruell foe.

He that love lik'ned unto fire knew well   5
His perfid'ous and wicked kind. For looke
But on this fire, how fine a thing it is
But touch it, and t'is then a cruell thing.
The world hath not a monster more to dread.
It ravens worse then beasts, and strikes more deepe   10
Then edgéd steele, and like the winde it flies:
And where it planteth his imperious feet,
Each force doth yeeld, all power giveth place.
Ev'n so this love, if we it but beheld,
In two faire eyes, and in a golden Tresse,   15
Oh how it pleaseth! Oh how then it seemes
To breathe out joy, and promise largely peace!
But if you it approach, and tempt it once,
So that it creepe and gather force in you,
Hircane no Tigres, Liby no Lyons hath,   20
Nor poisonous wormes, with teeth or stings so fierce,
That can surpasse, or equall loves disease;
More dreadfull then is hell, then death it selfe,
Sweete pitties foe, the minister of rage:
And to conclude, love voyd of any love.   25
Why speake I thus of love? Why blame him thus?
Is he the cause that the whole world in love,
Or rather love-dissembling, sinneth so?
Oh womans treacherie! That is the cause
That hath begotten love this infamy.   30
How ever love be in his nature good,
With them his goodnesse suddenly he leeseth.
They never suffer him to touch their hearts,
But in their faces onely build his bowre.
Their care, their pompe, and all their whole delight   35
Is in the barke of a bepainted face;
T'is not in them now faith with faith to grace,
And to contend in love with him that loves,
Into two breasts dividing but one will.
Now all their labour is with burnish'd gold   40
To die their haire, and tye it up in curles,
Therein to snare unwary lovers in.
O what a stinking thing it is to see them take
A Pencill up, and paint their bloudlesse cheekes:
Hiding the faults of nature and of time,   45
Making the pale to blush, the wrinkled plaine,

The blacke seem white, faults mending with farre worse.
Then with a paire of pincers do they pull
Their eye-browes till they smart againe.
But this is nothing, though it be too much,   50
For all their customes are alike to these.
What is it that they use which is not counterfeit?
Ope they their mouthes? They lie. Moove they their eyes?
They counterfeit their lookes. If so they sigh,
Their sighes dissembled are. In summe, each act,   55
Each looke, each gesture, is a verie lie.
Nor is this yet the worst. T'is their delight
Them to deceive ev'n most that trust them most;
And love them least that are most worthy love.
True faith to hate, worser then death it selfe: 60
These be the trickes that make love so perverse.
Then is the fault, faithlesse Corisca, thine?
Or rather mine, that have beleev'd thee so?
How many troubles have I for thy sake sustaind?
I now repent; nay, more I am ashamed.   65
Lovers, beleeve me, women once ador'd
Are worser than the griesly powers of hell.
Strait by their valure vaunt they that they are
The same you by your folly fashion them.
Let go these baser sighes, praiers and plaints,   70
Fit weapons for women and children onely.
Once did I thinke that praiers, plaints, and sighes
Might in a womans heart have stirréd up
The flames of love, but, tush, I was deceiv'd.
Then if thou wouldst thy mistresse conquer, leave   75
These silly toyes, and close thou up all love.
Do that which love and nature teacheth thee,
For modestie is but the outward vertue of
A womans face. Wherefore to handle her with modestie
Is a meere fault; she though she use it, loves it not.   80
A tender-harted Lover shalt thou not,
Corisca, ever find me more, but like a man
I will assaile and pierce thee through and through.
Twise have I taken thee, and twise againe
Thou hast escap'd (I know not how) my hands: 85
But if thou com'st the third time in my reach,
I'le fetter thee for running then away.
Th' art wont to passe these woods; I like a hound

Will hunt thee out. Oh, what a sweet revenge
I meane to take: I meane to make thee prove   90
What t'is unjustly to betray thy Love.   *Exit.*

CHORUS

Oh high and puissant law writ, rather borne
Within Joves mightie brest,
Whose ever sweet and lovely loving force,
Towards that good which we unseene suborne,
Our harts doth pull and wills doth wrest,   5
And ev'n natures selfe to it doth force;
Not onely our fraile corpce
Whose sense scarce sees is borne and dies againe,
As daily houres waxe and waine.
But ev'n inward causes, hidden seeds   10
That moves and governes our eternall deeds.
    If great with child the world do wondrous frame
So many beauties still;
And if within as farre as Sunne doth see
To the mightie Moone and starres Titanian fame   15
A living spright doth fill,
With his male valew this same vast degree,
If thence mans ofspring bee.
The plants have life, and beasts both good and bad,
Whether the earth be clad,   20
With floures, or nipt have her ill-feathered wing,
It still comes from thine everlasting spring.
    Nor this alone but that which hopes of fire
Sheds into mortall wights:
From whence starres gentle, now strait fierce are found   25
Clad in good fortunes or mishaps attire.
From whence lifes frailest lights
The houre of birth have, or of death the bound.
That which makes rise or else pulls downe
In their disturbd affects all humane will   30
And giving seems, or taking still.
Fortune, to whom the world would this were given
All from thy soveraigne bountie is deriven.
    Oh word inevitably true and sure
If it thy meaning is   35
Arcadia shall after so many woes

Finde out new rest and peace, new life procure;
If the fore-told-on blisse
Which the great Oracle did erst expose
Of the faire fatall marriage rose   40
Proceed from thee, and is thy heav'nly minde
Her fixéd place doth find;
If that same voice do not dissemble still,
Who hinders then the working of thy will?
    See loves and pitties foe, a wayward swaine,   45
A proud and cruell youth,
That comes from heaven, and yet with heav'n contends.
See then another Lover (faithfull in vaine)
Battring a harts chast truth,
Who with his flames perhaps thy will offends,   50
The lesse that he attends,
Pittie to's plaints: reward to his desart
More straungely flames in faith his hart.
Fatall this beautie is to him that it high prizeth,
Being destenied to him that it despizeth.   55
    Thus in it selfe, alas, divided stands
This heavenly power,
And thus one fate another justles still,
Yet neither conquered is, neither commands.
False humane hopes that towre   60
And plant a siege to th' Elementall hill,
Rebellious unto heavens will:
Arming poore thoughts like giant fooles againe,
Lovers and no Lovers vaine.
Who would have thought love and disdaine, blind things,   65
Should mount above the soveraigne starry wings.
    But thou that standst above both starres and fate,
And with thy wit divine,
Great mover of the skies, dost them restraine,
Behold: we thee beseech our doubtfull state   70
With desteny combine.
And fathers loving zeale, love and disdaine,
Mixe flame and frozen vaine.
Let them that shund to love, now learne to love,
Let not that other mone.   75
Ah, let not others blindest folly thus
Thy gently-promisde pittie take from us.
But who doth know? Perhaps this same that seemes

An unavoydable mischievous estate,
May prove right fortunate.   80
   How fond a thing it is for mortall sight
   To search into the eternall sunnes high light!

Act II Scene 1

ERGASTO. MIRTILLO.

[*Er.*] How I have searcht alongst the rivers side,
   About the meadowes, fountains, and the hils,
   To find thee out: which now I have, the gods be praisd.
Mir. Ah, that thy newes, Ergasto, may deserve
   This haste. But bringst thou life or death?   5
Er. This though I had I would not give it thee.
   That do I hope to give thee, though I have it not
   As yet. But fie, thou must not suffer griefe
   To overthrow thy sences thus. Live, man, and hope.
   But to the purpose of my comming now,   10
   Ormino hath a sister, knowst her not?
   A tall big wench, a merry-countnaun'st Nymphe
   With yealow haire, somewhat high-colouréd.
Mir. What is her name?
Er.   Corisca.
Mir.   I know her well,
   And heretofore have spoke with her.   15
Er. Then know that she (and see withall your lucke)
   Is now become (I know not by what priviledge)
   Companion to your beauteous Amarillis.
   I have discoveréd all your love to her,
   And this which you desire, and readily   20
   She me hath giv'n her faith to bring 't about.
Mir. O happie Mirtillo if this same prove true:
   But said she nothing of the meanes whereby?
Er. Nothing as yet, nor would she that conclude
   Untill she knew the manner of your love.   25
   How it began, and what hath hapt therein,
   That she might easilier spie into the hart
   Of your belovéd Nymphe, and better know
   How to dispose by praiers or by fraud
   Of her request. For this I came to you,   30
   And make me now acquainted from the head,

With all the historie of your deare Love.
Mir. So will I do, but yet, Ergasto, know
   This memorie (a bitter hopelesse thing)
   Is like a fire-brand tosséd in the winde,   35
   By which how much the fire increaseth still,
   So much the brand with blazing flame consumes.
   O piercing shaft made by some power divine!
   The which the more we seeke to draw it out,
   The faster hold it takes, the deeper roote.   40
   Well can I tell you that these Lovers hopes
   Are full of vanities and falshoods still;
   Loves fruit is bitter, though the roote be sweet.
   In that sweet time when dayes advantage get
   Above the nights, then when the year begins,   45
   This daintie pilgrim, beauties bright new sunne,
   Came with her count'nance like another spring,
   T' illuminate my then thrise happie soyle
   Of Pisa and Eglidis faire. Brought by her mother
   To see the sacrifices and the sports   50
   That celebrated in those solemne daics
   Were unto Jove. Where while she ment to make
   Her eye-sight blest with that same spectacle,
   She blest the spectacle with her faire eyes,
   Being loves greatest miracle beneath the skies.   55
   No sooner had I seene that face, but straight
   I burnt, defending not the formost looke,
   Which though mine eies into my brest directed
   Such an imperious beautie, as me thought did say,
   Mirtillo, yeeld thy hart, for it is mine.   60
Er. Oh in our brests what mighty power hath love?
   Ther's none can tell, save they the same which prove.
Mir. See how industrious love can worke ev'n in
   The simplest brests. A sister which I had
   I made acquainted with my thoughts, who was   65
   By chaunce companion to my cruell Nymphe,
   The time she staid in Pisa and Elide.
   Shee faithfull counsell and good aide me gave,
   She drest me finely in one of her gownes,
   Circling my temples with a periwig.   70
   Which gracefully she trimméd up with flowres.
   A quiver and a bowe hung at my side;
   She taught me furthermore to faine my voice

And lookes, for in my face as then there grew no haire.
This done, she me conducted where the Nimphe   75
Was wont to sport her selfe, and where we found
A noble troupe of maydens of Megara,
By blood or love allyéd to my goddesse.
Mongst whom she stood like to a princely Rose,
Among a heape of humble Violets.   80
We had not long bene there before uprose
One of the maydens of Megara, and thus bespake:
Why stand we idly still in such a time
When palmes and famous trophees are so rife?
Have not we armes counterfait fights to make   85
As well as men? Sisters, be rulde by mee:
Let's prove among our selves our armes in jest,
That when we come to earnest them with men,
We may them better use. Let's kisse, and strive
Who can kisse sweetliest among our selves;   90
And let this garland be the victors gaine.
All at the proposition laught; and all
Unto it strait agreed. Straigtway began
A sight confused: no signall we attended,
Which by her seene that first ordaind the sport,   95
She saies againe: Let's make her worthy judge
That hath the fairest mouth. All soone agreed,
And Amarillis chose, who sweetly bowing downe
Her beauteous eyes, in modest blushing staind,
Did show they were as faire within as th' were without.   100
Or that her face her rich-clad mouth envyed,
And would be cloath'd in pompous purple too,
As who should say, I am as faire as it.
Er. In good time did you chaunge into a Nymphe,
A happy token of good lucke to come.   105
Mir. Now did the beautious judge sit in her place,
According as the Megarence prescrib'd
Each went by lot to make due proofe of her
Rare mouth, that heavenly paragon of sweetnesse,
That blessed mouth that may be likened to   110
A perfum'd Indian shell of oriental pearle,
Op'ning the daintie treasure, mixt with hony sweet
And purple blush. I cannot (my Ergasto) tell
Th' inexplicable sweetnesse which I felt
Out of that kisse. But looke what Cypres canes   115

Or hives of Hybla have are nothing at all
Compar'd with that which then I tasted there.
Er. Oh happy theft, sweet kisse.
Mir.   Yea, sweet,
But yet not gracious, for it wanted still
The better part: love gave it, but love not   120
Return'd it backe.
Er.   But then how did you
When it was your lot to kisse?
Mir.   Unto those lips
My soule did wholy flie, and all my life
So shut therein, as in a litle space
It waxéd nothing but a kisse. And all   125
My other limmes stood strengthlesse, trembling still
When I approachéd to her lightning lookes;
Knowing my deed was theft and eake deceit,
I feared the majestie of her faire face;
But she assures me with a pleasing smile: 130
And puts me forward more, love sitting like
A Bee upon two fresh and daintie Roses close.
Kissing, I tasted there the honey sweet,
But having kist, I felt the lovely Bee
Strike through my hart with his sharp piercing sting.   135
And being wounded thus, halfe desperate,
I thought t' have bitten those manslaught'ring lips,
But that her odoriferous breath like aire divine,
Wak'ned my modestie and still my rage.
Er. This modestie molesteth Lovers still.   140
Mir. Now were the lotts fulfild, and ev'ry one
With heedfull minds the sentence did attend:
When Amarillis judging mine the best,
With her owne hands she crownes my tresses with
The gentle garland kept for victorie.   145
But never was shadelesse meadow drier parcht
Under the balefull fury of the heavenly dog,
Then was my hart in sunshine of that sweet,
Never so vanquisht as in victory.
Yet had I power to take the garland off,   150
And reach it her, saying, to you belongs
Alone the same. T'is due to you, that made
Mine good, by vertue of your mouth.
She gently took't and crownd her selfe therewith.

And with an other that she ware crownd mine.   155
T'is this I weare thus driéd as you see,
It will I carry to my grave with mee.
In deare remembraunce of that happie day.
But more for sign of my dead hopes decay.
Er. Thou pittie more then envy dost deserve,   160
That wert another Tantalus in loves delights,
That of a sport a torment true didst make.
Thou pai'st too deare for thy stolne delicates.
But did she ere perceive thy policies?
Mir. That know I not (Ergasto), yet thus much I know,   165
That in the time she made Elidis blest
With her sweet count'nance, she liberall was
Of pleasing lookes to mee. But thereof did
My cruell fates robbe me so sodeinly,
That I perceiv'd it not till they were gone.   170
When I drawne by the power of her beauteous looke
Leaving my home came hither where thou knowst
My father had this poore habítacle.
But now the day that with so faire a spring began,
Come to his western bound, thunders and lightens out,   175
Ah, then I saw these were true signes of death.
Now had (alas) my tender father felt,
My not-foreseene departure, and orecome
With griefe, fell sicke nigh hand to death,
Whereby I was constrainéd to returne.   180
Ah, that returne proovéd the fathers health,
But deadly sicknesse to the sonne: for in short time
I languishéd and pinéd quite away.
Which held me from the time the sunne had left
The bull, untill his entry into Capricorne.   185
And so had still, had not my pitious father sought
For counsaile to the Oracle, which said,
Onely Arcadia could restore my health.
So I returnd to see her that can heale
My bodies griefe (O Oracles false lye)   190
But makes my soule sicke everlastingly.
Er. Strange tale thou telst (Mirtillo) though 't be true.
The onely health to one that's desperate
Is to dispaire of health. And now t'is time
I goe communicate with our Corisca.   195
Go to the fountaine you; there stay for me;

Ile make what haste I can.
Mir. Goe happily,
The heavens (Ergasto) quit thy curtesie.

Act II Scene 2

DORINDA. LUPINO. SILVIO.

[*Dor.*] O fortunate delight, and care of my
Faire spightfull Silvio. Ah that I were
As deare unto thy cruell maister as thou art;
(Happie Melampo), he with that white hand,
That nippes my heart, thee softly stroking feeds. 5
With thee all day and all the night he is,
Whilst I that love him so, sigh still in vaine.
And that which greeves me worst, he gives thee still
Kisses so sweete, that had I one of them,
I should goe blest away; I cannot choose 10
But kisse Melampo. Now if th'happie starres
Of love sent thee to me because thou shouldst
Find out his steps, go'w whither me great love
Thee nature teacheth. But I heare a horne
Sound in these woods.
Sil. Vo ho ho, Melampo, ho. 15
Dor. If my desire deceive me not, that is the voice
Of my beloved Silvio, that calls his dogge;
He hath our labour sav'd.
Sil. Vohoho, Melampo, ho.
Dor. Doubtlesse tis he; happie Dorinda, heavens
Have sent him whom thou soughtst; t'is best I put 20
The dogge aside, so may I win his love.
Lupino!
Lup. What's your will?
Dor. Go hide thy self
In that same thicke, and take the dogge with thee.
Lup. I goe.
Dor. And stirre not till I call.
Lup. No more I will.
Dor. Go soone.
Lup. And call you soone, least hunger make 25
The dogge beleeve I am a shoulder of mutton, and so fall too.
Dor. Go, get you hence, hen-hearted wretch.

Sil. O wretched me, whither shall I goe
  To follow thee my deere, my faithfull dogge?
  The dales, the mountaines, I have sought with care,   30
  All weary now I am. Curst be the beast
  Thou didst pursue. But see, a Nymphe; perhaps
  She can tell newes of him. Out upon her!
  T'is she that's still so troublesome to me.
  I must dissemble. Faire and gracious Nymphe,   35
  Did you my good Melampo see to day?
Dor. I faire, good Silvio? Can you call me faire
  That am not faire a whit unto your eyes?
Sil. Or faire, or foule, did you not see my dogge?
  Answere to this, or I am quickly gone.   40
Dor. Stil thou art froward unto her that thee adores,
  Who would beleeve that in that smooth aspéct
  Were harbouréd such rugged thoughts. Thou through
  These savage woods and rocky hills pursu'st
  A beast that flies thee, and consum'st thy selfe   45
  In tracing out thy greyhounds steps: and me
  Thou shunst and dost disdaine that loves thee so.
  Ah, leave these does that runne so fast away,
  Take hold of my thy preordainéd pray.
Sil. Nymphe, I Melampo came to seeke, not to loose time,   50
  Farewell.
Dor.   Do not so shun me, cruell Silvio,
  I'le tell thee newes of thy Melampo, man.
Sil. Thou jests, Dorinda.
Dor.   Silvio, I protest
  By that deare love that me thy handmaid makes,
  I know where thy Melampo is that courst the doe.   55
Sil. How did he leese her?
Dor.   Both dog and doe are in my power.
Sil. Both in your power?
Dor.   Why doth it grieve you then
  That I them hold that do adore you soe?
Sil. Deare Dorinda, quickly give me him.
Dor. See, wav'ring child, am I not fortunate   60
  When a beast and a dogge can make me deare to thee?
Sil. Good reason too, but yet her Ile deceive.
Dor. What will you give me?
Sil.   Two guilded apples
  Which my mother gave me yesterday.

Dor. I want no apples, and perhaps I could   65
   Thee better-tasted give, didst thou not thus
   Disdaine my gifts.
Sil.   What wouldst thou have, a kid,
   A lambe? Ah, but my father gives me no such leave.
Dor. Nor kids, nor lambes do I desire; it is thy love,
   My Silvio, which I seeke.
Sil.   Wilt thou nought but my love?   70
Dor. Nought else.
Sil.   I give it thee. Now, my deare Nymphe,
   Give me my dog and doe.
Dor.   Ah, that thou knewst
   That treasures worth whereof thou seemst so liberall,
   Or that thy heart did answere to thy tongue.
Sil. Heare me, faire Nymphe, thou ever telst me of   75
   A certaine love; I know not what it is.
   Thou dost desire I should thee love, and so I do.
   As farre forth as I can, or understand;
   Thou callst me cruell and I know not crueltie.
Dor. Wretched Dorinda, how hast thou plast thy hopes   80
   In beautie feeling ne're a sparke of love?
   Thou lovely boy, art such a fire to me,
   And yet burnes not thy selfe. Thee under humane shape
   Of daintie mother did the *Cyprian* dame
   Bring forth; thou hast his arrowes and his fire.   85
   Well knowe my breast both burnt and wounded too,
   Get but his wings unto thy shoulders, and
   New *Cupid* shalt thou be, wer't not thy heart
   Is made of rocky frozen Isy shelfe,
   Thou wantest naught of love but love it selfe.   90
Sil. Tell me, what kind of thing is this same love?
Dor. If in thy face I looke (oh lovely boy)
   Then is this love a paradize of joy.
   But if I turne and view my spirit well,
   Then t'is a flame of deepe infernall hell.   95
Sil. Nymphe, no more words, give me my dog and doe.
Dor. Nay, give me first the love you promiséd.
Sil. Have I not giv'n it? What a stirre is here
   Her to content. Take it, do what thou wilt;
   Who doth forbid thee? What wouldst thou have more?   100
Dor. Thou sow'st thy seed in sand, wretched Dorinda.
Sil. What would you have? Why do you linger thus?

Dor. As soone as you have got what you desire,
   (Perfidious Silvio) you are gone from me.
Sil. No, trust me Nymphe.
Dor.   Give me a pledge.
Sil.   What pledge?   105
Dor. I dare not tell.
Sil.   And why?
Dor.   I am asham'd.
Sil. Are you asham'd to speake, and not asham'd
   It to receive?
Dor.   If you will promise me
   To give it, I will tell.
Sil.   I promise you.
Dor. (Silvio my deare) do you not understand me yet?   110
   I should have understood you but with halfe of this.
Sil. Thou art more subtill much then I.
Dor. I am more earnest, and lesse cruel much then thou.
Sil. To say the troath, I am no Prophet I;
   You must speake if you'le have me understand.   115
Dor. O wretch, one of those which thy mother gave to thee.
Sil. A blow on th' eare?
Dor.   A blow on th' ear to one that loves thee?
Sil. Sometime she maketh much of me with one of them.
Dor. Doth she not kisse you then?
Sil.   Nor she nor any else
   Doth kisse me. But perhaps youl'd have a kisse.   120
   You answere not, your blushing you accuseth.
   I am content, but give me first my dogge.
Dor. Y'have promist me?
Sil.   T'is true, I have promist thee.
Dor. And will you stay?
Sil.   Tush, what a stirre is here! I will.
Dor. Come forth, Lupino; Lupino, dost not heare?   125
Lup. Who calls? I come, I come; it was not I,
   It was the dogge that slept.
Dor.   Behold thy dogge
   More courteous then thy selfe.
Sil.   O happy me.
Dor. He in these armes that thou despisest so
   Did put himselfe.
Sil.   O my most deare Melampo.   130
Dor. Esteeming deare my kisses and my sighes.

Sil. I'le kisse thee thousand times, poore curre.
   Hast thou no harme in running, poore Melampo?
Dor. O happie dog, might I change lots with thee:
   Am I not brought unto an excellent passe.   135
   That of a dog I must be jealous thus?
   Lupino, go unto the hunting strait,
   Ile follow thee.
Lup.   Mistresse I go.   *Exit*

Act II Scene 3

SILVIO. DORINDA.

[*Sil.*] Is ought behind? Where is the Doe you promist me?
Dor. Will you her have alive or dead?
Sil. I understand you not.
   How's she alive; hath not my dog her kild?
Dor. But say the dog hath not.
Sil.   Is she alive?   5
Dor. Alive.
Sil.   So much more welcome she'is.
Dor. Onely shee's wounded in the hart.
Sil.   Thou mock'st:
   How can she live and wounded in the hart?
Dor. My cruell Silvio, I am that same Do,
   Without pursuit or conquest taken so.   10
   Quicke, if thou pleasest to accept of me,
   Dead, if thou dost despise my companie.
Sil. Is this the Do, the game you told me of?
Dor. This is the same. Ay me, why looke you so?
   Hold you a Nimph no dearer then a Do?   15
Sil. I neither hold thee deare nor like of thee:
   But hate thee, brute, vilde, lying filth.
                           Exit

Dor. Is this my guerdon, cruell Silvio?
   Ungratefull boy, is this all my reward?
   I gave Melampo and my selfe with him to thee,   20
   Hoping that thus thou wouldst not have denide
   The sunshine of thine eyes to me. I would
   Have kept thee and thy dog most faithful company.
   I would have wipte thy browes from toilefull sweat:
   Upon this lap that never taketh rest   25

Thou might'st have ta'ne thy rest. I would
Have carried all thy tew and and prov'd thy pray;
When beasts had wanted in the woods thou mightst
Have shot at me for one, and in this brest
Have uséd still thy tough-well-sinew'd bowe.   30
So as thou wouldst, I like thy servant might
Thy weapons carried have, or prov'd thy pray,
Making my brest both quiver and the marke
For those thy shafts. But unto whom speake I?
To him that heares me not, but's fled from me.   35
Flie where thou wilt, thee will I still pursue,
Ev'n into hell, if any hell can be
More painfull then my griefe, then thy great crueltie.

Act II Scene 4

CORISCA.

[*Cor.*] O how Fortune favours my disseignes
  More then I lookt for. She good reason hath,
  For I ne're askt her favour shamefastly.
  Great pow're she hath, and with good cause the world
  Calls her a puissant goddesse: yet must we not sit still,   5
  For sildome idle folkes prove fortunate.
  Had not my industry made me companion unto her,
  What would this fit occasion have availéd me
  To bring my purpose unto passe? Some foole
  Would have her rivall shund, and shew'd signes of   10
  Her jealousie, bearing an evil eye
  About, but that had beene ill done, for easilier
  May one keepe her from an open then a hidden foe.
  The cover'd rocks are those which do deceive
  The wisest marriners. Who cannot friendship faine,   15
  Cannot truly hate. Now see what I can do;
  I am not such an asse to thinke she doth not love,
  It might she make some other foole beleeve.
  But tush, I am the mistresse of this art. A tender wench,
  Scarce from the cradle crept, in whom love hath   20
  Still'd but the first drop of his sweet, so long
  Pursude and woo'd by a worthy friend,
  And worse, kist, and rekist, and yet not love:
  She is an asse that it beleeves. Ile not beleev't.

But see how Fortune favours me: Behold 25
Where Amarillis is her selfe. Ile make
As though I sawe her not, and stand aside.

Act II Scene 5

AMARILLIS. CORISCA.

[*Am.*] Deare blessed woods, and you the silent groves
    Of rest and peace, the harbour-houses true:
    How willingly I turne to visit you.
    And if my starres had so bene pleasde t'have let
    Me live unto my selfe, I with th' elizian fields, 5
    The happie gardeins of the demy gods,
    Would not have chang'd your gentle shadow spots.
    If I judge right, these worldly goods are nought
    But mischiefes, still the richest have least goods,
    And he possesseth most that is most poore. 10
    Riches are ever snares of libertie.
    What's fame of beautie worth in tender yeares?
    Or heavenly noblenesse in mortall blood?
    So many favours, both of heaven and earth,
    Fields large, and happie, goodly meadow plaines, 15
    Fat pastures that do fatter flocks present,
    If in the same the hart be not content.
    Happie that shepheardesse, whose scarcely knees
    A poore but yet a cleanly gowne doth reach;
    Rich in her selfe, onely in natures gifts, 20
    Who in sweet povertie, no poorenesse knowes,
    Nor feeles no tortures which this riches brings.
    Desire to have much nere doth her torment,
    If she be poore, yet is she well content.
    She natures gifts doth nurse with natures gifts, 25
    Making milke spring with milke, saucing her native sweet
    With hony of the Bee; one fountaine serveth her
    To drinke, to wash, and for her looking glasse.
    If she be well, then all the world is well.
    Let the cloudes rise, and thunder threat amaine, 30
    Her povertie doth all the feare prevent,
    If she be poore, yet is she well content.
    Finely the flocke committed to her charge
    Feeds on the grasse, the whilst her shepheard friend

Feeds on her eyes, not whom the starres, or men,   35
Her destenies, but whom affection chooseth.
Then in the shadow of a Mirtell tree,
Cherisht, she cherisheth againe; nor doth
She feele that heat which she discovers not:
Nor ever heat discover which she doth not feele.   40
Alwaies declaring troth of her intent,
If she be poore, yet is she well content.
True life that knowes not death before they die.
Ah, that I might my fortunes chaunge with theirs.
But see Corisca. Gods save you, good Corisca.   45
Cor. Who calleth me? Deare Amarillis, dearer then
   Mine eies, my life, whither go you alone?
Am. No further then you see, glad I have found you out.
Cor. You have her found that will not part from you.
   And ev'n now, thus was I thinking with my selfe,   50
   Were I her soule, how could she stay away so long?
   And therwithall you came, my deare, and yet
   You do not love your poore Corisca.
Am.   Why so?
Cor. Aske you why so and you a bride today?
Am. A bride?
Cor.   A bride, and yet from me you keep it.   55
Am. How should I utter that I do not know?
Cor. Yet will you faine?
Am.   You jest.
Cor.   T'is you that jest.
Am. And can it then be true?
Cor.   Most certaine true.
   Do you not know thereof?
Am.   I know I promist was,
   But know not that the marriage is so neare.   60
Cor. I heard it of my brother Ormin: and to say the troth,
   There is no other talke. But you looke pale.
   This newes perhaps doth trouble you.
Am.   It is
   Long since the promise past, and still my mother said
   This day it should revive.
Cor.   Unto a better life   65
   You shall revive, for this you should be merry;
   Why do you sigh? Let that poore wretch go sigh.
Am. What wretch?

Cor.   Mirtillo, whom ev'n now I found
   Readie to die: and surely he had died
   Had I not promist him this marriage to disturbe,   70
   Which though I onely for his comfort said,
   Yet were I fit to do it.
Am.   And did he give consent?
Cor. I, and the meanes.
Am.   I pray hou how?
Cor.   Easily:
   So you thereto disposéd be to yeeld.
Am. That could I hope, and would you give your faith   75
   Not to disclose it, I discover would
   A thought which in my heart I long have hid.
Cor. I disclose! Ground open first thy jawes
   And swallow me up by a miracle.
Am. Know then (Corisca) when I think I must   80
   Be subject to a child that hates, that flies from me,
   And hath no other sport but woods and beasts,
   And loves a dogge better then thousand Nimphs,
   I malecontented live halfe desperate.
   But dare not say so for respect I beare   85
   Unto mine honestie, unto my faith
   Which to my father, and what worser is,
   Which to our puissant goddesse I have giv'n.
   If by thy helpe my faith, my life both sav'd,
   I might divide me from this heavie knot,   90
   Then shouldst thou be my health, my veric life.
Cor. If so for this thou sigh'st, good reason thou,
   Deare Amarillis hast. How oft he said
   A thing so faire to one that can despise it?
   So rich a Jemme to one that knowes it not;   95
   But you too craftie are to tell the troth,
   What let's you now to speake?
Am.   The shame I have.
Cor. Sister, you have a mischievous disease;
   I'had rather have the poxe, the fever, or the fistula;
   But trust to me, you'le quickly leave the same: 100
   Once do but master it, and then t'is gone.
Am. This shamefastnesse that nature stamps in us
   Cannot be mastered, for if you seeke
   To hunt it from your hart, it flies into your face.
Cor. O Amarillis, who (too wise) conceales   105

Her ill, at last great folly she reveales.
Hadst thou but at the first descoveréd
This thought to me, thou hadst bene lose ere this.
Now trie Coriscaes art, you could not have
Entrusted you into more subtil faithfull hands.   110
But when you shall be freéd by my helpe
From this same captive husband, will you not
Provide you of another Lover then?
Am. At better leysure we will thinke of that.
Cor. Trust me you cannot faithfull Mirtillo.   115
You know there is not at this day a swaine
For valew, honest troth and beautie, worthier
Of your affection. And you will let him die,
Without so much as saying so. Yet heare him once.
Am. How better t'were to give him peace and stab   120
The roote of such desire as hath no hope.
Cor. Give him this comfort yet before he die.
Am. It rather double will his miserie.
Cor. Leave that to him.
Am.   But what becomes of me,
If ever it be knowne?
Cor.   Small hurt thou hast.   125
Am. And small t'shalbe before my name it do endaunger.
Cor. If you may faile in this, then in the rest
I you may faile. *Adiew.*
Am.   Nay stay, Corisca.
Heare me but speak.
Cor.   No, not a word, unlesse
You promise me.
Am.   I promise you, so you   130
Do tie me to nought else.
Cor.   To nothing else.
Am. And you shall make him thinke I knew not of it.
Cor. Ile make him think it was by chance.
Am.   And that I may
Depart assoone as I thinke good.
Cor.   Assoone
As you have heard him speake.
Am.   And that he shall   135
Quickly dispatch.
Cor.   So shall he do.
Am.   And that

He come not neare me by my darts length never.
Cor. O what a toyle t'is to reforme your simplenesse:
   All parts saving his tongue wee'le surely tie.
   Will you ought else?
Am.   No, nothing else.
Cor.   When wil you do't?   140
Am. When you think good; give me but so much time
   I may go home and heare more of this marriage.
Cor. Go. But take heed you do it warily.
   But heare what I am thinking on. Today
   About noone time among these shadow trees   145
   Come you without your Nimphs; here you shall find
   Me to that end; with me shalbe Nerine,
   Aglaure, Elisa, Phillis, and Licoris, all mine owne,
   As wise as faithfull, good companions.
   Her may you now (as often you have done)   150
   Play at blind buffe. Mirtill will easily thinke
   That for your sport and not for him you came.
Am. This pleaseth me, but yet I would not have
   Your Nimphs to heare the words Mirtillo speakes.
Cor. I understand, and well advisde; let me alone;   155
   I'le make them vanish when I see my time:
   Go, and forget not now to love your poore Corisca.
Am. How can I chuse but love her in whose hands
   I have reposde my life.   *Exit Am.*
Cor.   So she is gone.
   Small force will serve to batter downe this rocke,   160
   Though she have made defence to my assault,
   Yet will she never his abide. I know too well
   How hartie praiers of a gracious Love
   Can tempt a tender wenches hart. Yet with this sport
   I'le tye her so, shee'le scarcely think it sport.   165
   I'le by her words, will she or nill she, spie
   And pierce into the bowels of her hart,
   I'le make me mistresse of her secrets all.
   Then I'le conduct her so that she shall thinke
   Her most unbrideled love and not my art   170
   Hath brought her to play this wretched part.

Act II Scene 6

CORISCA. SATIR.

[*Cor.*] O I am dead.
Sa.   And I alive?
Cor.   Ah turne,
   My Amarillis, turne againe, I taken am.
Sa. Tush, Amarillis heares thee not; be quiet now.
Cor. Oh me, my heare.
Sa.   I have hunted thee so long
   That at the last th' art falne into my snare.   5
   This is the roabe, sister, this is the heare.
Cor. Speake you to me, Satir?
Sa.   I, ev'n to thee.
   Are you not that same famous Corisca, that
   Excellent mistresse of lyes, that at so deare a rate
   False hopes, fain'd lookes, and lying words dost sell,   10
   That hast betraied me so many waies, perfidious Corisca?
Cor. I am Corisca, gentle Satir, but not now
   So pleasing to thine eyes as I have bene.
Sa. I, gentle wicked wretch, I was not so
   When me thou lefst to follow Coridon.   15
Cor. I left thee for another.
Sa.   See, see a wonder,
   This newes indeed. But when I stole
   Faire Lillaes bowe, Cloris scarfe, Daphnes rich roabe,
   And Silvias buskins, then thou promi'st me
   Thy love thou gav'st another should be my reward.   20
   The daintie garland which I gave to thee,
   Thou gav'st to Nisus. And when me thou mad'st
   To watch so many frostie nights, both in
   The cave, the woods, and by the river side,
   And ever mockedst me, was I not gentle then?   25
   Beleeve me, now thou shalt me pay for all.
Cor. Thou stranglest me as if I were a dogge.
Sa. Now see if thou canst runne away againe.
   Thy pollicies shall not availe thee now.
   If but thy head hold on, t'is vaine to strive.   30
Cor. Good Satir, give me leave to speak to thee.
Sa. Speak then.
Cor.   How can I speake? Let me go!
   Upon my faith I will not runne away.

Sa. What faith, oh faithlesse woman hast? Dar'st thou
    Yet speak of faith to me? Ile carry thee   35
    Into the darkest cave this mountaine hath,
    Where never Sunne nor humane steppe approach't;
    I'le hide the rest there; thou with my delight
    And with thy scorne shalt feele what I wil do with thee.
Cor. And canst thou be so cruel to that haire   40
    For which thou oft hast sworne t'were sweet to die,
    And that thou coudst not suffer too much ill for me?
    Oh heavens, oh fates, whom shall a woman trust?
Sa. Ah, wicked, thinkst thou to deceive me yet?
    Canst thou yet tempt me with thy subtilties?   45
Cor. Oh, gentle Satir, do not make a scorne
    Of her that thee adores. If so thy hart
    Be not of marble made, behold me at
    Thy feete; if ever I offended thee (O Idole of
    My soule) I pardon crave. By these same strong   50
    And more then manlike knees which I embrace,
    By that same love thou sometime bar'st to me,
    By that same sweenesse which wont'st to draw,
    Thou said'st, out of mine eyes, calling them starres,
    Now wretched fountaines of these bitter teares,   55
    I pray thee pittie me; let me but go.
Sa. The wretch hath almost mov'd me; should I but trust
    Affection onely I were overcome.
    But to be short, I will not trust thee. Strive no more.
    For all this humblenesse thou are Corisca still.   60
Cor. Oh me, my head, stay, yet do not deny
    Me one poore favour yet.
Sa.   What favour's that?
Cor. Heare me but once.
Sa.   Thou think'st with fainéd words
    And forgéd teares to mollifie my heart.
Cor. Ah, curteous Satir, what wilt thou make of me?   65
Sa. Wee'le trie.
Cor.   No pittie then?
Sa.   No pittie I.
Cor. Art thou resolv'd of this?
Sa.   I am resolv'd.
    Hast thou now made an end of all thy charmes?
Cor. Oh villaine, indiscreet, unseasonable:
    Halfe a man, halfe a goat, and all a beast: 70

Dryed *Carogne,* defect of wicked nature.
Dost thou beleeve Corisca loves not thee?
It is most true. What should I love in thee:
This goodly bunch of that beslavered beard,
These goatlike eares, that stinking toothlesse cave? 75
Sa. Oh witch, are these to me?
Cor.   These are to thee.
Sa. Ribald to me?
Cor.   Halfe goat to thee.
Sa.   And do not I
With these my hands thrust out thy bitches tongue?
Cor. I, if thou durst.
Sa.   A silly woman in my hands,
Dares brave me, dares despise me thus? Well I'le.... 80
Cor. Villaine, what wilt thou do?
Sa.   I'll eate thee quick.
Cor. Where be thy teeth?
Sa.   Oh heavens, who can endure!
I'le pay you home, come on.
Cor.   I will not come.
Sa. That will I see.
Cor.   Spite of thy hart I will not.
Sa. Come on, wee'le see who hath the stronger, thou 85
The necke or I the armes. Nay, soft and faire.
[*Cor.*] Well, let us see.
Sa.   Go too.
Cor.   Satir, hold fast.
Farewell, I would thy necke were broke.
                                        Exit Cor.
Sa. O me, my head, my backe, my side! Oh what
A fall is this! I scarce can turne my selfe. 90
And is she gone and left her head behind?
Unusuall wonder! Nimphs and shepheards, come,
Behold a witchcraft tricke of one that's fled
And lives without a head! How light it is!
It hath no braines; there commeth out no blood. 95
Why looke I so? Oh, foole, she gone without a head!
Thou art without a head that seest not
How thou are mockt. Treacherous, perfidious witch,
Is't not inough th'ast made thy hart to lie,
Thy face, thy words, thy laughter and thy lookes 100
But that thy haire must lie? Poets, behold

Your native gold, your amber pure, that you
So fondly praise, for shame your subject chaunge;
In steed whereof, sing me a witches subtiltie,
That robbeth sepulchres and rotten heads   105
To dress her owne. As well you may go praise
Megeraes viprous monstrous haires. Lovers,
Behold, and be ashaméd wretches now;
Make this the meanes your sences to recover
That are insnar'd in such without more plaints.   110
But why stay I to publish out her shame?
This haire my tongue so famous made erewhile,
I will go prove to make againe as vile.   [*Exit*]

CHORUS

   Great was her fault and errour sure
That did occasion all our teene:
Who loves great lawes holy and pure
(Breaking her faith) did violate
And thereby did illuminate   5
The mortall rage of our immortal queene,
That neither teares nor blood
Of many harmlesse soules have done us good.
So faith to every vertue-roote
The ornament of every foole well borne,   10
In heaven hath surely set his foote,
That worthily are faithlesse held in scorne.
So nature truth would ever happie make,
Ev'n for the true almightie makers sake.
Blind mortalls, you that have so deep desire   15
To get and to possesse
A guilded carkasse of a painted tire,
That like a naked shadow walkes on still,
Seeking her sepulchre by gesse:
What love, or rather fond will,   20
Hath witcht your hart dead beautie to pursue?
Rich treasures are loves follies found. The true
And lively love is of the soule:
All other subjects want what love requires,
Therfore they not deserve these amorous desires.   25
The soule because it onely loves againe,
Is onely worthie of this loving paine.

It is a pretie thing to kisse
The delicate vermilion Rose
Of some faire cheeke; they have prov'd that blisse   30
(Right happie Lovers) so will say. Yet those
Will say againe, kisses are dead and vaine
Where beautie kist restores it not againe.
The strokes of two inamour'd lips are those
Where mouth on mouth loves sweetest vengeance showes.   35
Those are true kisses where with equall wills
We ever give and take againe our fills.
Kisse but a curious mouth, a daintie hand,
A breast, a brow, or what you can demand,
You will confesse no part in woman is,   40
Save for sweet mouth that doth deserve a kisse,
By which two soules with lively spirits meet,
Making live rubies kindly entergreet;
So mongst themselves those sowly sprightfull kisses
Do enter-speake, and in a little sowne   45
Great things bewray, and sweetest secret blisses
To others hidden, to themselves well knowne.
Such joy, nay, such sweet life doth loving prove,
Soule knit to soule by th' earthly knot of love,
Kisses that kisses meet do paint unmov'd   50
Th' incounters of two harts, loving belov'd.

Act III Scene 1

MIRTILLO.

[*Mir.*] O Spring, the gentle childhood of the yeare,
   Mother of floures, fresh hearbs, and fresh desires,
   Thou turn'st againe, but with thee do not turne
   The happie dayes of my delightfull joyes:
   Thou turnst, thou turnst, but with thee turnst nought else   5
   Save of the losse of my dear treasures lorne
   The miserable wretched memorie.
   Thou art the same thou wert, so fresh, so faire,
   But I am not as I was wont to be,
   So deare to other eyes. Oh bitter sweets of love,   10
   Much worser t'is to leese you once possest,
   Then never to have you enjoy'd at all,
   Much like the griefe to chaunge a happie state.

The memorie of any good that wasts,
Consumes it selfe as th' other is consum'd.   15
But if my hopes be not as is their use,
Of brittle glasse, or that my deep desire
Make not my hope much greater then the truth,
Here shall I see the sun-beames of mine eyes.
Here if I be not mockt I shall her see,   20
Stay her quick feete at sound of my lament.
Here shall my greedie eyes after long fast
Receive sweet foode from her divinest looke.
Here will she turne her sov'raigne lights on mee,
If not gentle, yet cruell will they bee,   25
If not the meanes to breed mine inward joy,
So fierce, yet as I die to mine annoy.
O happie day, sigh'd for long time in vaine,
If after times so clouded with complaints,
Love, thou dost graunt me sight of her faire eies,   30
I meane made bright as is the morning Sun,
Hither Ergasto sent me, where he said
Corisca and my beauteous Amarillis
Would be together playing at blind man buffe:
Yet here see I none blind, save my blind will,   35
That wandring seekes her sight by other meanes
But findes it not. O poyson to my food,
This long delay blindeth my heart with feare.
My cruell desteny will never chaunge.
Each houre, each moment that a Lover staies   40
Expecting his contentment seemes a world.
But who doth know? Perhaps I staid too long,
And here Corisca hath attended mee.
Ay me! If this be true, then welcome death.

Act III Scene 2

AMARILLIS. MIRTILLO. CHORUS OF NIMPHS. CORISCA.

[Am.] Behold the buffe!
Mir.   Behold indeed! Ah sight.
Am. Why stay ye now?
Mir.   Ah, voice that hast at once
   Both wounded me and healéd me againe!
Am. Where bee ye? What do ye? Lisetta you

That hath so desir'd this sport, where are you now?   5
Where is Corisca? And where be the rest?
Mir. Now may't be truly said that love is blinde,
And hath a scarfe that bindeth up his eyes.
Am. Come, list to me! Guide me cleare of these trees;
There set me in the plaine; you round about   10
A circle make and so begin the play.
Mir. What shall I do? I see not how this sport
Can do me good, nor I Corisca see, that is
The load-starre of my hopes. Heavens, aide me.
Am. Why, are ye come? Think ye nought else to do   15
But blind mine eies? Where are ye? Let's begin!
*Cho. Nim. Blind love, I do not trust to thee,
That makes desires full of obscuritie.
Thou hast small sight and lesser troath,
Unhappie they that trust thine oath.   20
Blind or not blind, thou tempst in vaine,
For I can shift me in this plaine.
Blind, thou dost see through Argos eies,
Blind, thou best-sighted, safely ties.
Now that I am at libertie,   25
I were a foole to trust to thee.
In jest nor earnest I'le not stay,
Because thou kill'st when thou dost play.*
Am. But ye play too far off; ye should touch me.
Mir. O mightie Gods! What do I see? Am I   30
In heaven or earth? Y' have no such harmonie.
*Cho. Nim. But you that blind and faithlesse prove,
That calleth me to play this houre,
Behold I play, and with my hand
Hit your backe and by you stand.*   35
*I play and round about you run,
And for I trust not you I shun.
Here am I now and there againe,
Whilst you take me, you strive in vaine.
The reason is my heart is free,*   40
Therefore you cannot handle mee.
Am. I thought I had Licoris caught, and I
Have got a tree. I heare you laugh full well.
Mir. Oh would I were that tree. Methinkes I see Corisca
Hidden in yonder shrubs; she nods to mee,   45
Tis ev'n she, she beckens still to mee.

Cho. Nim. Free harts have ever feet to fly,
  And so (entising powre) have I.
  Yet will you tempt me in to traine?
  In faith (sweet) no: t'is all in vaine.   50
  The reason is my hart is free,
  Therefore you cannot handle mee.
Am. I would this tree were burn'd; now had I thought
  I had Elisa ta'en.
Mir.   Yet doth Corisca point;
  She threatens me; sh' would have me put my selfe   55
  Among these Nimphes.
Am.   Belike thus I all day
  Must play with trees.
Cor.   I must spite of my hart
  Go out and speake. Why staist thou, fearfull wretch,
  Untill she come into thy armes? Let her take thee,
  Give me thy dart (foole); go and meet with her.   60
Mir. How ill agrees my hart with my desire!
  Th' one dares so little, th' other seekes so much.
Am. T'is time I turne againe unto the sport,
  I almost weary am. Fie, fie: you make
  Me run too much; in faith y'are too blame.   65
Cho. Nim. Now looke about, triumphant powre,
  That the worlds tribute dost devoure.
  Now bearst thou mocks and many a bat,
  And like an Owle th' art wondred at.
  About whom birds flocke thicke and round,   70
  Whilst them she strives in vaine to wound.
  So art thou, love, this instant tide.
  Laught at and mockt on every side.
  Some hit thy backe, and some thy face,
  Sparing thee neither time nor place.   75
  It will not boote thee spread thy wings,
  Nor that thy pinions whistling flings.
  Catch how thou wilt, thou getst not mee,
  The reason is my hart is free.
           (Amarillis takes Mirtillo now.)
  Him thou hast caught, it is no wonder,   80
  For love holds all his sences under.
           Exeunt Cho. Nim.

Act III Scene 3

AMARILLIS. MIRTILLO. CORISCA.

[*Am.*] In faith, Auglaura, I have catcht you now.
  Will you be gone? Nay, soft, Ile hold you fast.
Cor. Trust me, had I not unawares to him
  Thrust him on her, this labour had bene lost.
Am. What, not a word? Are you she or not she?   5
Cor. Here do I take this dart, and in this grove
  I turne me to observe what followeth.
Am. So now I know; Corisca, are you not?
  T'is so you are, so great and have no haire,
  I could have wisht no better match then this.   10
  And since you ti'de me, do untie me too,
  Quickly, my hart, and I will pay thee with
  The sweetest kisse thou ever hadst. Why stai'st?
  Me thinkes your hands do shake. Put to your teeth,
  If with your nailes you cannot do the deed.   15
  How tedious y' are! Let me alone,
  My selfe will rid me of this trouble soone:
  But see how many knots have made me sure.
  Ah, that I may but make you play this part.
  So now I see. Ay me, what do I see?   20
  Let me alone (traytor) ay, wretched me.
Mir. Stand still, my soule.
Am.   Let me alone I say,
  Dare you thus offer force to Nimphs? Aglaure,
  Elisa, treachours, where are you become?
  Let me alone!
Mir.   Behold, I let you go.   25
Am. This is Coriscaes craft; well, keep you that
  Which you have not deserv'd
Mir.   Why flie you hence?
  (Cruell) behold my death, behold this dart
  Shall pierce my wofull brest.
Am.   What will you do?
Mir. That which perhaps grieves you (most cruell Nimph).   30
  That any else beside your selfe should do.
Am. Oh me, me thinkes I am halfe dead.
Mir. But if this worke belong alone to you,
  Behold my brest; here, take this fatall dart.
Am. Death you have merited. But tell me who   35

Hath made you boldly thus presume?

Mir.   My love.

Am. Love is no cause of any villian-act.

Mir. Love, trust me, t' was in me. I made me respective:
  And since you first laid hold on me, lesse cause
  You have to call my action villanie.   40
  Yea, ev'n when I by so commodious meanes
  Might be made bold to use the lawes of love,
  Yet did I quake a Lover to be found.

Am. Cast not my blind deeds in my teeth I pray.

Mir. My much more love makes me more blind then you.   45

Am. Prayers and fine conceits, not snares and thefts,
  Discreetest Lovers use.

Mir.   As savadge beast
  With hunger hunted, from the woods breakes forth
  And doth assaile the stranger on his way,
  So I that onely by your beauteous eyes   50
  Do live; since that sweet foode me have forbad,
  Either your crueltie or else my fate,
  A starvéd Lover issuing from those woods
  Where I have suffered long and wretched, fast,
  Have for my health assaid this strategeme   55
  Which loves necessitie upon me thrust.
  Now blame not me (Nimph cruell) blame your selfe,
  For praiers and conceits, true loves discretion
  As you them call, you not attend from me;
  You have bereav'd with shunning me the meanes   60
  To love discreetly.

Am.   Discreetly might you do
  To leave to follow that which flies you so;
  In vaine you know you do pursue me still.
  What is't you seeke of me?

Mir.   Onely one time
  Daine but to heare me, ere I wretched die.   65

Am. T'is well for you, the favour that you aske
  You have alreadie had: now get you hence.

Mir. Ah, Nimph, that which I have already said
  Is but a drop of that huge ample sea
  Of my complaints; if not for pittie sake,   70
  Yet for your pleasure now heare (cruell) but
  The latest accents of a dying voice.

Am. To ease your mind and me this cumber rid,

I graunt to heare you, but with this condition,
Speake small, part soone, and never turne againe.   75
Mir. In too too small a bundle (cruell Nimphe)
You do commaund me binde my huge desires,
Which measures but by thought nought cou'd containe.
That I you love, and love more then life,
If you deny to know, aske but these woods   80
And they will tell, and tell you with them will
Their beasts, their trees and stones of these great rocks
Which I so oft have tender made to melt
At sound of my complaints. But what make I
Such proofe of love where such rare beautie is?   85
See but how many beauteous things the skies containe,
How many dresse the earth in brave attire,
Thence shall you see the force of my desire.
For as the waters fall, the fire doth rise,
The ayre doth flie, the earth lies firmely still,   90
And all these same the skies do compasse round.
Ev'n so to you as to their chiefest good,
My soule doth flie, and my poore thoughts do run
With all affection to your lovely beauties.
He that from their deare object would them turne   95
Might first turne from their usuall course the skie,
The earth, the ayre, the water, and the fire,
And quite remoove the earth from off his seate.
But why commaund you me to speake but small?
Small shall I tell, if I but tell you shall   100
That I must die, and lesse shall dying doo,
If I but see what is my ruine too.
Ay me, what shall I do which may out-last
My miserable love? When I am dead,
Yet, cruell soule, have pitie on my paines.   105
Ah faire! Ah deare! Sometime so sweete a cause
Why I did live whilst my good fates were pleasd.
Turne hitherward those starry lights of love,
Let me them see once meeke and full of pitie
Before I die. So may my death be sweet.   110
As they have bene good guides unto my life,
So let them be unto my death, and that
Sweet looke which first begat my love, beget
My death: let my loves *Hesperus* become
The ev'ning starre of my decaying day.   115

But you obdurate, never pitie feele,
Whil'st I more humble, you more haughtie are.
And can you heare me and not speake a word?
Whom do I speake too (wretch) a marble stone?
If you will say nought else, yet bid me die,   120
And you shall see what force your words will have.
Ah, wicked love, this is a miserie extreame,
A Nymph so cruell, so desirous of my death,
Because I aske it as a favour, scornes to give it,
Arming her cruell voyce in silence so,   125
Least it might favour mine exceeding wo.
Am. If I as well to answere as to heare
    You promis'd had, just cause you might have found
    To have condemn'd my silence for unjust.
    You call me cruell, imagining perhaps   130
    By that reproofe more easily to drawe
    Me to the contrary. No, know (Mirtillo)
    I am no more delighted with the sound
    Of that desertlesse and dislikéd praise
    You to my beautie give, then discontent   135
    To heare you call me cruell and unjust.
    I graunt this crueltie to any else a fault,
    But to a lover vertue t'is and honestie,
    Which in a woman you call crueltie.
    But be it as you would blame-worthy fault   140
    To be unkinde to one that loves, tell me,
    When was Amarillis cruell unto you?
    Perhaps when reason would not give me leave
    To use this pitie: yet how I it us'd
    Your selfe can judge, when you from death I sav'd: 145
    I meane when you among a noble sort of maides,
    A lustfull Lover in a womans cloathes
    Banded your selfe, and durst contaminate
    Their purest sports, mingling mong kisses innocent,
    Kisses lascivious and impure, which to remember   150
    I am asham'd. But heavens my witnesse are,
    I knew you not, and after I you knew,
    I scornd your deed, and kept my soule untoucht
    From your lasciviousnesse, not suffering at all
    The venome there to runne to my chaste heart.   155
    You violated nothing save th' outside
    Of these my lips. A mouth kist but by force

Spits out the kisse, and kills the shame withall.
But tell me you, what fruite had you receiv'd
Of your rash theft, had I discovered you   160
Unto those Nymphes? The Thracian *Orfeus* had not bene
So lamentably torne on Ebers bankes
Of *Bacchus* dames as you had bene of them,
Had not you help'd her pittie, whom you cruell call.
That pittie which was fit for me to give, I ever gave;   165
For other, t'is in vaine you either aske or hope:
If you me love, then love my honestie,
My safetie love, and love my life withall.
Thou art too farre from that which thou desir'st,
The heavens forbid, the earth contraries it;   170
Death is the punishment thereof. And above all
Mine honestie defies forbidden acts:
Then with a safer keeper or her honours floure
A soule well-borne will ever scorne to have.
Then rest in peace (Mirtillo) give ore this suite,   175
Get thee farre hence to live if thou bee'st wise.
T' abandon life for peevish griefe or smart
Is not the action of a valiant hart.
From that which pleaseth vertue, t'is t' abstaine,
If that which pleaseth breeds offence againe.   180
Mir. To save ones life is not within his power,
    That hath his soule forsaken and giv'n ore.
Am. One arm'd in vertue conquereth all desire.
Mir. Vertue small conquest gets where love tryumphes.
Am. Who cannot what he would will what he can.   185
Mir. Oh, loves necessitie no lawes endures.
Am. Distance of place may heale your wound againe.
Mir. In vaine one flies from that his hart doth harbour.
Am. A new desire an old will quite displace.
Mir. Had I another hart, another soule.   190
Am. Time will at last clearly this love consume.
Mir. I, after love hath quite consum'd my life.
Am. Why then your wounds will not be cur'd at all?
Mir. Never till death.
Am.   Till death? Well, heare mee now,
    And looke my words be lawes unto your deeds   195
    Howbee't I know to die is the more usual voice
    Of an inamour'd tongue, then a desire
    Or firme conceit his soule hath entertain'd,

Yet if by chaunce such a straunge folly hath
Possest thy minde, know then thy death will be   200
Death to mine honour as unto thy life.
Now if thou lov'st me, live and let it be
A token of thy wit henceforth thou shun
To see me, or to seeke my company.
Mir. O cruell sentence! Can I without life   205
    Live, thinke you then? Or can I without death
    Find end unto my torment and my griefe?
Am. Well now t'is time you go (Mirtillo) hence!
    Yow'le stay too long. Go, comfort your selfe
    That infinit the troupe of wretched Lovers is.   210
    All wounds do bring with them their severall paine,
    Nor can you onely of this love complaine.
Mir. Among these wretches I am not alone; but yet
    A miserable spectacle am onely I,
    Of dead and living, nor can live nor die.   215
Am. Well, go your waies
Mir.   Ah, sad departure,
    End of my life; go I from you, and do not die?
    And yet I feele the verie pangs of death,
    That do give life unto mine exstasie,
    To make my hart immortally to die.   [*Exit Mirtillo*]   220

Act III Scene 4

AMARILLIS.

[*Am.*] Oh Mirtillo! Oh, my dearest soule,
    Could'st thou but see into her hart whom thou
    Call'st cruell Amarillis, then wouldst thou say
    Thou hadst that pittie which thy hart desires.
    Oh mindes too much infortunate in love!   5
    What bootes it thee, my hart, to be belov'd?
    What bootes it me to have so deare a Love?
    Why should the cuell fates so disunite
    Whom love conjoines, and why should traiterous love
    Conjoyne them whom the destenies do part?   10
    Oh happie savadge beasts whom nature gives
    No lawes in love, save verie love it selfe.
    Inhumane humane law, that punish'st
    This love with death, if't be so sweet to sin,

And not to sin so necessary bee,   15
Imperfect nature that repugneth law,
Or law too hard that nature doth offend.
But tush, she loves too litle that feares death,
Would gods death were the worst that's due to sin.
Deare chastitie, th' inviolable powre   20
Of soules well-borne, that hast my amorous will
Retein'd in chaines of holy rigour still:
To thee I consecrate my harmlesse sacrifize.
And thou, my soule (Mirtillo) pardon me,
That cruell am where I should piteous bee.   25
Pardon her that in lookes and onely words
Doth seeme thy foe, but in my heart thy friend.
If thou wouldst be reveng'd, what greater paine
Wouldst thou inflict, then this my cruel griefe?
Thou art my heart, and shall be spite of heaven   30
And earth; when thou dost plaine and sigh, and weep,
Thy teares become my bloud, thy sighes my breath:
And all thy paines they are not onely thine,
For I them feele, and they are turnéd mine.

Act III Scene 5

CORISCA. AMARILLIS.

[*Cor.*] Hide you no more, my Amarillis, now.
Am. Wretch I discoveréd am.
Cor.   I all have heard;
  Be not afraid; did I not say I lov'd you,
  And yet you are afraid, and hides your selfe
  From her that loves you so. Why do you blush?   5
  This blushing is a common fault.
Am. Corisca, I am conquer'd I confesse.
Cor. That which you cannot hide you wil confesse.
Am. And now I see too weake a thing doth prove
  A womans heart t'encounter mightie love.   10
Cor. Cruel unto Mirtillo, but more cruel to your selfe.
Am. It is no crueltie that springs of pitie.
Cor. Cicute and Aconite do grow from holsome rootes.
  I see no difference twixt this crueltie
  That doth offend, and pitie helping not.   15
Am. Ah me, Corisca!

Cor.   These sighes, good sister,
   Are but weakenesse of your heart. Th' are fit
   For women of small worth.
Am.   I could not be
   Thus cruell but I should love, cherish hopelesly.
   Therefore to shun him shewes I have compassion   20
   Of his ill and mine.
Cor.   Why hopelesly?
Am. Do you not know I am espows'd to Silvio,
   And that the law each woman doomes to death
   That violates her faith?
Cor.   Oh simple foole,
   Is this the let? Which is more auncient among us,   25
   Dianaes lawe or loves? This in our breasts
   Is bred and growes with us, Nature her selfe
   With her owne hands imprints in our hearts breasts:
   And where this law commands, both heav'n and earth obey.
Am. But if the other law do take my life,   30
   How can loves law restore it me againe?
Cor. You are too nice; were ev'ry woman so,
   Had all such straight respects, good times farewell;
   Small practisers are subject to this paine.
   The lawe doth never stretch unto the wise: 35
   Beleeve me, should blame-worthy all be slaine,
   The countre then would soone proove womanlesse.
   It needfull was, theft should forbidden bee
   To them that closely could not cover theft.
   This honestie is but an art to seeme so;   40
   Let others as they list beleeve, Ile thinke so still.
Am. These are but vanities (Corisca); t'were best
   Quickly to leave that which we cannot hold.
Cor. And who forbids thee, foole? This life's too short
   To passe it over with one onely love: 45
   Men are too sparing of their favours now,
   (Whether't be for want, or else for frowardnesse)
   The fresher that we are, the dearer still.
   Beautie and youth once gone w'are like Bee hives
   That hath no honey, no, nor yet no waxe   50
   Let men prate on, they do not feele our woes,
   For their condition differs much from ours,
   The elder that they grow, they grow the perfecter.
   If they loose beauty, yet they wisedome gaine.

But when our beautie fades that oftentimes   55
Conquers their greatest witts, strait fadeth all our good;
There cannot be a vilder thing to see
Then an old woman. Therefore ere thou age attaine,
Know me thy selfe, and use it as thou shouldst.
What were a Lion worth did he not use his strength?   60
What's a mans wit worth that lies idly by?
Ev'n so our beautie proper strength to us
As force to Lyons, wisedome unto men,
We ought to use whilst it we have. Time flies
Away and yeares come on; our youth once lost   65
We like cut flowres never grow fresh againe.
And to our hoary haires love well may runne,
But Lovers will our wrinkled skinnes still shunne.
Am. Thou speakest this (Corisca) me to trie,
Not as thou think'st, I am sure. But be assur'd   70
Except thou show'st some meanes how I may shun
This marriage bonds, my thought's irrevocable,
And I resolvéd am rather to die
Then any way to spot my chastitie.
Cor. I have not seene so obstinate a foole;   75
But since you are resolv'd I am agreed.
But tell me do you thinke your Silvio is
As true a friend to faith as you to chastitie?
Am. Thou mak'st me smile. Silvio a friend to faith?
How can that be? Hee's enemy to love.   80
Cor. Silvio an enemy to love? O foole,
These that are nice, put thou no trust in them:
Loves theft is never so securely done
As hidden under vaile of honestie,
Thy Silvio loves (good Sister) but not thee.   85
Am. What goddesse is she? For she cannot bee
A mortal wight that lighted hath his love.
Cor. Nor goddesse, nor a Nimph.
Am.   What do you tell?
Cor. Know you Lisetta?
Am.   She that your cattell keeps?
Cor. Ev'n she.
Am.   Can it be true?
Cor.   That same's his hart.   90
Am. Sure hee's provided of a daintie Love.
Cor. Each day he faines that he on hunting goes.

Am. I ev'ry morning heare his curséd horne.
Cor. About noone-time when others busie are,
    He his companions shuns, and comes alone   95
    By a backe way unto my garden, there,
    Where a shadow hedge doth close it in,
    There doth she heare his burning sighes, his vowes,
    And then she tells me all, and laughes at him.
    Now heare what I thinke good to doo. Nay, I   100
    Have don't for you alreadie. You know the law
    That tyes us to our faith doth give us leave,
    Finding our spowses in the act of perfidie,
    Spite of our friends the marriage to denie,
    And to provide us of an other if we list.   105
Am. That know I well; I have examples two,
    Leucipp to Ligurine, Armilla to Turingo,
    Their faith once broke, they tooke their owne again.
Cor. Now heare! Lisetta by my appointment hath
    Promist to meet th' unwary Lover here   110
    In this same Cave, and now he is the best
    Contented youth that lives, attending but the houre.
    There would I have you take him. Ile be there
    To beare you witnesse of't, for else we worke
    In vaine; so are you free from this same noisome knot   115
    Both with your honour, and your fathers too.
Am. Oh brave invention, good Corisca, what's to do?
Cor. Observe my words. In midst of this same cave
    Upon the right hand is a hollow stone,
    I know not if by Art or nature made,   120
    A little Cave all linde with Ivy leaves,
    To which a litle hole aloft gives light,
    A fit and thankfull receptacle for loves theft.
    Prevent their comming and attend them there:
    Ile haste Lisetta forward, and as soone   125
    As I perceive your Silvio enter, so will I:
    Step you to her, and as the custome is,
    Weele carry both unto the Priest, and there dissolve
    This marriage knot.
Am.   What, to his father?
Cor. What matter's that? Think you Montanus dare   130
    His private to a publike good compare?
Am. Then, closing up mine eyes, I let my selfe
    Be ledde by thee, my deare, my faithfull guide.

Cor. But do not stay now, enter me betime.
Am. I'le to the Temple first, and to the Gods   135
   My prayers make, without whose aide no happy end
   Can ever sort to mortall enterprise.
Cor. All places (Amarillis) temples are,
   To hearts devout; you'le slacke your time too much.
Am. Time's never lost in praying unto them   140
   That do commaund the time.
Cor.   Go then, dispatch.

                                              [Exit Amarillis]

   Now if I erre not, am I at good passe,
   Onely this staying troubles me, yet may it helpe;
   I must goe make new snares to traine in Coridon.
   Ile make him thinke that I will meet him there,   145
   And after Amarillis send him soone,
   Then by a secret way Ile bring *Dianaes* Priests:
   Her shall they finde, and guiltie, doome to death.
   My rivall gone, Mirtillo sure is mine,
   See where he comes. Whilst Amarillis stayes   150
   Ile somewhat trie him. Love now once inspire
   My tongue with words, my face with heav'nly fire.

Act III Scene 6

MIRTILLO. CORISCA.

[Mir.] Here weeping sprights of hell, new torments heare,
   New sorts of paine, a cruell mind behold
   Included in a looke most mercifull;
   My love more fierce then the infernall pit,
   Because my death cannot suffice to glut   5
   Her greedie will, and that my life is but
   A multitude of deathes commaund me live,
   That to them all my life might living give.
Cor. Ile make as though I heard him not; I heare
   A lamentable voyce plaine hereabouts,   10
   I wonder who it is, oh my Mirtillo.
Mir. So would I were a naked shade or dust.
Cor. How feele you now your selfe after your long
   Discourse with your so dearly lovéd Nymph?
Mir. Like a weake sick man that hath long desir'd   15
   Forbidden drinke, at last gets it unto his mouth

And drinks his death, ending at once both life and thirst.
So I long sicke, burn't and consuméd in
This amorous drought, from two faire fountaines that
Ice do distill from out a rockie braine   20
Of an indurate heart,
Have drunke the poyson that my life will kill,
Sooner then halfe of my desire fulfill.
Cor. So much more mightie waxeth love as from
  Our heart the force is he receives (deare Mirtillo)   25
  For as the Beare is wont with licking to give shape
  To her mishapen brood, that else were helplesse borne,
  Ev'n so a Lover to his bare desire,
  That in the birth was shapelesse, weake and fraile,
  Giving but forme and strength begetteth love,   30
  Which whilst t'is young and tender, then t'is sweet,
  But waxing to more yeares, more cruell growes,
  That in the end (Mirtillo) an inveterate affect
  Is ever full of anguish and defect.
  For whilst the mind on one thought onely beates,   35
  It waxeth thicke by being too much fixt,
  So love that should be pleasure and delight,
  Is turn'd to melancholy, and what worser is,
  It proves at last, or death, or madnesse at the least:
  Wherefore wise is that heart that often changeth love.   40
Mir. Ere I change will or thought, chang'd must my life
  Be into death, for though the beautious Amarillis
  Be most cruell, yet is she all my life.
  Nor can this bodies bulke at once containe
  More then one heart, more then one soule retaine.   45
Cor. O wretched shepheard, ill thou knowst to use
  Love in his kind. Love one that hates thee, one
  That flies from thee, fie man, I had rather die.
Mir. As gold in fire, so faith in griefe's refinde,
  Nor can (Corisca) amorous constancie   50
  Shewe his great power, but thorough crueltie.
  This onely rests amongst my many griefes,
  My sole content doth my heart burne or die,
  Or languish ne're so much, light arc the paines,
  Plaints, torments, sighes, exile, and death it selfe,   55
  For such a cause, for such a sweet respect.
  That life before my faith shall broken bee,
  So worse then death I hold inconstancie.

Cor. O brave exploit, Lover magnanimous,
    Like an enragéd beast or sencelesse rocke,   60
    There cannot be a greater damnéd plague,
    More mortall poyson to a soule in love,
    Then is this faith. Unhappie is that heart
    That let it selfe be guld with vaine fantasmes
    Of this erronious and unseasonable   65
    Disturber of these amorous delights.
    Tell me, poore man, with this thy foolish vertue of constancie,
    What lov'st thou in her that doth thee despise?
    Lov'st thou the beautie that is none of thine?
    The joy thou hast not? The pittie thou wantst?   70
    The reward thou dost not hope for? If thou deem'st right,
    Th' art mad to hunt thus that thou canst not have.
    Lift up thy selfe (Mirtillo) happily thou wantst
    Some choice of friends, thou finds none to thy mind.
Mir. More deare to me is paine for Amarillis,   75
    Then any joy a thousand else can give.
    If me my fates forbid her to enjoy,
    For me then die all other kinds of joy.
    I fortunate in any other kinde of love?
    No, though I would I could not;   80
    Nor though I could I would not.
    And if I thought in any time henceforth
    My will would wish or power obtaine the same,
    I would desire of heav'n and love at once
    Both will and power might quite be ta'ne away.   85
Cor. Wilt thou then die for her that thee disdaines?
Mir. Who pitie not expects doth feare no paines.
Cor. Do not deceive thy selfe, perhaps thou think'st
    Shee doth dissemble in this deepe despight,
    And that she loves thee well for all this showe.   90
    Oh, that thou knewst what unto me shee ever sayes.
Mir. All these are trophees of my truest faith,
    With which I will triumph over her cruell will,
    Over my paines, and my distresséd chance,
    Over worlds fortune, and over death it selfe.   95
Cor. (What would he do, did he but know her love?)
    How I bewaile thee, wretched phrensie man:
    Tell me, didst thou e're any love besides?
Mir. She was my first, and she my last shall be.
Cor. For ought that I can see you never try'd   100

Love but in cruell moodes, but in disdaine.
Oh, if you had but prov'd him one time kind,
Prove him but so, and you shal see how sweet a thing
It is t'enjoy a gratefull Nymph; shee'le you adore.
Shee'le make your Amarillis bitter to your taste.   105
How deare a thing it is wholy to have
What you desire, and be nought bard thereof;
Here your Nymph sight to coole your scalding sighs,
And after say (my deere) all that you see is yours.
If I be faire, I am onely faire for you;   110
Onely for you I cherish these my cheekes,
My lockes, my brest, you deare hearts onely lodge.
But this (alasse) is but a brooke to that
Great Sea of sweets which we in love might taste,
Which none can utter save by proofe.   115
Mir. Thousand times blest that under such a star is borne.
Cor. Here me (Mirtillo)—how like I was t'have said
     My heart—a Nymph as gentle as the winde
     Doth blow upon, with haire of glistering gold,
     As worthy of your love as you of hers,   120
     Praise of these woods, love of a thousand hearts,
     By worthy youthes in vaine sollicited,
     You, onely, loves more then her heart, her life,
     If you be wise do not dispise her then.
     She like a shadow to thy selfe will be,   125
     A faithfull follower of thy footsteps ever,
     One at thy word, obedient at thy becke,
     All houres of day and night at thy commaund.
     Do not forsake this rare adventure then,
     No pleasure in this earth so sweet as this,   130
     It will not cost a teare, no not a sigh.
     A joy accommodated to thy will,
     A sweetnesse temp'red sweetly to thy taste,
     Is't not a treasure worth the having (man)?
     Leave then the feet of flying hopelesse trace,   135
     And her that followes thee, scorne not t'embrace.
     I feed you not with hopes of vanitie,
     If you desire to see her, you shall see her straight.
Mir. My hart's no subject for these loves delights.
Cor. Prove it but once, and then returne againe   140
     Unto thy solitary griefe, so may'st thou see
     What are those joyes that in loves pleasures bee.

Mir. A taste corrupted, pleasant things abhors.

Cor. Be not you cruel yet to rob her life,
   That on your eyes depends, you know what t'is   145
   To beg with povertie; if you desire
   Pitie your selfe, do it not her denie.

Mir. What pitie can he give that none can get?
   In summe I am resolv'd whilst here I live,
   To keepe my faith to her how ere she prove,   150
   Cruell or pitifull, or how she will.

Cor. (Oh truly blind, unhappie sencelesse man)
   To whom preserv'st thou faith? Trust me I am loth
   T' augment thy griefe, but for the love I beare thee
   I cannot choose. Thinkst Amarillis is unkind   155
   For zeale she to religion beares?
   Or unto chastitie? Thou art a foole,
   The roome is occupied, and thou must weepe
   Whilst others laugh. What! Now th' art dumbe.

Mir. Now stands my life in midst twixt life and death,   160
   Whilst I in doubt do stand, if to beleeve,
   Or not beleeve; this makes me so amaz'd.

Cor. You'le not beleeve me then?

Mir.   Oh if I do
   Straight shall you see my miserable end.

Cor. Live, wretched man, live and revengéd bee.   165

Mir. Oh, no, it is not true, it cannot bee.

Cor. Well, theres no remedie; I must rehearse
   That which will vexe thy heart. Seest thou that cave?
   That is the true custodian of her faith
   And her religion. There thee to scorne she laughes,   170
   There with thy torments doth she sauce the joyes
   Of thy thrise happie rivall. There, to be plaine,
   Thy faithfull Amarillis oft is wont
   To dally in the armes of a base shepheard slave.
   Go sigh, preserve thy faith; there's thy reward.   175

Mir. Dost thou tell true, Corisca? May I beleeve thee?

Cor. The more thou seek'st, the worse thou findest still.

Mir. But hast thou seene this thing, Corisca?

Cor. I have not seen't, yet may'st thou if thou wilt;
   For even this day is order ta'ne this houre,   180
   That they may meete. Hide thee but somewhere here,
   And thou shalt see her first go in, then he.

Mir. Then comes my death.

Cor.   See where she comes,
   Softly descending by the Temples way. Seest thou her?
   Do not her stealing feete bewray her stealing heart?   185
   Attend thou here and thou shalt see th' effect.
Mir. Since I am here, the truth I now will see,
   Till then, my life and death suspended bee.

Act III Scene 7

AMARILLIS.

[Am] Let never mortall enterprise be ta'ne in hand
   Without this heavenly counsell; halfe confusde
   And doubtfull was my heart when I went hence
   Unto the Temple, whence thankes be to heaven
   I do well comforted and well dispos'd returne.   5
   Methought to my pure prayers and devout,
   I felt a spright celestiall moove within me
   Hartning my thoughts, that as it were did say,
   What fear'st thou, Amarillis? Be assur'd.
   So will I goe assur'd, heav'ns be my guide,   10
   Favour, fair Mother of love, her pure desseignes
   That on thy succour onely doth depend.
   Queene of the triple skie, if e're thou prov'dst
   Thy sunnes hotte fire, take pitie then of mine.
   Guide hither, curteous goddesse, that same swaine   15
   With swift and subtill feet that hath my faith.
   And thou, deare Cave, into thy bosome take
   Me, loves handmaid, and give me leave there to
   Accomplish my desires. Why do I stay?
   Here's none doth see or heare. Enter secure.   20
   Oh Mirtillo, couldst thou but dream to find me here.

Act III Scene 8

MIRTILLO.

[Mir.] What, am I blind, or do I too much see?
   Ah, had I but bene borne without these eyes,
   Or rather not at all had I bene borne.
   Did spitefull fates reserve me thus alive
   To let me see so bad, so sad a sight?   5

Mirtill, thy torments passe the paines of hell.
No; doubt no more: suspend not thy beliefe;
Thine eies, thine eares, have seene, have heard it true.
Thy love an other ownes, not by the lawe
Of earth that bindes her unto any one,   10
But by loves lawe that tyes her sole to thee.
O cruell Amarillis, was't not inough
To kill me, wretch, but thou must scorne me too?
That faithlesse mouth that sometime grac't my joies,
Did vomit out my hatefull name, because   15
She would not have it in her heart to be
A poore partaker of her pleasures sweet.
Why stay'st thou now? She that did give me life
Hath ta'n 't away, and giv'n't an other man:
Yet wretch thou liv'st, thou dost not die. O die   20
Mirtillo, die to thy tormenting griefe,
As to thy joy thou art alreadie dead.
Die, dead Mirtillo, finish't is thy life.
Finish thy torment too: fleet wretched soule
Through this soure constrain'd and wayward death.   25
Tis for thy greater ill that thus thou livst.
But what? And must I die without revenge?
First will I make him die that gives me death,
Desire to live so long I will retaine
Till justly I have that Usurper slaine.   30
Yeeld Griefe unto Revenge: Pittie to Rage,
Death unto life, till with my life I have
Reveng'd the death another guiltles gave.
This Steele shall not drinke mine unvengéd blood,
My hand shall rage ere it shall pitteous bee.   35
What ere thou art that joyst my comfortes all,
I'le make thee feele thy ruine in my fall,
I'le place me heere ev'n in this very Grove,
And as I see him but approach the Cave,
This Dart shall sodaine wound him in his side.   40
It shalbe cowardlike to strike him thus;
I'le challenge him to single combat. I,
Not so, for to this place so knowne and usd,
Shepheards may come to hinder us, and worse,
May search the cause that moov'd me to this fight,   45
Which to deny were wickednesse, to faigne
Will make me faythlesse held; and to discover

Will blot her name with endlesse infamie.
In whom albeit I like not what I see,
Yet what I lov'd I do, and ever shall.   50
But what hope I to see th' adult'rer die
That robd her of her honor, me my life?
But if I kill him, shall not then his blood
Be to the world a token of this deed?
Why feare I death since I desire to die?   55
But then this murder once made plaine, makes plaine
The cause whereby she shall incurre that infamie.
I'le enter then this Cave, and so assayle him,
I so, that pleaseth me, I'le steale in softly,
So that she shall not heare me. I beleeve   60
That in the secretst and the closest part
I gather by her wordes I shall her finde;
Therefore I will not enter in too farre.
A hollow hole there is made in a Rocke,
The left side cover'd all with Yvie leaves;   65
Beneath th' other asscent there will I stand.
And time attend t' effect what I desire:
I'le beare my dead foe to my lyving foe;
Thus of them both I shalbe well reveng'd.
Then with this selfe same Dart Ile pierce this brest,   70
So shall there be three pier'st without reliefe,
First two with Steele, the third with deadly griefe.
(Fierce) she shall see the miserable end
Of her belov'd, and her betrayéd friend.
This Cave that should be harbour of her joyes,   75
Of both her loves, and that which more I crave,
Of her great shame, may prove the happy grave.
And you the steppes that I in vaine have followed,
Could you me speed of such a faythfull way?
Could you direct me to so deare a Bowre?   80
Behold I follow you. O Corisca, Corisca,
Now hast thou told too true, now I beleeve thee.

Act III Scene 9

SATYRE.

[Sat.] Doth this man then beleeve Corisca, following her steps
Into the Cave of *Ericina*? Well, hee's mad,

He knowes her not; beleeve mee he had need
Have better hold of her ingagéd fayth
Then I had of her heare. But knottes more stranged   5
Then gaudy guiftes on her he cannot tie.
This damnéd Whoore hath sold her selfe to him,
And here shee'le pay the shamefull markets price.
Shee is within, her steps bewray the same,
This falles out for her punishment, and thy revenge.   10
With this great overstanding stone close thou the Cave,
Goe then about, and fetch the Priest with thee:
By the hill way which few or none do know,
Let her be executed as the law commaunds,
For breach of marriage troth, which she to Coridon   15
Hath plighted, though she ever it conceal'd
For feare of me; so shall I be reveng'd
Of both at once. I'le leese no farther time:
From off this Elme I'le cut a bough, with which
I may more speedely remove this stone! Oh, how great it is!   20
How fast it stickes. I'le digge it round about.
This is a worke in deed! Where are my wonted forces?
Oh perverse Starres, in spight of you I'le moov't.
Oh *Pan Liceus,* helpe me now, thou wert a lover once;
Revenge thy love disdaind, upon Corisca.   25
So, in the name of thy great power, it mooves.
So, in the power of thy great name, it falles.
Now is the wicked Foxe ta'ne in the trappe.
Oh that all wicked Women were with thee within,
That with one fire they might be all destroyd.   30

CHORUS

How puissant art thou, Love,
Natures miracle, and the Worlds wonder!
What savadge nation, or what rusticke hart
Is it that of thy power feeles no part?
But what Wit's so profound can pull a sunder   5
That powers strength?
Who feeles those flames thy fire lightes at length,
Immoderate and vaine,
Will say, a mortall spright, thou sole dost raigne
And live, in the corporall and fleshly brest.   10
But who feeles after how a lover is

Wak'néd to Vertue, and how all those flames
Do tremble out at sight of honest shames,
(Unbrid'led blust'ring lustes brought downe to rest)
Will call thee Spright of high immortall blisse,   15
Having thy holy receptacle in the soule.
Rare miracle of humane and divine aspécts,
(That blind) dost see, and Wisedome (mad) corrects,
Of sence and understanding intellects,
Of reason and desire confus'd affects.   20
Such Emperie hast thou on earth,
And so the heavens above dost thou controule.
Yet (by your leave) a wonder much more rare,
And more stupendious hath the world then you,
For how you make all wonders yeeld and bow   25
Is easely knowne. Your powers do berthe
And being taken from vertue of a woman faire.
O woman, guift of the high heavenly skie,
Or rather his who did their spangled gowne
So gorgious make unto our mortall eye.   30
What hath it which a Womans beautie push not downe?
In his vast brow a monstrous Ciclop-like,
It onely one eye hath,
Which to beholding gazers gives no light,
But rather doth with terrour blindnesse strike.   35
If it do sigh or speake, t'is like the wrath
Of an enragéd Lion that would fight:
And not the skies alone but even poore fieldes
Are blasted with the flames his lightning weildes.
Whilst thou with Lampes most sweete,   40
And with an amorous angelicke light
Of two Sunnes visible that never meete,
Dost alwayes the tempesteous, troubled spright
Of thy beholder quiet and delight:
Sound, motion, light, that beautie doth assume,   45
State, daintinesse, and valew do aright
Mixe such a harmony in that faire sight,
That skyes themselves with vanitie presume;
If lesse then Paradice those skies do shine
To Paragon with thee (thing most devine)   50
Good reason hath that soveraigne creature (nam'd
A Man) to whom all mortall thinges do bow,
If thee beholding, higher cause allow

And yeeld to bee.
What though he rule and triumph truely fam'd,   55
It is not for high powers more worth do see
In him then is in thee,
Either of scepter or of victorie:
But for to make thee farre more glorious stand,
Because the Conqueror thou dost commaund: 60
And so 't must bee, for mans humanitie
Is subject still to Beauties deitie.
   Who will not trust this, but contrary saith,
   Let him behold Mirtilloes wondrous fayth:
   Yet Woman to thy worth this is a staine,   65
   Love is made love so hopelessly and vaine.

Act IV Scene 1

CORISCA.

[Cor.] So fixéd was my hart and whole intent
  In bringing of this Deere unto the bow,
  That I forgotten had my dearest heire
  That brutish villaine robd me of: Oh how I grievd,
  With such a price to purchace mine escape.   5
  But t' was of force to get out of the handes
  Of that same senceles beast, who though he have
  Lesse hart then any Conny hath, yet might he do
  Me many injuries and many skornes.
  I always him despisd: whilst he had blood   10
  In any of his vaines (like a Horse-leach)
  I suckt him still. Now doth it grieve him that
  I have giv'n o're to love him still; just cause he had.
  If one could love a most unlovely Beast,
  Like hearbes that earst were got for holsome use,   15
  The juice drawne out, they rest unprofitable,
  And like a stinking thing we them despise:
  So him (when I had what so ere was good suckt out
  From him) now should I use, but throw the saples trunke
  Unto the dunghill heape? Now will I see   20
  Yf Coridon be gotten close into the Cave.
  What newes is this I see? Sleepe I or do I wake?
  I am assurd this Caves mouth erst was ope,
  How close tis shut! How is this auncient Stone

Rould downe? Was it an Earthquake since?   25
Yet would I know if Coridon were there.
With Amarillis, then car'd I little for the rest.
Certaine hee's there, for tis a good while since
Lisetta gave him word. Who knowes the contrary?
T' may be Mirtillo, movéd with disdaine,   30
Hath done this deed; hee, had hee but my minde,
Could onely have perform'd this rare exployte.
Well by the Mountaines way will I go see,
And learne the troth of all how it hath past.

Act IV Scene 2

DORINDA. LINCO.

[Dor.] Linco, I am assur'd thou knowst me not.
Lin. Who would have thought that in these rusty rags
    Gentle Dorinda had been ever hid.
    Were I some Dogge, as I but Linco am,
    Unto thy cost I should thee know too well.   5
    What do I see?
Dor.   Linco, thou seest great love,
    Working effectes both strange and miserable.
Lin. One like thy selfe, so soft, so tender yet,
    Thou wert but now (as one would say) a babe
    And still me thinkes it was but yesterday   10
    Since in mine armes I had thee, little wretch,
    Ruling thy tender cryes, and taught thee too
    To call thy Father Dad, thy Mother Mamme:
    When in your house I was a Servant hir'd,
    Thou that so like a fearefull Doe wast wont   15
    To feare each thing before thou feltst this love,
    Why, on a sodaine thee would scare each blast,
    Each Bird that stird a bush, each Mouse that from
    Her hole did run, each Leafe would make thee start,
    Now wandrest all alone by hills, by woodes,   20
    Fearing no Beast that hauntes the Forrestes wilde?
Dor. Wounded with Love, who feares another hurt?
Lin. Love had great power, that could not onely thee
    Into a Man, but to a Wolfe transforme.
Dor. O Linco, could'st thou but see here within,   25
    There should'st thou see a lyving Wolfe devoure

My wretched soule like to a harmeles Lambe.
Lin. And who's that Wolfe? Silvio?
Dor.   Ah, thou hast said.
Lin. Thou, for he is a Wolfe, hast changd thy selfe
  Into a Wolfe; because no humane lookes   30
  Could moove his love, perhaps this beastes yet mought.
  But tell me, where had'st thou these cloathes so ragd?
Dor. I'le tell thee true; to day I went betime
  There where I heard that Silvio did intend
  A noble hunting to the savage Boore,   35
  At Erimanthus foote, where Elicet
  Puts up his head, not farre off from the lawnd,
  That from the hill is sever'd by discent,
  I found Melampo, my faire Silvioes Dogge,
  Whose thirst I thinke had drawne him to that place.   40
  I that each thing of Silvio hold full deare,
  Shade of his shape, and footsteps of his feete,
  Much more the Dogge which he so dearely lov'd,
  Him straightway tooke, and hee without adoo,
  Like to some gentle Cade, came quietly with mee.   45
  Now whilst I cast this Dogge to reconvey
  Home to his Lord and mine, hoping to make
  A conquest of his love by guift so deare,
  Behold he comes seeking his footsteps out,
  And heere he stayes. Deare Linco, I will not   50
  Leese further time in telling every thing
  That twixt us past, but briefly to dispatch.
  After a heape of faignéd vowes and wordes,
  The cruell Boy fled from me straight away
  In irefull mood with his thrice-happy Dogge,   55
  And with my deare and sweetest sweete reward.
Lin. Oh desperate Silvio! Oh cruell Boy!
  What didst thou then? Disdain'st thou not his deed?
Dor. As if the heate of his disdaine had been
  Of love unto my hart the greatest fire,   60
  So by his rage increaséd my desire:
  Yet still pursuing him unto the chace,
  Keeping my broken way, I Lupus met,
  Heere thought I good with him to change my cloathes,
  And in his servile habite me to hide,   65
  That mongst the Swaines I for a Swaine might passe,
  And at my pleasure see my Silvio.

Lin. Went'st thou to hunt in likenesse of a Woolfe,
   Seene by the Dogges, and yet returned'st safe?
   Dorinda, thou hast done inough.
Dor.   Linco,   70
   No wonder t'is, the Dogges could do no harme
   Unto their Maisters preordeynéd pray.
   There stood I by the Toyles amongst a sort
   Of neighbour Shepheards come to see the sport,
   Rather to see the huntsman then the game.   75
   At every motion of the savadge Beast
   My hart did quake. At each of Silvioes actes
   My soule stept out, push't on with all her will;
   But my chiefe hope the fearefull sight disturb'd
   Of that immeasurable Boore in force,   80
   Like as the rav'nous strength of sodaine storme
   In little time bringes trees and rockes to ground,
   So by his tuskes bedew'd with blood and foame,
   We see Dogges slaine, Staves broke, and wounded men,
   How many times did my poore blood desire   85
   For Silvioes blood to combat with the Boore.
   How often times would I have stept to make
   My brest a buckler for my Silvioes brest,
   How often sayd I in my selfe, excuse,
   Excuse the daintie lapp of my deare Love;   90
   So to my selfe spake I with praying sighes,
   Whilst he his Dogge, all arm'd with hardned skin,
   Lets loose against the Beast, who waxéd proud
   Of having made a wretched quarries sight
   Of wounded Shepheardes and Dogges slaine outright.   95
   Linco, I cannot tell this Dogges great worth,
   And Silvio loves him not without good cause.
   Looke how an angry Lyon entertaines
   The poynted hornes of some undaunted Bull,
   Sometime with force, sometime with pollicie,   100
   And fastens at the last his mightie pawes
   So on his backe as no powre can remov't.
   So strong Melamp' avoyding craftely
   The Boores swift strokes and mortall wounding blowes,
   At last taints on his eare, which first he shakes   105
   And afterward so firmely him he holdes,
   As his vast sides might wounded be at ease:
   The dismall token of a deadly stroke,

Then Silvio, invocating *Phoebes* name,
Direct this blow (sayd he) and here I vow   110
To sacrifize to thee his gastly head.
This sayd, from out his quiver of pure gold
He takes a speedy Shaft, and to his eare
He drawes his mighty Bow, and straight the Boore
Betweene his necke and shoulder wounded, dyes.   115
I free'd a sigh, seeing my Silvio safe.
Oh, happy beast that mightst thy life so leave,
By him that hartes from humane breastes doth reave.
Lin. But what became of that same fearefull beast?
Dor. I do not know, because I came away   120
For feare of being seene. But I beleeve
That solemnly they meane to carry it
Unto the Temple, as my Silvio vow'd.
Linc. And meane you not to change these rustie cloathes?
Dor. Yes, wis full faine, but Lupine hath my Gowne,   125
And promised t'attende me at this Spring,
But him I misse; deare Linco, if thou lov'st me
Goe seeke him in these Woods; he is not farre;
I'le rest me in the meane time by this Den,
For weerinesse makes me to sleepe desire,   130
Nor would I home returne in this attire.
Linc. I go, and stirre not you till I returne.

Act IV Scene 3

CHORUS. ERGASTO.

[*Cho.*] Shepheardes, have you not heard our Demi-God,
Montanus worthy sonne of *Hercules* discent,
Hath slaine the dreadfull Boore, that did infest
All Arcady, and now he doth prepare
To satisfie his Vowes; if we will thankefull bee   5
For such a benefite, lets go and meete him,
And give him all the reverence that we can.
Er. Oh dolefull fortune! Oh most bitter chaunce!
Immedicable wounde, Oh mornefull day!
Cho. What voyce of horror and of plaint heare wee?   10
Er. Starres foomen to our good, thus mocke you us?
Did you so high our hopes lift up, that with
Their fall you might us plague the more?

Cho. This seemes Ergasto, and t'is surely hee.
Er. Why do I Starres accuse? Accuse thy selfe   15
   That brought'st the Yron to Loves Anvile so,
   Thou didst it strike, thou mad'st the sparkes fly out
   From whence this fire growes so unquenchable.
   But heavens do know my pittie brought me to 't.
   Oh haples Lovers, wretched Amarillis,   20
   Unfortunate Titirus, childles father,
   Sad Montanus, desolate Arcadia:
   Oh miserable we; and to conclude,
   All that I see, speake, heare, or thinke, most miserable.
Cho. What wretched accident is this that doth containe   25
   So many miseries? Gow' Shepheards, Gow'!
   Lets meete with him. Eternall heavenly powers,
   Will not your rage yet cease? Speake, good Ergasto,
   What lamentable chaunce is this thou plainst?
Er. Deare friendes, I plaine us all the ruine of Arcadia.   30
Cho. What's this?
Er.   The prop of all our hopes is downe.
Cho. Ah, speake more plaine.
Er.   Daughter of Titirus,
   The onely branch of her decaying stocke,
   Hope of our health, which to Montanus sonne
   Was by the heavens promist and destenied,   35
   Whose marriage should have freed Arcadia,
   Wise Amarillis, Nimph celestiall,
   Patterne of honor, flowre of chastetie—
   My heart will not give me leave to speak—
Cho.   Why, is she dead?
Er. Nay, doom'd to death.
Cho.   Ay me, what's this?   40
Er. Nay, worse, with infamie.
Cho.   Amarillis infamous!
Er. Found with the adult'rour, and if hence ye go not soone,
   Ye may her see, led captive to the Temple.
Cho. Oh rare but wicked valure of this female sexe!
   Oh, chastetie, how singuler thou art;   45
   Scarce can a man say any woman's chast,
   Save she that ne're was try'd; unhappy age:
   But curteous Shepheard, tell us how it was.
Er. This day betime you know Montanus came
   With th' haples father of the wretched Nimph,   50

Both by one selfe devotion led, which was
By pray'rs to haste the marriage to good end.
For this the Sacrifizes offered were,
Which solemnly perform'd with good aspéctes;
For never were there seene intrailes more faire,⁣ 55
Nor flames more bright, by which the blind Divine
Moovéd, did to Montanus say: This day
With Amarillis shall your sonne be wed.
Goe quickly and prepare the marriage feast.
Oh, blindly done, blind Prophets to beleeve, 60
The fathers and the standers by were glad,
And wept, their hartes made tender with this joye.
Titirus was no sooner gone, but straight we heard
And saw unhappy fearefull signes, the messengers
Of sacred ire; at which so sodaine and so fierce, 65
Each stood amaz'd; the Priestes incloséd were
Within the greater Cloysture, we without,
Weeping were saying holy pray'res, when loe
The wicked Satyre audience earnest craves
Of the chiefe Priest: and for this was my charge, 70
I let him in, to whom he thus begins,
Fathers, if to your Vowes the Incense and
The Sacrifizes be not answerable,
If on your Aulters purely burne no flames,
Woonder not, for in *Ericinaes* Cave, 75
A treacherous Nimph prophanes your holy Lawes,
And in adultry her fayth doth breake.
Come Ministers with me, wee'le take in the fact.
A while th' unhappy father breathes, thinking he had
Found out the cause of this so dismall signes, 80
Straight he commaundes chiefe Minister Nicander go
With that same Satyre, and captivd to bring
Them to the Temple both: him straight accompanied
With all our troupe of under Ministers;
The Satyre by a darke and crooked way, 85
Conductes into the Cave: the young man scar'd
With our torch-light, so sodainely assail'd,
Assayes to fly unto that outward issue,
But it the Satyre closéd hath too fast.
Cho. What did you then?
Er.   I cannot tell you how 90
Amaz'd we were to see her that we taken had

To be Titirus daughter, whom no sooner we
Had layd hold on, but out Mirtillo steps,
And throwes his Dart, thinking to wound Nicander:
And had the steele hit as he did direct,   95
Nicander had been flaine: but shrinking backe,
Whether by chaunce or wit, he shund the harme.
But the strong Dart pierced his hayrie cloathes,
And there stucke fast, Mirtillo not being able
It to recover, captive taken was.   100
Cho. What's come of him?
Er.   He by an other way is led.
Cho. What shall he do?
Er.   To get more out of him
Besides; perhaps he shall not skotfree scape,
For having so offended our high Priest;
Yet would I could have comforted the wretch.   105
Cho. Why could you not?
Er.   Because the Law forbids
Us under Ministers to speake with guiltie folkes:
For this I came about, and left the rest,
Provoking heavens with teares and prayers devout,
To turne away this dreadfull storme from us.   110
And so pray yee, and therewithall, farewell.
Cho. So shall we do; had we but once performd
Our duetie unto Silvio, eternall Gods
In pittie, not in furie, shew your selves supreame.

Act IV Scene 4

CORISCA.

[Cor.] Now crowne my temples with triumphant Bayes,
Victorious temples, this day happely
I combatéd have in the field of Love,
And vanquishéd: this day both heaven and earth,
Nature and Art, Fortune and Destenie,   5
Both friendes and enemies have fought for mee.
The wicked Satyre whom I hated so,
Hath helpt me much: for it was better that
Mirtillo should, then Coridon, be ta'ne,
To make her fault more likely and more ill.   10
What though Mirtillo taken be, hee'le soone be free;

To her alone the punishment is due.
O solemne victorie, Oh famous triumph,
Dresse me a Trophee, amourous deceites;
You in this toung, in this same precious brest   15
Are above Nature most omnipotent.
Why stay I now? T'is time for me to go;
Untill the Law have judg'd my rivall dead,
Perhaps the Priest may draw the troth from mee:
Fly then, Corisca, daunger t'is to ly,   20
For them that have no feete wherewith to fly.
I'le hide me in these woodes untill I may
Returne t'enjoy my joyes; happy Corisca,
Who ever saw a braver enterprise?

Act IV Scene 5

NICANDER. AMARILLIS.

[*Nic.*] Hee had a hart most hard, or rather had
   No hart at all, nor any humane sence,
   That did not pittie thee, poore wretched Nimph,
   And felt no sorrow for thy miserie:
   Onely to see a Damsell captivate,   5
   Of heavenly countenance and so sweete a face,
   Worthy the world should to thee consecrate
   Temples and Sacrifices, led to the Temple
   For a Sacrifice, surely t'were a thing
   That with dry eyes I thinke none could behold.   10
   But who knowes how and wherefore thou wert borne?
   Titirus daughter, Montan'es daughter in law
   That should have been, and that these two are they
   Which do uphold Arcadia, and that thy selfe
   A daintie Nimph, so faire of forme,   15
   The naturall confines of this thy life,
   Approachest now so neare the boundes of death.
   Hee that knowes this, and doth not plaine the same,
   He is no man but beast, in humane shape.
Am. If that my fault did cause my wretchednesse,   20
   Or that my thoughtes were wicked, as thou thinkst
   My deed, lesse greevous would my death be then.
   For it were just my blood should wash the spots
   Of my defiléd soule, heavens rage appease,

And humane justice justly satisfie;   25
Then could I quiet my afflicted sprights,
And with a just remorse of well-deservéd death,
My senses mortifie, and come to death.
And with a quiet blow passe foorth perhaps
Unto a life of more tranquilitie.   30
But too too much, Nicander, too much griev'd
I am, in so young yeeres, Fortune so hie,
An Innocent, I should be doom'd to die.
Nic. Ah pleasd it heavens we had gainst thee offended,
Not thou offended gainst the heavenly powers.   35
For we, alas, with greater ease might have
Restor'd thee to thy violated name
Then thou appeasd their violated powers.
But I see not who thee offended hath,
Saving thy selfe. Tell me, wert thou not found   40
In a close place with the Adulterer, alone,
With him alone? Wert thou not promised
Unto Montanus sonne? Hast thou not broke thy fayth?
How art thou innocent?
Am.   I have not broke
The Law, and I am innocent.
Nic.   Thou hast not broke   45
The law of Nature happely (*Love if thou likest*)
But humane law and heavens thou hast transgrest,
(*Love lawfully.*)
Am.   Both heavens and men have er'd to me,
If it be true that thence our haps do come;
For is it reason in my destenie,   50
I beare the paine that's due to other's faultes?
Nic. Peace, Nimph; came up thy toung in wilfull rage,
Let loose; do not condemne the Starres, for wee
Our selves procure us all our miserie.
Am. I none accuse in heav'n, but my ill fates.   55
And worse then them is shee, that mee deceiv'd.
Nic. Then blame thy selfe, that hast deceiv'd thy selfe.
Am. I was deceiv'd, but by an others fraude.
Nic. T'is no deceite, to whom deceite is deare.
Am. Then you I see condemne me for unchast?   60
Nic. I say not so; aske but your deedes, they'le tell.
Am. Deedes often are false tokens of the hart.
Nic. The deedes we see; we cannot see the hart.

Am. See what you will, I'am sure my hart is cleare.
Nic. What led you then into the Cave alone?   65
Am. Simplicitie, and my too much beliefe.
Nic. Trust you your Chastitie unto your Love?
Am. I trusted my false friend, and not my Love.
Nic. What friend was that, your amorous desire?
Am. Orminoes sister, who hath me betrayde.   70
Nic. Sweet trecherie, to fall into your love.
Am. I knew not of Mirtilloes comming, I.
Nic. Why did you enter then? And to what end?
Am. Let it suffize, not for Mirtilloes sake.
Nic. You are condemn'd except y'have better proofe.   75
Am. Let her be askéd of my innocencie.
Nic. What, shee that was the occasion of your fault?
Am. Shee that betray'd mee; will you not her beleeve?
Nic. What fayth hath she that was so faythlesse then?
Am. I by our Goddesse *Cinthiaes* name will sweare.   80
Nic. Thy deedes have mard the credite of thine oath.
   Nimph, to be plaine, these are but dreames; and waves
   Of muddy water cannot wash cleane, nor guilt hartes
   Speake troth; thou should'st have kept thy chastitie
   As dearely as the apple of thine eye.   85
Am. And must I then thus (good Nicander) die?
   Shall none me heare, nor none my cause defend?
   Thus left of all, depriv'd of every hope,
   Onely accompanied with an extreame
   Unhappy Funerall, pitty that not helpes mee.   90
Nic. Nimph, be content, and since thou wert so fond
   In sinning, be more wise in suffering punishment.
   Direct thine eyes to heav'n; thence art thou come,
   And thence doth come all good or ill that haps,
   As from a Fountaine doth a streame descend: 95
   And though to us it ill do seeme, as ev'ry good
   Is mingled with some ill, yet there t'is good.
   Great *Jove* doth know, to whom all thoughtes are knowne.
   So doth our Goddesse whom we worshyp heere,
   How much I grieve for thee; and if I have   100
   Piers't with my wordes thy soule, like a Phisicion I
   Have done, who searcheth first the wound
   Where it suspected is; be quiet then,
   Good Nimph, and do not contradict that which
   Is writ in heav'n above of thee.   105

Am. O cruell sentence, whether writ in heav'n
   Or earth! In heav'n it is not writ,
   For there mine innocencie is knowne; but what
   Availes it since I needes must die? Ah too, too hard,
   And too, too bitter cupp. Ah, good Nicander,   110
   For pittie sake make not such hast with mee
   Unto the Temple! Stay, Oh stay a little while!
Nic. O Nimph, to whom death is so greevous now,
   Each moment seemes a death; it is thine ill to stay.
   Death hath not so much harme, as feare thereof;   115
   Thou sooner dead, thy paine is sooner past.
Am. Some helpe may come, deare father: father, now
   Dost thou leave me, now leave thine onely child?
   Wilt thou not helpe me yet before I die?
   Do not deny me yet thy latest kisse.   120
   One blade shall wound both brestes, and out of mine
   Thy blood must streame. Oh father! Oh sweete name!
   Sometime so deare which I ne're calld in vaine,
   Make you your onely daughters marriage thus,
   A morninges Bride, an evening Sacrifize?   125
Nic. Nimph, do not thus torment thy self and me,
   T'is time I lead you to the Temple now,
   My duetie t'is, I may not slacke it so.
Am. Deare Woods, farewell, my dearest Woods, farewell,
   Receive my latest sighs untill my soule   130
   By cruell wound from this my body free,
   Returne to seeke your lovéd shadowes out.
   For Innocentes can not be doom'd to hell,
   Nor mongst the blesséd can despayrers dwell.
   O Mirtillo, wretched was that day   135
   That first I saw thee, and thy sight did please,
   Since I my life must leave, more deare to thee
   Then thine, which prooves the occasion of my death.
   Wilt thou beleeve that she is doom'd to death
   For thee, that cruell ever was to thee,   140
   To keepe me innocent? For mee too bold,
   For thee too little daring was my will; how ever t'was,
   I faultles die, fruitles, and without thee
   My deare, I die, my deare Mirtillo.
Nic.   Surely shee
   Is dead, and in Mirtilloes loved name her life   145
   Hath finishéd; her love and griefe the blade

Prevented hath; come, helpe to hold her up;
Shee lyveth yet, I feele her hart doth throb.
Carry her to the Fountaine here hard by,
Fresh water may restore her stonied sprights,   150
But were it not a deed of pittie now,
To let her die of griefe, and shun the blade.
No, let us rather succour now her life,
Wee do not know what heav'ns will do with her.

Act IV Scene 6

CHORUS OF HUNTSMEN.
CHORUS OF SHEPHEARDS WITH SILVIO.

Cho. Hu. O glorious child of great *Alcides* race,
  That Monsters kilst, and Wild-bestes dost deface.
Cho. Sh. O glorious child, who Erimantus Boore
  Hast overthrowne, unconquerable thought.
  Behold his head, that seemes to breath out death,   5
  This is the Trophee of our Demi-God,
  Helpe, Shepheardes, helpe, to celebrate his name,
  And with solemnitie his deedes to grace.
Cho. Hu. O glorious child of great *Alcides* race,
  That Monsters kilst, and Wild-bestes dost deface.   10
Cho. Sh. O glorious child, by whom the fertile plaines,
  Depriv'd of tillage, have their good regaind.
  Now may the Plough-man goe securelie, and
  Sow both his Seede, and reape his Harvest in.
  These ougly teeth can now no more them chace.   15
Cho. Hu. O glorious child of great *Alcides* race,
  That monsters kilst, and wild Beastes dost deface.
Cho. Sh. O glorious child, how thou dost couple still
  Pittie with fortitude. *Cinthia*, behold
  Thy humble Silvioes vow; behold this head,   20
  That here and here in thy despight is armd
  With white and crooked tuskes, envying thy hornes.
  Thou puissant Goddesse, since thou didst direct
  His shaft, the price of his great victorie
  Is due to thee: hee famous by thy grace.   25
Cho. Hu. O glorious child of great *Alcides* race,
  That monsters kilst, and wild Beastes dost deface.

Act IV Scene 7

CORIDON.

[*Cor.*] Untill this time I never durst beleeve
  That which the Satyre of Corisca said,
  Imagining his tale had been but fordg'd
  Maliciously to worke me injurie:
  Far from the troth it seemd to me that place,   5
  Where she appoynted I with her should meete,
  (If that be true which was on her behalfe,
  Delivered me by young Lisetta late)
  Should be the place to take th' Adultrour in.
  But see a signe that may confirme the same,   10
  Ev'n as he told mee, so it is in deed.
  Oh what a Stone is this, which shuts up thus
  The huge mouth of this Cave! Oh Corisca,
  All in good time I have found out your guiles,
  Which after so long use, at last returne   15
  With damage to your selfe. So manie lies,
  So many trecheries, must needes presage
  Some mortall disadventure at the least,
  To him that was not madd, or blinde with love.
  T'was good for mee I stayde away so long,   20
  Great fortune that my father me detain'd
  So with a tedious stay, as then me thought.
  Had I kept time but as Lisetta bad,
  Surely some strange adventure had I had.
  What shall I doe? Shall I attir'd with spleene   25
  Seeke with outragious furie for revenge?
  Fie no, I honour her too much; so bee
  The case with reason waighd, it rather would
  Have pittie and compassion then revenge.
  And shall I pittie her that me betrayes?   30
  Shee rather doth betray her selfe, that thus
  Abandons mee, whose fayth to her was pure,
  And give her selfe in pray
  To a poore Shepheard straunger vagabond,
  That shall to morrow be more perfidious then shee.   35
  Should I, according to the Satyres counsell, her accuse,
  Of the fayth broken, which to mee shee swore?
  Then must shee die. My hart's not halfe so base;
  Let her then live for mee: or to say better,

Let her die unto mee, and live unto others: 40
Live to her shame, live to her infamie;
Since she is such, she never can in me
Kindle one sparke of fearefull jealowsie.

Act IV Scene 8

SILVIO. [ECCHO].

[*Sil.*] O Goddesse, that no Goddesse art, but of
  An idle people, blinde and vaine, who with
  Impurest mindes and fond Religion,
  Hallowes the Aulters and great Temples too.
  What, sayd I Temples? Wicked Theaters   5
  Of beastly deedes, to colour their dishonest actes
  With titles of thy famous Deitie,
  Because thy shames in others shames made lesse,
  Let lose the raines of their lasciousnesse.
  Thou foe to Reason, plotter of misdeedes,   10
  Corrupter to our soules, calamitie
  To the whole worlde; thou daughter of the Sea,
  And of that treacherous monster rightly borne,
  That with the breath of hope dost first intice
  These humane brestes, but afterward dost moove   15
  A thousand stormes of sighes, of teares, of plaintes.
  Thou mayst be better calld Mother of tempestes and
  Of rage, then Mother of Love.
  To what a miserie hast thou throwne downe
  Those wretched Lovers? Now mayst thou vaunt thy selfe   20
  To be omnipotent, if thou canst save
  That poore Nimphs life, whom with thy snares thou hast
  Conducted to this miserable death.
  O happy day I hallowd my chast minde
  To thee, my onely Goddesse, *Cinthia*,   25
  Such power on earth to soules of better sort,
  As thou art light in heav'n above the Starres.
  Much better are those studious practises
  Then those which *Venus* unchast servantes use.
  Thy servantes kill both Beares and ougly Boores,   30
  Her servantes are of Beares and Boores still slaine.
  Oh Bowe and matchles Shaftes, my power and my delight,
  Vaine fantastive Love, come proove thyne armes,

Effeminate with mine: but fie, too much
I honour thee, poore weake and wreckling child,   35
And for thou shalt me heare, I'le speake aloud.
A rod to chastise thee will be inough, ... ynough.
What are thou, *Eccho*, that so soundes againe?
Or rather Love, that answerest louldly so . . . . y so.
I could have wisht no better match; but tell   40
Me then, art thou (by heaven) hee . . . . eaven hee.
The sonne of her that for *Adonis* did
So miserably burne, in whom nought good is? . . . . Goddesse.
A Goddesse? No, the Concubine of *Mars*,
In whom lasciousnesse doth wholly lye, ... wholly a lye. 45
O fine, thy tongue doth clacke against the winde,
Wilt thou come foorth? Thou dost but darkly dare, . . . y dare.
I helde thee for a coward still; art thou a bastard or
Dost thou that title bravely skorne? . . . . y skorne.
O God, then art thou *Vulcanes* sonne, by that   50
Lame Smith begot . . . . God.
A God? Of what? Of Winds, madd with base mearth . . . earth.
God of the earth? Makes thou thy loves to rue? . . . . t'rue.
With what dost thou still punish those that strive,
And obstinately do contende with Love? . . . . with Love. 55
Nay soft, when shall crook't Love (tell me, good foole)
Enter my brest? I warrent t'is too straight . . . . straight.
What, shall I fall in love so sodainely? . . . . sodainely.
What is her name that I must then adore? . . . . Dore.
Dorinda, foole, thou canst not speake out yet,   60
But dost not thou meane her? . . . . ee'n her.
Dorinda whom I hate, but who shall force my will? . . . . . I will.
What weapons wilt thou use? Perhaps thy Bow . . . . . thy Bow.
My Bow? Not till it be by thy leawd folly broken . . . . . broken
My broken armes incounter me, and who   65
Shall breake them? Thou? . . . . thou.
Fie, fie, thou art drunke; goe sleepe, goe sleepe; but stay,
These marvailes must be done; but wheare? . . . . heare.
O foole, and I am gone, how thou art loden with
Wit-robbing Grapes that grew upon the Vine . . . . Divine. 70
But soft, I see, or els mee thinkes I see
Something that's like a Woolfe in yonder Grove.
T'is sure a Woolfe. How monstrous great it is.
This day for me is destenied to prayse:
Good Goddesse, with great favours dost thou shew   75

To triumph in one day over two Beastes.
In thy great name, I loose this shaft, the swiftest and
The sharpest which my Quiver holdes.
Great Archeresse, direct thou my right hand,
And here I vow to sacrifize the spoyles   80
Unto thy name. O daintie blow, blow falne
Ev'n where my hand and eye it destenyed.
Ah that I had my Dart, it to dispatch
Before it get into the Woodes away.
But heere be Stones, what need I any else?   85
Heere's scarcely one, I need none now: heere is
Another Shaft will peirce it to the quicke.
What's this I see? Unhappie Silvio!
I'have shot a Shepheard in a Wolvish shape.
O bitter chaunce! O ever miserable!   90
Mee thinkes I know the wretch, ti's Linco that
Doth hold him up. Oh deadly shaft! Oh most
Unhappie Vow! I guiltie of anothers blood!
I thus the causer of anothers death!
I that have been so liberall of my life,   95
So large a spender of my blood for others health?
So, cast away thy weapons, and go live
All glorilesse. But see where he doth come,
A great deale lesse unhappy then thy selfe.

Act IV Scene 9

LINCO. SILVIO. DORINDA.

[*Lin.*] Leane thou thy selfe (my Daughter) on this arme.
    Unfortunate Dorinda.
Sil.   Oh mee! Dorinda? I am dead.
Dor. O Linco, Linco, Oh, my second father!
Sil. It is Dorinda sure: Ah voyce; ah sight.
Dor. Dorinda to sustaine, Linco, hath been   5
    A fatall office unto thee; thou hardst
    The first cryes that I ever gave on earth,
    And thou shalt heare the latest of my death;
    And these thine Armes that were my Cradle once,
    Shall be my Coffin now.
Lin.   O child, more deare   10
    Then if thou wert mine owne. I cannot speake,

Griefe hath my wordes dissolvéd into teares.

Sil. Oh earth, hold ope thy jawes and swallow mee.

Dor. Oh stay both pace and plaint (good Linco) for
 The one my griefe, my wound the other doth increase.   15

Sil. Oh what a hard reward, most wretched Nimph,
 Hast thou receivéd for thy wondrous Love!

Lin. Be of good cheere, thy wound not mortall is.

Dor. I, but Dorinda mortall wilbe quickly dead.
 But dost thou know who t'is hath wounded me?   20

Lin. Let us care for the sore, not for the offence,
 For never did Revenge yet heale a wound.

Sil. Why stay I still? Shall I stay whilst they see me?
 Have I so bold a face? Fly, Silvio, fly
 The punishment of that revengefull sight,   25
 Fly the just edge of her sharpe cutting voice.
 I cannot fly; fatall necessitie doth hold
 Me heere, and makes me seeke whom most
 I ought to shunne.

Dor.   Why, Linco, must I die
 Not knowing who have given me my death?   30

Lin. It Silvio is.

Dor.   I'st so?

Lin.   I know his shaft.

Dor. Oh happie issue of my lives last end,
 If I be slaine by such a lovely friend.

Lin. See where he is, with countenance him accusing.
 Now heavens be praysd, y'are at good passe.   35
 With this your bowe and shaftes omnipotent;
 Hast thou not like a cunning Wood-man shot?
 Tell me, thou that of Silvio livst, was it not I
 That shot this daintie shoote? Oh Boy too wise,
 Hadst thou beleev'd this foolish agéd man,   40
 Had it not better been? Answere me, wretch.
 What can thy life be worth, if shee do die?
 I know thou'lt say thou thoughtst t'have shot a Woolfe,
 As though it were no fault to shoote
 Not knowing (careless and wandring child) if t'were   45
 A man or beast thou shotst at. What Heardsman, or
 What Ploughman dost thou see attyr'd in other cloathes?
 Ah Silvio, Silvio, who ever soweth witt so greene,
 Doth ever reape ripe fruite of ignorance.
 Thinke you (vaine Boy) this chaunce by chaunce did come?   50

Never without the powers devine did such like happen.
Heaven is enrag'd at your supportlesse spight
To love and deepe despising so humane affectes.
Gods will not have companions on the earth,
They are not pleasd with this austeritie: 55
Now thou art dumbe, thou were not wont t'indure.

Dor. Silvio, let Linco speake, he doth not know
What sov'raignetie thou o're Dorinda hast,
In life and death by the great power of Love.
If thou hast shot me, thou hast shot thine owne.   60
Thou hitst the marke that's proper to thy shaft,
These handes that wounded me have follow'd right
The ayme of thy faire eyes. Silvio, behold her whom
Thou hatest so, behold her as thou wouldst.
Thou wouldst me wounded have, wounded I am.   65
Thou wish't me dead, I ready am for death.
What wouldst thou more? What can I give thee more?
Ah, cruell Boy, thou never wouldst beleeve
The wound by thee Love made; canst thou deny
That which thy hand hath done? Thou never sawst   70
The blood mine eyes did shed; seest thou this then
That gusheth from my side; but if with pittie now
All gentlenesse and valoure be not spent,
Do not denie me, cruell soule, I pray,
At my last gaspe, one poore and onely sigh: 75
Death should be blest, if thou but thus wouldst say,
Goe rest in peace, poore soule, I humbly pray.

Sil. Ah, my Dorinda, shall I call thee mine,
That art not mine, but when I thee must loose?
And when thou hast thy death received by mee,   80
Not when I might have giv'n thee my life.
Yet will I call thee mine, that mine shalt bee
Spight of my fortune; and since with thy life
I cannot have thee, I'le have thee in death:
All thou seest in me is ready for revenge: 85
I kilde thee with these weapons, with the same
I'le kill my selfe. I cruell was to thee,
I now desire nothing but crueltie.
I proudly thee despis'd; upon my knees
I humbly thee adore, and pardon crave.   90
But not my life. Behold my Bowe, my Shaftes,
Wound not mine eyes or handes, th'are innocent.

But wound my brest, monster to pittie, foe
To love; wound me this hart that cruell was
To thee; behold, my brest is bare.   95
Dor. Silvio, I wound that brest? Thou hadst not need
  Let it be naked to mine eyes, if thou desirest
  I should it wound. O daintie, beauteous rocke,
  So often beaten by the waves and windes
  Of my poore teares and sighes in vaine; and is it true,   100
  Thou pittie feelst? Or am I, wretch, but mockt?
  I would not this same Alablaster skin
  Should me deceive, as this poore Beastes hath thee.
  I wound thy brest? T'is well, Love durst do so.
  I aske no more revenge then thou shouldst love.   105
  Blest be the day wherein I first did burne,
  Blest be my teares and all my martirdomes.
  I wish thy prayse, and no revenge of thee.
  But, curteous Silvio, that dost kneele to her,
  Whose Lord thou art, since mee thou needes wilt serve,   110
  Let thy first service be to rise when I thee bid.
  The second, that thou liv'st: for mee, let heavens
  Worke their will; in thee my hart will live.
  As long as thou dost live, I cannot die.
  But if it seeme unjust my wound should be   115
  Unpunishéd, then breake this cruell Bowe,
  Let that be all the mallice thou dost show.
Sil. Oh curteous doome; and so't shalbe;
  Thou deadly Wood shalt pay the price of others life;
  Behold, I breake thee, and I render thee   120
  Unto the Woodes, a trunke unprofitable.
  And you my Shaftes that piercéd have the side
  Of my faire Love, because you brothers bee,
  I put you both togither, and deliver you,
  Roddes armd in vaine, and vainely featheréd.   125
  T'was true Love tolde me late in *Ecchoes* voyce,
  O powerfull tamer both of Gods and men,
  Late enemie, now Lord of all my thoughtes,
  If thou esteemest it glory to have mollified
  A proude obdurate hart, defende me from   130
  The fatall stroke of death! One onely blow
  Killing Dorinda, will me with her kill.
  So cruell death, if cruell death she prove,
  Will triumph over thee, triumphant love.

Lin. So wounded both, yet woundes most fortunate,   135
   Were but Dorindaes sownd. Let's soone go seeke
   Some remedie.
Dor.   Do not, good Linco, lead
   Me to my fathers house in this attire.
Sil. Shall my Dorinda go to other house
   Then unto mine? No sure: alive or dead   140
   This day I'le marrie thee.
Lin.   And in good time,
   Since Amarillis hath lost life and marriage too.
   O blessed couple! O eternall Gods!
   Give two their lives, giving but one her health.
Dor. Silvio, I weary am; I cannot hold me on   145
   My wounded side.
Sil.   Be of good cheere,
   Thou shalt a burthen be to us most deare.
   Linco, give me thy hand.
Lin.   Hold, there it is.
Sil. Hold fast, and with our armes wee'le make a seate
   For her. Sit there, Dorinda, and with thy right hand   150
   Hold Lincoes necke, and with thy left close mine.
   Softly, my hart, for rushing of thy wound.
Dor. O now, mee thinkes I am well.
Sil.   Linco, hold fast.
Lin. Do not you stagger, but go forward right;
   This is a better triumph then a head.   155
Sil. Tell me, Dorinda, doth thy wound still pricke?
Dor. It doth; but in thine armes, my lovelie treasure,
   I hold ev'n pricking deare, and death a pleasure.

CHORUS

   O sweete and golden age, when Milke
   Unto the tender World was meate:
   Whose Cradle was the harmelesse Wood,
   Their dearer partes, whose grasse like silke,
   The Flockes untoucht, did joy to eate.   5
   Nor feard the World the spoyle of blood,
   The troublous thoughts that do no good
   Did not then make a cloudy vaile
   To dimme our sunnes eternall light.
   Now Reason being shut up quight,   10

Cloudes do our Wits skies over-haile;
   From whence it is straunge landes we seeke for ease,
   Ploughing with huge Oake trees the Ocean seas.
This bootlesse superstitious voyce,
This subject profit lesse then vaine   15
Of toyes, of titles, and of sleight,
Whom the mad World through worthlesse choyce
Honor to name doth not disdaine,
Did not with tyranny delight
To rule our mindes, but to sustaine   20
Trouble for troth, and for the right
To maintaine fayth a firme decree
Amongst us men of each degree,
Desire to do well was of right.
   Care of true Honor, happy to be named,   25
   Who what was lawfull pleasure to us framed.
Then in the pastures grovy shade,
Sweete Carroles and sharpe Madrigales
Were flames unto deare lawfull Loves.
There gentle Nimphes and Shepheards made   30
Thoughts of their wordes, and in the dales
Did *Himen* joyes and kisses move,
Farre sweeter and of more behove;
True lovers onely did enjoy
Loves lively Roses and sweete Flowers,   35
Whilst Wily-craft found alwayes showers,
Showers of sharpe will, and wills annoy:
   Were it in woodes or Caves for quiet rest,
   The name of Husband still was likéd best.
False wicked World, that courtest still   40
With thy base mercenary name
The soules chiefe good, and dost entice
To nourish thought of newfound Will,
With likelihoodes restraind againe.
Unbridling ever secret vice,   45
Like to a Net layde by device
Among faire Flowers and sweete spread Leaves,
Thou cloathst vilde thoughtes in holy weedes,
Esteeming seeming goodnesse deedes,
By which the life with Art deceives.   50
   Nor dost thou care (this Honor is thy act)
   What theft it be, so Love may bide the fact.

But thou, great Honour, great by right,
Frame famous spirits in our hartes;
Thou true Lord of each Noble brest.   55
O thou that rules Kinges of might,
Once turne thee into these our partes,
Which wanting thee, cannot be blest.
Make them from out their mortall rest,
With mightie and with powerfull stinges,   60
Who by a base unworthy will
Have left to work thy pleasure still,
And left the worth of antique thinges.
Let's hope our ills a truce will one day take,
And let our hopes not waver, no, nor shake: 65
Let's hope the setting sunne will rise againe,
And that the skyes when they most darke appeare,
Do draw (though cover'd) after wishéd cleare.

Act V Scene 1

URANIO. CARINO.

[*Ura.*] The place is ever good, where any thrives,
    And every place is native to the wise.
Car. True (good Uranio) I by proofe can tell,
    That young, did leave my fathers house, and sought
    Strange places out, and now turne home gray hear'd,   5
    That earst departed hence with golden lockes;
    Yet is our native soyle sweete unto him
    That hath his sence: Nature doth make it deare,
    Like to the Adamant, whom though the Mariner
    Carry farre hence, sometime where as the Sunne   10
    Is borne, and sometime where it dyes; yet still
    The hidden vertue wherewith it beholdes
    The Northern Pole it never doth forgoe.
    So he that goes farre from his native soyle,
    And often times in straungerland doth dwell,   15
    Yet he retaines the love he to it bore.
    O my Arcadia, now I greet thy ground,
    And welcome, good Uranio, for t'is meete
    You do partake my joyes, as you have done my toyle.
Ura. I may pertake your toyle, but not content,   20
    When I remember how farre hence I left

My house and little houshold off: well may I rest
My limbes, but well I wot my hart will mone,
Nor save thy selfe, could any thing have drawne
Me from Elidis now; yet I know not   25
What cause hath made you travaile to this place.
Car. Thou knowst, my deare Mirtillo, whom the heavens
    Have giv'n me; for my Sonne came hither sicke,
    Heere to get health, according to the Oracle,
    Which sayd onely Arcadia could restore it him.   30
    Two monthes he hath been heere, and I not able to
    Abide that stay went to the Oracle
    To know of his returne, which answered thus,
    Returne thou to thy Countrey, where thou shalt
    Live merrily with thy Mirtillo deare,   35
    Heavens have determined great thinges of him;
    Nor shalt thou laugh but in Arcadia.
    Thou, then my deare companion, merrie bee,
    Thou hast a share in all my good, nor will
    Carino smile, if my Uranio grieve.   40
Ura. All labours that I for Carino take
    Have their reward; but for to short the way,
    I pray you tell what made you travaile first.
Car. A youthfull love I unto Musicke bore,
    And greediness of forraine fame, disdayning that   45
    Arcadia onely should me prayse, made me
    Seeke out Elide and Pisa famous so,
    Where I saw glorious Aegon crowned with Bayes,
    With Purple next to Vertue evermore;
    So that he *Phebus* seem'd; when I devout   50
    Unto his powre did consecrate my Lute.
    Then left I pisa and to Micene went,
    And afterwardes to Argos, where I was
    At first, adoréd like a God: but twilbe too,
    Too troublesome to tell the storie of my life.   55
    I many fortunes tride, sometime disdaind,
    Sometime respected like a power devine,
    Now rich, then poore; now downe, then up aloft.
    But in the change of place, my fortuncs never changd;
    I learnd to know and sigh my former libertie.   60
    And leaving Argos, I returnéd to
    My homely Bowre I in Elidis had:
    Where (Gods be prays'd) I did Mirtillo buy,

Who since, hath comforted all mine annoyes.
Ura. Thrise happie they who can conteine their thoughts   65
   And not through vaine and most immoderate hope,
   Leese the sweete tasted fruite of moderate good.
Car. Who would have thought t'have waxéd poore in gold?
   I thought t'have found in royall Pallaces
   People of more humanitie, then heere,   70
   Which is the noble ornament of worthy sprightes;
   But I (Uranio) found the contrarie:
   People in name and wordes right curteous,
   But in good deedes most scarce, and Pitties foes:
   People in face, gentle and pleasant still;   75
   But fiercer then th'outragious swelling Sea.
   People with countenaunce all of charitie,
   But throughly Covetous, and fraught with Envie:
   The greater showes they make, the lesse troth they meane:
   That which is vertue otherwhere is there but vice: 80
   Uprightest deedes, true love, pittie sinceere,
   Inviolable fayth, of hand and hart,
   A life most innocent; these they esteeme
   But cowards still, and men of sillie wittes:
   Follies and vanities that are ridiculous,   85
   Coosonage, lying, theft, and rapine clad
   In holinesse, by others downefalles and their losse,
   Rich still to grow, to builde their reputation
   On others infamie, to lay fine snares
   To trap the innocent; these are the vertues of that place.   90
   No merrit worth, reverence of age,
   Of law, or of degree, no raines of shame,
   Respect of love or blood, nor memorie
   Of any good received: and to conclude,
   Nothing so reverend, pure, or just can be,   95
   That seemes forbidden to these gulfes of pride,
   Of honour so ambitious, so covetous
   Of getting still. Now I that alwayes liv'd
   Unwarie of their snares, and in my forehead had
   All my thoughts written, my hart discoveréd;   100
   You well may judge, I was an open marke
   To the suspicious shaftes of envious folkes.
Ura. What can be happie in that caytive land
   Where Envie ever Vertue doth commaund?
Car. If since I travailéd, my Muse had had   105

As good a cause to laugh as t'had to weepe,
Perhaps my stile would have been fit t'have sung
The armes and honours of my noble Lord,
So that he needed not to have envyed
The brave Meonian trumpet of Achilles fame.   110
I might have made my countries browes been girt
With happie Laurell too. But too inhumane is this age,
And too unhappie guift of Poetrie.
The Swans desire a quiet nest, a gentle ayre,
Pernassus never knew this byting care.   115
Who quarrels with his fate and fortune still,
His voyce must needes be hoarse, his song but ill:
But now t'is time to seeke Mirtillo out.
Oh how this Countrey's chaungd! I scarcely know't.
But Straungers never want a guide that have a tongue,   120
We will enquire to the next harbour house,
Where thou thy wearie limmes mayst well repose.

Act V Scene 2

TITIRUS. NUNTIO.

[*Tit.*] Which plaine I first (my child) of thee? Thy life
Or honestie? Ile plaine thine honestie,
Because thy fire (though mortall) honest was:
And in thy steed my life I'le plaine and spend
Of thy life and thine honestie to see an end.   5
O Montane, onely thou with thy devices
And ill-cund Oracles, and with thy love,
And proud despiser of my daughter, to this end
Hast brought my child. Oh doubtfull Oracles,
How vaine you bee? And honestie gainst love   10
In youthful hartes a weake defence doth prove;
A woman whom no match hath ever sought
Is evill guarded from this common thought.
Nun. If dead he be not, or that through the ayre
No windes have carried him, him might I finde.   15
But see him now, when least I thought I should.
O late for mee, for thee too quickly found,
Except the newes were better that I bring.
Tit. Bringes thou the weapon that hath slaine my child?
Nun. Not this, but lesse. But how heard you this newes?   20

Tit. Why lives she then?
Nun.   She lives, and may do still,
  For in her choyce it is to live or die.
Tit. Oh blest be thou that liftes me up from death.
  But how is she unsafe, since at her choyce it is
  To live or die?
Nun.   Because she will not live.   25
Tit. She will not live? What madnesse makes her thus?
Nun. Anothers death; and if thou dost not move her,
  Shee is so bent, as others send in vaine
  Their praying wordes.
Tit.   Why stay we? Let us goe!
Nun. What, soft and faire, the Temples gates are shut,   30
  And know you not how it unlawfull is
  For any one save *sacerdotall* foote,
  To touch the sacred ground, untill such time
  The Sacrifize unto the Aulters come,
  Adornéd with the Sanctuarie rites?   35
Tit. How if shee 'ffect her purpose in the while?
Nun. She cannot, for shee's kept.
Tit.   In the meane time
  Then tell truely how all this is come to passe?
Nun. Thy mournefull child now come before the Priest
  With lookes of feare and griefe, that teares brought foorth,   40
  Not onely from us by, but by my troth,
  Ev'n from the pillors of the Temples selfe
  And hardest stones that seemd to feele the same,
  Was in a trice accus'd, convic't, condemn'd.
Tit. O wretched child, and why was she condemn'd?   45
Nun. Because the groundes of her defence were small.
  Besides, a certaine Nimph, whom she did call
  In testimonie of her innocence,
  Was absent now, and none could finde her out.
  And fearefull signes, and monstrous accidents   50
  Of horrour in the Temple proov'd the doubt,
  As dolorous to us, as strange and rare,
  Not seene since we did feele heavenly ire
  That did revenge Amintas love betrayde,
  The first beginning of our miserie.   55
  Diana swet out blood, the Earth did shake,
  The sacred Cave did bellow out unwonted howling
  And dire deadly cries.

Withall, it breath'd out such a stinking mist,
As *Plutoes* impure kingdome hath no worse.   60
And now with sacred order goes the Priest
To bring thy daughter to her bloodie ende,
The whilst Mirtillo (wondrous thing to tell)
Offer'd by his owne death, to give her life,
Crying, unbind those handes (unworthie stringes)   65
And in her steed that should be sacrifizd
Unto *Diana*, draw me to the Aulters
A Sacrifize to my faire Amarillis.
Tit. O admirable deede of faythfull love,
   And noble hart.
Nun.   Now heare a miracle: 70
Shee that before so fearefull was to die,
Chaung'd on the sodaine by Mirtilloes wordes,
Thus answeres with a bold undaunted hart:
Think'st thou (my deare) then by thy death to gaine
Life to her death, that by thy life doth live.   75
O Miracle unjust! On Minister, on on, why do you stay?
Leade me foorthwith unto mine end. Ile no such pittie I,
Mirtillo replies, Live, cruell pitteous love,
My hart his spightfull pittie doth reprove:
To me it longes to die. Nay, then to me   80
(She answers) that by Law condemnéd am.
And heere anew begins a wondrous strife,
As though that life were death, and death were life.
(O soules well borne) O couple worth of
Eternall honour, never dying prayse: 85
O living, and o dying glorious lovers.
Had I so many tongues, so many voyces,
As Heaven hath eyes, or Ocean sea hath sandes;
All would be dumbe and hoarse in setting out
Their wondrous and incomprehended prayse.   90
Eternall Childe of heaven, O glorious Dame,
That mortall deedes enchroniclest to time,
Write thou this Historie, and it infold
In solid Diamond with wordes of gold.
Tit. But what end had this mortall quarrell then?   95
Nun. Mirtillo vanquisheth? O rare debate,
Where dead on lyving getts the victorie!
The Priest speakes to your Child, be quiet, Nimph,
We cannot change this doome, for he must die

That offers death, our Law commaunds it so.   100
And after bids your Daughter should be kept,
Least griefes extreame should bring her desperate death.
Thus stood the state when Montane sent me for thee.
Tit. In sooth tis true, sweete scented Flowers shall cease
To dwell on Rivers bankes, and Woodes in Spring   105
Shall be without their Leaves, before a Mayde
Adorn'd with youth shall set sweete Love at naught.
But if we stay still heere, how shall we know
When it is time unto the Church to go?
Nun. Heere best of all, for in this place, alas,   110
Shall the good Shepheard sacrifizéd be.
Tit. And why not in the Church?
Nun.   Becasue there where
The fault is done, the punishment must be.
Tit. And why not in the Cave? There was the fault.
Nun. Because to open skyes it must be hallow'd.   115
Tit. And how knowst thou all these misteriall rites?
Nun. From the High-priest, who from Tireno had them,
For true Amintas and untrue Locrine,
Were sacrifizéd so. But now tis time to goe;
See where the sacred Pompe softly descendes: 120
Twere well done of us by this other way
To go unto the Temple to thy daughter.

Act V Scene 3

CHORUS OF SHEPHEARDS. CHORUS OF PRIESTES.
MONTANUS. MIRTILLO.

[*Cho. Sh.*] Oh daughter of great *Jove*, sister of *Phebus* bright,
Thou second *Titan*, to the blinder world that givest light;
Cho. Pri. Thou that with thy well temper'd vitall ray,
Thy brothers wondrous heate doth well allay,
Which mak'st sweete Nature happely bring foorth   5
Rich firtile birthes of Hearbes, of Beastes, of Men:
As thou his heate doth quench, so calme thine ire
That sets Arcadiaes wretched hartes on fire.
Cho. Sh. O daughter of great *Jove*, sister of *Phebus* bright,
Thou second *Titan*, to the blinder world that givest light.   10
Mon. Yea, sacred Priestes, the Aulters ready make,
Shepheardes devout, reiterate your soundes,

And call upon the name of our great Goddesse.
Cho. Sh. O daughter of great *Jove*, sister of *Phebus* bright,
   Thou second *Titan*, to the blinder world that givest light.   15
Mon. Now Shepheards stand aside, nor you my servants
   Come not neare, except I call for you.
   Valiant young man, that to give life els where,
   Abandonest thine owne, die comforted thus farre:
   T'is but a speedie sigh, which you must passe;   20
   For so seemes death to noble-minded sprightes;
   That once perform'd, this envious age,
   With thousandes of her yeeres shall not deface
   The memorie of such a gentle deed,
   But thou shalt live the example of true fayth,   25
   But for the Law commaundes thee sacrifiz'd
   To dye without a word, before thou kneelst,
   If thou hast ought to say, say it, and hold thy peace
   For ever after that.
Mir. Father, let it be lawfull that I call thee so,   30
   For though thou gav'st not, yet thou tak'st my life.
   My bodie to the ground I do bequeath, my soule
   To her that is my life. But if she die,
   As she hath threatnéd [so] to do; aye mee,
   What part of me shall then remaine alive?   35
   Oh death were sweete, if but my mortall parts
   Might die, and that my soule did not desire the same.
   But if his pittie ought deserves that dyes,
   For soveraigne pittie, then, courteous father,
   Provide she do not die; and with that hope   40
   More comforted, Ile pay my destenies;
   Though with my death you me from her disjoyne,
   Yet make her live, that she may me retaine.
Mon. Scarse I containe from teares: o frayle mankind!
   Be of good cheare, my sonne; I promise thy desire;   45
   I sweare it by this head, this hand take thou for pledge.
Mir. Then comforted, I die all comforted:
   To thee, my Amarillis, do I come,
   Soule of the faythfull Shepheard, as thine owne
   Do thou receive, for in thy lovéd name   50
   My wordes and life I will determine straight:
   So now to death I kneele, and hold my peace.
Mon. On, sacred Ministers, kindle the flame
   With Frankensence and Mirrhe, and Incense throw thereon

That the thicke vapoure may on high ascend.   55
Cho. Sh. Oh daughter of great *Jove*, sister of *Phebus* bright,
Thou second *Titan*, to the blinder world that givest light.

Act V Scene 4

CARINO. MONTANO. NICANDER. MIRTILLO.
CHORUS OF SHEPHEARDS.

[*Car.*] What Countrymen are here, so bravely furnishéd
  Almost all in a Liverie? Oh what a show
  Is heere? How rich, how full of pomp it is!.
  Trust mee, I thinke it is some Sacrifize.
Mon. Reach mee (Nicander) the golden Bason,   5
  That containes the juice of *Bacchus* fruite.
Nic. Behold, t'is ready here.
Mon.   So may this faultles blood
  Thy brest (Oh sacred Goddesse) mollifie,
  As do these falling droppes of Wine extinguish
  This blasing flame. So, take the Bason, there;   10
  Give me the silver Ewer now.
Nic.   Behold, the Ewer.
Mon. So may thine anger cease with that same faithles Nimph
  Provok't, as doth this fire this falling streame extinguish.
Car. This is some Sacrifize, but where's the holocaust?
Mon. Now all is fit; there wantes nought but the end.   15
  Give me the Axe.
Car.   If I be not deceiv'd,
  I see a thing that by his backe seemeth a man:
  He kneeles: he is perhappes the holocaust,
  O wretch tis so, the Priest holdes him by th'ead.
  And hast thou not, unhappy countrey yet   20
  After so many yeeres heavens rage appeasd?
Chor. Sh. O daughter of great *Jove*, sister of *Phebus* bright,
  Thou second *Titan*, to the blinder world that givest light.
Mon. Revengefull Goddesse, that for private fault
  Dost publicke punishment on us inflict,   25
  (Whether it be thy onely will, or els
  Eternall providence immutable commaund)
  Since the infected blood of Lucrine (false)
  Might not thy burning justice then appease,
  Drinke now this innocent and voluntarie Sacrifize,   30
  No lesser faythfull then Amintas was,

That at thy sacred Aulters in thy dire revenge I kill.
Cho. Sh. O daughter of great *Jove*, sister of *Phebus* bright,
    Thou second *Titan*, to the blinder world that givest light.
Mon. Oh, how I feele my hart waxe tender now,   35
    Binding my senses with unusuall maze:
    So both my hart not dares, my handes unable are
    To lift this Axe.
Car.   Ile see this wretches face,
    And then depart; for pittie will not let me stay.
Mon. Perhaps against the Sunne my strength doth faile,   40
    And tis a fault to sacrifize against the Sunne,
    Turne thou thy dying face toward this hill.
    So now, tis well.
Car.   O wretch! What do I see?
    My sonne Mirtillo. Is not this my sonne?
Mon. So now I can.
Car.   It is even so.
Mon.   Who lets my blow?   45
Car. What dost thou, sacred Priest?
Mon.   O man prophane,
    Why hast thou held this holy Axe? How darest
    Thou thy rash handes impose upon the same?
Car. O my Mirtillo, how camst thou to this?
Nic. Goe, dotard old and foolish insolent.   50
Car. I never thought t'have thee imbracéd thus.
Nic. Patch, stand aside, thou mayst not handle thinges
    Sacred unto the Gods, with handes impure.
Car. Deare to the Gods am also I, that by
    Their good direction hither came even now.   55
Mon. Nicander, cease, heare him, and turne him hence.
Car. Then, courteous Priest, before thy sword doth light
    Upon his necke, why dyes this wretched Boy?
    I, by the Goddesse thou ador'st, beseech thee tell.
Mon. By such a heavenly power thou conjur'st mee,   60
    That I were wicked, if I thee denied.
    But what wil't profit thee?
Car.   More then thou think'st.
Mon. Because he for an other willing is to die.
Car. Dye for an other? Then I for him will dye.
    For pittie then, thy falling blow direct,   65
    In stead of his, upon this wretched necke.
Mon. Thou dotest, friend.

Car.   And will you me denie
  That which you graunt another man?
Mon.   Thou art
  A Stranger man.
Car.   How, if I were not so?
Mon. Nor could'st thou, for he dyes but by exchange.   70
  But, tell me, what art thou? Thy habite shewes
  Thou art a Stranger, no Arcadian borne.
Car. I an Arcadian am.
Mon.   I not remember
  That I ever saw thee earst.
Car.   Heere was I borne,
  Carino cald, and father of this wretch.   75
Mon. Art thou Mirtilloes father then? Thou com'st
  Unluckily both for thy selfe and mee.
  Stand now aside, least with thy fathers teares,
  Thou makest fruitlesse, vaine our Sacrifize.
Car. If thou a father wert?
Mon.   I am a father man,   80
  A tender father of an onely sonne:
  Yet were this same my Silvioes head, my hand
  Should be as ready for't as t'is for this:
  For he this sacred habite shall unworthy weare
  That to a publique good his private doth preferre.   85
Car. O let me kisse him yet before he dye.
Mon. Thou mayst not, man.
Car.   Art thou so cruell, sonne,
  Thou wilt not answere thy sad father once?
Mir. Good father, hold your peace.
Mon.   O wretched, wee
  The holocaust contaminate, O Gods.   90
Mir. The life you gave, I cannot better give
  Then for her sake, who sole deserves to live.
Mon. Oh, thus I thought his fathers teares would make
  Him breake his scilence.
Mir.   Wretch, with errour have
  I done; the law of scilence quite I had forgot.   95
Mon. On Ministers, why do we stay so long?
  Carry him to the Temple back to th' holy Cell,
  There take againe his voluntary vow,
  Then bring him backe, and bring new Water too,
  New Wine, new Fire: dispatch, the sunne growes low.   100

Act V Scene 5

MONTANUS. CARINO. DAMETAS.

[*Mon.*] But thanke thou heavens, thou agéd impudent,
   Thou art his father! If thou were not, well,
   (I sweare by this same sacred habite on my head I weare)
   Thou shouldst soone taste how ill I brooke thy boldnes,
   Why, knowst thou who I am? Knowst thou that with   5
   This Rodd I rule affayres both humaine and divine?
Car. I cry you mercie, holy sacred Priest.
Mon. I suffered thee so long, till thou grow'st insolent.
   Knowest thou not Rage that Justice stirreth up,
   The longer t'is delayde, the greater tis?   10
Car. Tempestius furie never waignéd rage
   In brestes magnanimus, but that one blast
   Of Generous effect could coole the same.
   But if I can not grace obtaine, let mee
   Finde justice yet; you can not that denie.   15
   Lawmakers be not freéd from the Lawes.
   I aske you justice, justice graunt me then;
   You are unjust, if you Mirtillo kill.
Mon. Let me then know how I can be unjust.
Car. Did you not tell me it unlawfull was   20
   To sacrifize a Strangers blood?
Mon.   I told you so,
   And told you that which heavens did commaund.
Car. He is a Stranger you would sacrifize.
Mon. A Stranger, how? Is he not then thy sonne?
Car. Let if suffize, and seeke no further now.   25
Mon. Perhappes because you not begot him heere.
Car. Oft he least knowes that most would understand.
Mon. Heere we the kindred meane and not the place.
Car. I call him Stranger, for I got him not.
Mon. Is he thy sonne, and thou begots him not?   30
Car. He is my sonne, though I begotst him not.
Mon. Didst thou not say that he was borne of thee?
Car. I sayd he was my sonne, not borne of mee.
Mon. Extremitie of griefe hath made thee madd.
Car. If I were madd, I should not feele my griefe.   35
Mon. Thou art or madd or els a lying man.
Car. A lying man will never tell the trueth.
Mon. How can it be sonne and not-sonne at once?

Car. The sonne of love, and not of nature hee's.

Mon. Is he thy sonne? He is no Stranger then;   40
  If not, thou hast no part at all in him:
  Father or not, thus thou convincéd art.

Car. With wordes and not with trueth, I am convin'st.

Mon. His fayth is doubted that his wordes contraries.

Car. Yet do I say thou dost a deed unjust.   45

Mon. On this my head, and on my Silvioes head,
  Let my injustice fall.

Car.   You will repent it.

Mon. You shall repent, if you my duetie hinder.

Car. I call to witnesse men and Gods.

Mon.   Gods you
  To witnesse call that you despiséd have.   50

Car. Since you'le not heare me, heare me, heaven and earth.
  Mirtill a straunger is, and not my sonne;
  You do prophane your holy sacrifice.

Mon. Heavens aide me from this Bedlam man.
  Who is his father since hee's not your sonne?   55

Car. I cannot tell you; I am sure, not I.

Mon. See how he wavers; is he not of your blood?

Car. Oh no.

Mon.   Why do you call him sonne?

Car. Because I from his cradle have him nourisht still,
  And ever lov'd him like my sonne.   60

Mon. Bought you him? Stole you him? Where had you him?

Car. A courteous straunger in Elidis gave me him.

Mon. And that same straunger, where had he the childe?

Car. I gave him.

Mon.   Thou mov'st at once disdaine and laughter
  First thou him gav'st, and then hadst him in gift.   65

Car. I gave him that which I with him had found.

Mon. And where had you him?

Car.   In a lowe hole,
  Of daintie Mirtle trees upon Alpheus banke;
  And for this cause Mirtillo I him call'd.

Mon. Here's a fine tale! What, have your woods no beasts?   70

Car. Of many sorts.

Mon.   How scapte he being devour'd?

Car. A speedie Torrent brought him to this hole,
  And left him in the bosome of a litle Ile,
  On every side defended with the streame.

Mon. And were your streames so pitifull they drownd him not?   75
  Your Rivers gentle are that children nurse.
Car. Laid in a cradle like a litle ship,
  With other stuffe the waters wound together,
  He was safe brought by chance unto this hole.
Mon. Laid in a cradle?
Car.   In a cradle laid.   80
Mon. And but a childe?
Car.   I, but a tender childe.
Mon. How long was this agoe?
Car.   Cast up your count;
  Is it not nineteene yeares since the great floud?
  So long t'is since.
Mon.   Oh, how I feele a horror shake
  My bones.
Car.   He knowes not what to say: 85
  Oh wicked act, orecome, yet will not yeeld,
  Thinking t'outstrip me in his wit, as much
  As in his force; I heare him murmur,
  Yet he nill bewray that he convincéd is.
Mon. What interest had the man you speake of in   90
  That child? Was he his sonne?
Car.   I cannot tell.
Mon. Had he no better knowledge then of it then thus?
Car. Nor that know I.
Mon.   Know you him if you see him?
Car. He seem'd a shepheard by his cloaths and face;
  Of middle stature, of blacke haire his beard,   95
  And eye-browes were exceeding thicke.
Mon.   Shepheards,
  Come hither soone.
Dam.   Behold, we are readie here.
Mon. Which of these did he resemble then?
Car. Him whom you talke withall he did not onely seeme,
  But tis the same, though't be twentie yeares agoe,   100
  Hath not a whit alter'd his auncient looke.
Mon. Stand then aside; Dametas, stay with me.
  Tell me, know'st thou his man?
Dam.   Me seemeth so,
  But yet I know not where.
Car.   Him can I put in minde.
Mon. Let me alone. Stand you aside a while.   105

Car. I your commaundement willingly obey.
Mon. Now answere me, Dametas, and take heed
  You do not lye; tis almost twentie yeares
  Since you return'd from seeking out my child,
  Which the outragious River bare away: 110
  Did you not tell me you had search'd in vaine
  All that same countrey which Alpheus waters?
Dam. Why aske you this?
Mon.   Did not you tell me him
  You could not finde?
Dam.   I graunt I told you so.
Mon. What child then was it (tell me) which you gave   115
  Unto this stranger which did know you here?
Dam. Will you I should remember what I did
  So long agoe? Old men forgetfull are.
Mon. Is not he old? Yet he remembers it.
Dam. Tush, he doth rather dote!
Mon.   That shall we see;   120
  Come hither, straunger, come.
Car.   I come.
Dam.   Oh that
  Thou wert as farre beneath the ground.
Mon.   Tell me,
  Is this the shepheard that gave thee the gift?
Car. This same is he.
Dam.   What gift is't thou speak'st of?
Car. Dost not remember in the temple of Olimpick *Jove*,   125
  Having had answere of the Oracle,
  And being readie to depart, I met with thee,
  And ask'd thee of the Oracle, which thou declaredst;
  After I tooke thee home unto my house,
  Where didst thou not give me an Infant childe,   130
  Which in a cradle thou hadst lately found?
Dam. And what of that?
Car.   This is that very child,
  Which ever since I like mine owne have kept,
  And at these Aultars must be sacrific'd.
Dam. Oh, force of Destiny!
Mon.   Yet wilt thou faine?   135
  Is it not true which he hath told thee here?
Dam. Oh were I dead as sure as it is true.
Mon. And wherfore didst thou give an others goods?

Dam. Oh, maister, seeke no more; let this suffice.
Mon. Yet wilt thou hold me off and say no more?   140
   Villaine, thou dyest if I but aske againe!
Dam. Because the Oracle foretold me that the child
   Should be in danger on his fathers hands
   His death to have if he returnéd home.
Car. All this is true, for this he told me then.   145
Mon. Ay me, it is too manifest; the case is cleare.
Car. What resteth then? Would you more proofe then this?
Mon. The proofe's too great; too much have you declar'd;
   Too much I understand; O Carino, Carino,
   How I change griefe and fortunes now with thine,   150
   How thy affections now are waxen mine.
   This is my sonne, oh most unhappie sonne
   Of a more wretched father. More savadge was
   The water in him saving then in running quite away,
   Since at these sacred Aulars by the fathers hands   155
   Thou must be slaine, a wofull sacrifice,
   And thy poore bloud must wash thy native soyle.
Car. Art thou Mirtilloes father then? How lost you him?
Mon. The deluge ravisht him, whom when I lost,
   I left more safe; now found, I leese him most.   160
Car. Eternall providence, which with thy counsell hast
   Brought all these occurrents to this onely point;
   Th' art great with childe of some huge monstrous birth;
   Either great good or ill thou wilt bring forth.
Mon. This t'was my sleepe foretold, deccitfull sleepe.   165
   In ill too true, in good too lying still.
   This was th'unwonted pitie, and the sudden horror that
   I felt to stay the axe and shake my bones:
   For nature sure abhorres a stroke should come
   From fathers hands, so vilde abhominable.   170
Car. Will you then execute the wicked sacrifice?
Mon. By other hands he may not at these Altars die.
Car. Why, will the father murder then the sonne?
Mon. So bids our law, and were it pietie to spare
   Him since the true Amyntas would not spare himselfe?   175
Car. O wicked Fates, me whither have ye brought?
Mon. To see two fathers soveraigne pitie made a homicide,
   Yours to Mirtillo, mine unto the Gods;
   His father you denying for to bee,
   Him thought to save, and him you lost thereby;   180

Thinking and seeking, I to kill your sonne,
Mine owne have found, and must mine owne go kill.
Car. Behold the monster horrible this Fate brings forth.
O cruell chance (Mirtillo) o my life!
Is this that which the Oracle told of thee?   185
Thus in my native soyle hast thou me happy made?
O sonne of me, poore old and wretched man,
Lately my hope, my life, now my dispaire and death.
Mon. To me, Carino, leave these wofull teares;
I plaine my bloud: my bloud, why say I so,   190
Since I it shead? Poore sonne, why got I thee?
Why wert thou borne? Did the milde waters save thy life,
The cruell father might the same bereave?
Sacred immortal powers, without whose deep insight
No wave doth stirre in seas, no blast in skies,   195
No leafe upon the earth; what great offence
Have I committed, that I worthy am
With my poore off-spring for to warre with heaven?
If I offended have, oh, yet my sonne:
What hath he done you cannot pardon him?   200
O *Jupiter*, the great disdainfull blast
Would quickly suffocate my agéd sence,
But if thy thunderbolts will not, my weapon shall.
The dolorous example Ile renew,
Of good Amyntas, our belovéd Priest;   205
My sonne amaz'd shall see his father slaine,
Ere I a father will go kill my sonne:
Die thou, Montane, tis onely fit for thee;
O powers, I cannot say whether of heaven or hell,
That agitate with grief dispairefull mindes,   210
Behold your fury; thus it pleaseth you.
I nought desire save onely speedie death;
A poore desire my wretched life to end
Some comfort seemes to my sad spright to send.
Car. Wretched old man, as greater flames do dimme   215
The lesser lights, even so the sorrow I
Do of thy griefe conceive hath put out mine.
Thy case alone deserveth pittie now.

Act V Scene 6

TIRENIO. MONTANUS. CARINO.

[*Tir.*] Softly, my sonne, and set thy feet secure,
  Thou must uphold me in this rugged way,
  Thou art my bodies eye, I am thy mindes,
  And when thou com'st before the Priest, there stay.
Mon. Is't not the reverend Tirenio which I see,   5
  Who blind on earth, yet seeth all in heaven?
  Some great thing moves him thus; these many years
  I sawe him not out of his holy Cell.
Car. God grant he bring us happie newes.
Mon. Father Tirenio, what's the newes with you?   10
  You from the temple? How comes this to passe?
Tir. To you I come for news, yet bring you news.
  How oft blind eyes do aide the inward sight,
  The whilst the minde untraveld with wilde sights,
  Withdrawes into it selfe, and Linceus eyes   15
  Doth set a worke in sightlesse sences blinde.
  We may not, Montane, passe so lightly ore
  The unexpected things that heavenly mixture tempers
  with humane,
  Because the Gods do not converse on earth,
  Nor partly hold with mortall men at all.   20
  But all these workes so great, so wonderfull,
  Which the blind world to blinder chance ascribes,
  Is nothing but celestiall counsell talke,
  So speake th' eternall powers amongst themselves,
  Whose voices though they touch not deafened eares,   25
  Yet do they sound to hearts that understand.
  O foure, o six times happy he that understands it well,
  The good Nicander, as thou didst command,
  Stayes to conduct the holy sacrifice,
  But I retaind him by an accident   30
  That's newly falne: the which (I know not) all
  Unwonted and confus'd, twixt hope and feare,
  Dulleth my sence. I cannot understand, and yet the lesse
  I comprehend, the more I do conceive.
Mon. That which you know not, wretch, I know too well,   35
  But tell me can the Fates hide ought from thee
  That piercest to the deep'st of Destinies?
Tir. If (sonne) the use divine of light propheticall

Were natures gift and not the gift of heaven,
Then might'st thou see as well as I that Fates   40
Secrets sometime denie our working mindes;
This onely tis that makes me come to thee,
That I might better be inform'd who tis
That is discovered father to the youth
That's doom'd to die (if I Nicander understand).   45
Mon. That father you desire to know am I.
Tir. You, father of our Goddesse sacrifice!
Mon. I am the wretched father of that wretched sonne.
Tir. Of that same faithful shepheard that to give
      Life to an other gives himselfe to death?   50
Mon. His that by death giveth an other life,
      Yet by that death kills him that gave him life.
Tir. And is this true?
Mon.   Behold my witnesse here.
Car. That which he saith is true.
Tir.   And who art thou?
Car. I am Carino, his father thought till now.   55
Tir. Is this the childe the floud so bare away?
Mon. The very same.
Tir.   And for this then dost thou,
      Montanus, call thy selfe a wretched father?
      O monstrous blindnesse of these earthly mindes,
      In what a darke, profound and mystie night   60
      Of errors be they drowned? When thou, o heavenly sonne,
      Dost not enlighten them: Montanus, thou
      Art blinder in thy minde then I of eyes,
      That dost not see thy selfe the happiest father
      And dearest to the gods that ever yet did child beget.   65
      This was the secret which the Fates did hide.
      This is that happy day, with so much bloud,
      So many teares we did expect.
      This is the blessed end of our distresse.
      O thou, Montanus, turne into thy selfe!   70
      How is the famous Oracle forgot,
      Printed i' the hearts of all Arcadia:
      No end there is to that which you offends,
      Till two of heavens issue love unite,
      The teares of joyes so satisfie my heart   75
      I cannot utter it. No end there is,
      No end there is to that which you offends,

Till two of heavens issue love unite,
And for the auntient fault of that false wight,
A faithfull shepheards pitie make amends.   80
Tell me, Montanus, is not this thy sonne
Heavens issue? Is not Amarillis so?
Who hath united them but holy love?
Silvio by parents force espowséd was
To Amarillis, whom he hated still;   85
If thou the rest examine, you shall plainly see
The fatall voyce onely Mirtillo ment.
For since Amyntas chance, where have we seene
Such faith in love that might coequall this?
Who since Amyntas willing was to die   90
For any Nymph, onely Mirtill except.
This is that faithfull Shepheards pitie, which deserves
To cancell that same auncient error of Lucrine.
With this deed is the heavens ire appeaz'd,
Rather then with the sheading humane bloud,   95
Rendring unto th' eternall justice, that
Which female treacherie did take away.
Hence t'was no sooner he unto the temple came,
There to renew his vow, but straight did cease
All those prodigious signes; now did   100
The holy Image sweat out bloud no more,
Nor shooke the ground, nor any noise nor stinch
Came from the Cave, save gracious harmony,
And odours. O sweet mightie providence,
O heavenly Gods, had I all words, all hearts,   105
All to thy honour would I consecrate.
But to my power Ile render you your due.
Behold upon my knees, o heavenly powers,
I praise your name; how much am I oblig'd
That you have let me live untill this day!   110
An hundred yeares I have alreadie worne,
And never yet was life so sweet as now:
I but begin to live, now am I borne againe.
Why leese I time with words that unto deeds is due?
Helpe me up, sonne; without thee can I not   115
Upraise these weake and feeble members, sonne.
Mon. Tirenio hath wak't such joy in me,
    United yet with such a myracle
    As I scarce feele I joy, nor can my soule

Confounded shewe me high reteinéd mirth,   120
O gracious pitie of the highest Gods.
O fortunate Arcadia, o earth,
More happie then all earths beneath the sunne,
So deare's thy good, I have forgot mine owne,
And my beloved sonnes, whom twise I lost,   125
And twise againe have found; these seeme a drop
To the huge waves of thy great good: o dreame,
O blessed dreame, celestiall vision rather.
Arcadia now thou waxest bright againe.
Tir. Why stay we, Montane, now? Heavens not expect   130
   A sacrifice of rage, but thankes and love;
   In stead of death our Goddesse now commaunds
   Of marriage knot a sweet solemnitie:
   But say, how farr's to night?
Mon.   Not past one houre.
Tir. Then to the Temple turne, where let thy sonne   135
   Espowséd be to Amarillis straight, whom he may leade
   Unto his fathers house before the sunne be set,
   So heavens commaund. Come, gow, Montanus, gow.
Mon. Take heed, Tirenio, we do not violate
   Our holy law; can she her faith now give   140
   Unto Mirtillo, which she Silvio gave?
Car. And unto Silvio may she give her faith,
   So said thy servant was Mirtillo call'd,
   Though I more lik'd Mirtillo him to name.
Mon. That's very true; I did revive his name   145
   In this my younger sonne.
Tir. That doubt's well clear'd; now let us goe.
Mon. Carino, go with us; this day Mirtillo hath
   Two fathers found, Montane a sonne, and thou a brother.
Car. In love, Mirtilloes father, and your brother;   150
   In reverence, a servant to you both.
   And since you are so kinde to me, I pray you then
   Bid my companion welcome for my sake.
Mon. Most welcome both.
Car.   Eternall heavenly powers,
   How diverse are your high untroden waies   155
   By which your favours do on us descend
   From those same crook't deceitfull pathes whereby
   Our thoughts would faine mount up into the sky!

Act V Scene 7

CORISCA. LINCO.

[*Cor.*] Linco, belike the spightfull Silvio
   When least he ment, a Lover is become,
   But what became of her?
Lin.   We carried her
   To Silvioes house, whose mother her embrac't
   With teares of joy or griefe, I know not whether;   5
   Glad that her sonne is waxt a loving spowse,
   But sory for the Nymphs mishap, and that
   She is a stepdame evill funishéd
   Of two daughters in law, playning one dead,
   An other wounded.
Cor.   Is Amarillis dead?   10
Lin. She must die straight, for so doth fame report,
   For this I goe to comfort old Montanus,
   Who leesing one sonnes wife, hath found an other.
Cor. Then doth Dorinda live?
Lin.   Live? It'were well
   Thou wert so well.
Cor.   Her wound not mortall was?   15
Lin. Had she bene dead, yet Silvioes cunning would
   Have her reviv'd.
Cor.   What Art her heal'd so soone?
Lin. From top to toe Ile tell the wondrous cure.
   About the wounded Nymph stood men and women,
   Each with a ready hand, but trembling heart.   20
   But faire Dorinda would not any should
   Save Silvio touch her, saying that the hand
   Which was her hurt should be her remedie.
   Silvio, his mother, and I stay'd there alone,
   Working with counsell too, one with his hand.   25
   Silvio, when gently he had wip'd away
   The bloudie streames that stain'd her Ivory flesh,
   Assayes to draw the shaft out of the wound,
   But the vilde steale yeelding unto his hand,
   Left hidden in the wound the harmfull head.   30
   Hence came the griefe, for t'was impossible
   With cunning hand, or daintie instrument,
   Or other meanes, to draw it out from thence.
   Opening the wound perhaps with wider wound

He might have found the steele with other steele. 35
So mought he do, or so he must have done,
But too, too pitious, and too loving now
Was Silvioes hand for such; like cruell pitie
By such hard meanes love never healeth wounds.
Although it seem'd to her that paine it selfe 40
Was pleasant now betweene her Silvioes hands.
He not amaz'd sayes thus: this head shall out,
And with lesse paine than any will beleeve.
I put it there, and thought I be not able straight
To take it out, yet with the use of hunting 45
I will restore the losse I have by hunting.
I do remember now an hearbe that is well knowne
Unto the savadge Goate when he is wounded
With some Huntsmans shaft: this they to us,
Nature to them bewray'd, and t'is hard by. 50
All suddenly he parts unto a neighbour hill,
And there a bundle gathers, straight to us
He comes, and out he drawes the juyce thereof,
And mingles it with vervine seed, and roote
Of Centaures bloud, making a playster soft, 55
Which on the wound he laies. Vertue myraculous,
The pain straight ceas'd, the bloud was quickly staid,
The steele straightaway without or toile or paine,
The workmans hand obeying, issues out.
And now her strength returnes to her againe, 60
As though she had not suffered wound at all.
Nor was it mortall, for it had untoucht
Both left the bones and bellies outward runne,
And onely pierst into the muscolous flanke.
Cor. Great vertue of an hearb, but much more great 65
For fortune of a woman hast thou tolde.
Lin. That which betweene them past when this was done,
Is better to be gess'd at then be told.
Dorinda sure is well, and with her side
Can serve her selfe to any use she likes. 70
Thou think'st she hath endur'd more wounds by this,
But as the piercing weapons divers are,
So are the wounds: of some the griefe is sharpe,
Of some t'is sweet; one healing waxeth sound,
The lesse an other heales, the sounder t'is. 75
In hunting he to shoote such pleasure found,

That now he loves he cannot choose but wound.
Cor. Still thou will be that amorous Linco.
Lin. In mind but not in force, my dear Corisca,
   Greene bloomes desire within this agéd tronke. 80
Cor. Now Amarillis hath resign'd her life,
   I will go see what dear Mirtillo doth.

Act V Scene 8

ERGASTO. CORISCA.

Er. O day of wonders, day all love, all grace,
   All joy, O happie land, O heavens benigne.
Cor. See where Ergasto is, he comes in time.
Er. Now all things joyfull are, the earth, the ayre,
   The skies, the fire, the world, and all things laugh. 5
   Our joyes have pierc'd the lowest hell, nor is
   There any place that not partakes our blisse.
Cor. How jocond is this man!
Er.   O happy woods
   That often sigh'd and wept our wofull case.
   Enjoy our joyes, and use as many tongues 10
   As leaves that leape at sound of these sweet windes,
   Which fill'd with our rejoycings calmely smile,
   Sing they the sweet adventures of these friends.
Cor. He speakes of Silvio and Dorinda sure;
   Well, we must live; teares are no sooner ebb'd, 15
   But straight the floud of joy comes huffing in;
   Of Amarillis not a word he speakes
   Onely takes care to joy with them that joy.
   Why, tis well done, for else this humane life
   Would still be full of sighes; whither away, 20
   Ergasto, go'st so pleasantly, unto some marriage?
Er. Even so, but hast thou heard the happy chance
   Of the two fortunate Lovers? Is't not rare, Corisca?
Cor. To my contentment even now I heard it all
   Of Linco, and t'doth somewhat mittigate 25
   The griefe I for my Amarillis feele.
Er. Why Amarillis? Of whom think'st thou I speake?
Cor. Of Silvio and Dorinda, man.
Er. What Silvio? What Dorinda? Thou know'st nought;
   My joy growes from a higher nobler roote. 30

I Amarillis and Mirtillo sing,
The best contented subjects of loves ring.
Cor. Why, is not Amarillis dead?
Er.   How dead?
I tell thee shee's a bright and merrie Bride.
Cor. Was she not then condemnéd unto death?   35
Er. She was condemn'd, but soone releast againe.
Cor. Telst thou me dreames or dreaming do I heare?
Er. Thine eies shall tell thee if thou'lt stay a while;
    Soone shalt thou see her with her faithfull friend
    Come from the Temple, where they plighted have   40
    Their marriage troth, and so go to Montanus house
    To reape sweet fruit of their long amorous toiles.
    O hadst thou seene (Corisca) the huge joy,
    The mightie noyse of joyfull voyces and
    Th' innumerable troupes of men and women,   45
    Thou should'st have seene, old, young, sacred and prophane,
    But litle lesse then mad or drunke with mirth.
    With wonder who ranne not to see the Lovers?
    Each reverence to each, them embracéd there.
    Some prais'd their pitie, some their constancie.   50
    Some prais'd the gifts that *Jove*, and some that nature gave.
    The hills, the dales, the meadowes did resound
    The glorious name of faithfull Shepheard;
    From a poore Shepheard to become so soone
    A Demy-god, and in a moment passe   55
    From life to death, the neighbour-obsequies
    To chaunge for unexpected and dispaired nuptialls.
    This is somewhat (Corisca) but not halfe
    Her to enjoy for whom he sought to die,
    Her that disdaind to live if he had dy'de,   60
    This is fortune, this is such a sweet
    As thought prevents, and yet thou art not glad.
    Is not thy Amarillis then as deare to thee,
    As my Mirtillo is to mee?
Cor. Yes, yes, Ergasto, see how glad I am.   65
Er. O hadst thou seene but Amarillis when
    She gave Mirtill her hand for pledge, and tooke
    His hand againe, thou easily hadst perceiv'd
    A sweet but unseene kisse: I could not say
    Whether she tooke it, or she gave it him.   70
    Her cheekes would have the purest colour stain'd

Purple or Roses, Art or nature brings,
How modestie was arm'd in daintie shield
Of sanguine beautie, with force of that stroke
Unto the strikor turned, whilst she all nice   75
Seemed as though she fled, but to recover force
Shee might more sweetly encounter that same blow,
Leaving it doubtfull if this kisse were given or ta'ne,
With such a wondrous Art it graunted was.
This taken sweet was like an action mixt   80
With rapine and with yeelding both at once,
And so courteous that it seem'd to crave
The very thing that it denying gave:
Such a retrait, and such a speedlesse flight,
As mend the pace of the pursuers might.   85
O sweetest kisse, I cannot stay, Corisca,
I goe directly I to finde a wife:
For mongst the joyes there is no pleasure sure,
If gentle love do not the same procure.
Cor. If he say true, then thou, Corisca, hast lost all.   90

Act V Scene 9

CHORUS OF SHEPHEARDS. CORISCA. AMARILLIS. MIRTILLO.

Cho. Sh. Come, holy Himeneus, *come this even*
According to our vowes, and to our songs,
Dresse thou these Lovers as them best belongs.
Both t'one and t'other of the seed of heaven,
Knit thou the fatall knot this blessed eaven.   5
Cor. Ah me, it is too true; this is the fruite
   Thou from thy store of vanities must reape.
   O thoughts, o my desires, no lesse unjust
   Then false and vaine. Thus of an innocent
   I sought the death to have my beastly will;   10
   So bloudie cruell was I then, so blinde.
   Who opens now mine eyes? Ah, wretch, I see
   My fault most foule that seem'd felicitie.
Cho. Sh. Come, holy Himeneus, *come this even*
According to our vowes, and to our songs,   15
Dresse thou these Lovers as them best belongs.
Both t'one and t'other of the seed of heaven,
Knit thou the fatall knot this blessed eaven.

See faithfull Shepheard, after all thy teares,
All thy distresses, whither thou art come;   20
Is not this shee from thee was ta'ne away
By lawe of heaven and earthe? By cruell fate?
By her chaste will? And by thy poore estate?
By her faith given an other man, and by her death,
Behold, Mirtillo, now shee's onely thine.   25
This face, these eyes, this breast, these daintie hands,
All that thou seest, hear'st, and feel'st, so often sought
In vaine by thee, are now rewards become
Of thine undaunted faith, yet thou art dombe.
Mir. How can I speak? I scarce know if I breathe, 30
Nor what I see, I scarce beleeve I see:
Let Amarillis you that pleasure give,
In her alone my soules affections live.
Cho. Sh. Come, *holy* Hymeneus, *come this even*
According to our vowes, and to our songs,   35
Dresse thou these Lovers as them best belongs
Both t'one and t'other of the seed of heaven,
Knit thou the fatall knot this blessed eaven.
Cor. What do ye now with me, trecherous toies,
Vilde frenzies of the body, spots of the soule? 40
You long inough have me betrayéd here,
Go, get you to the earth, for earth you are,
You weare th' armes erst of lascivious love,
Trophies of chastitie now may you prove.
Cho. Sh. Come, *holy* Himeneus, *come this even* 45
According to our vowes, and to our songs
Dresse thou these Lovers as them best belongs
Both t'one and t'other of the seed of heaven,
Knit thou the fatal knot this blessed eaven.
Cor. Why triflest thou (Corisca)? Now's fit time 50
Pardon to impetrate, fear'st thou thy paine?
Be bold, thy paine cannot be greater then thy fault.
Beauteous and blessed couple, of the skies
And earth belov'd, since to your glorious fate
This day hath meekely bow'd all earthly force, 55
Good reason she do bow that gainst the same
Hath set a worke all of her earthly force.
Now, Amarillis, I will not denie
I did desire the same which you desir'd,
But you enjoy it, for you worthy were. 60

You do enjoy the loyalst man alive.
And you, Mirtillo, do enjoy the chastest Nymph
That ere the world hath bred. Beleeve you me,
For I a whetstone was unto your faith,
And to her chastitie. But courteous Nymph, before   65
Your anger do discend on me, behold
Your husbands face; there shall you finde the force
Both of my fault, and of your pardon too:
For in the vertue of such worthinesse,
You cannot choose but cause of pardon finde.   70
Besides you felt, alas, the selfesame fire
That did inflame unfortunate desire.
Am. I do not onely pardon thee, Corisca, but
   I count thee deare, th' effect beholding not the cause.
   For fire and sword, although they wounds do bring,   75
   Yet those once heald, to us so whole th'are deare;
   Howsoever now thou prov'st or friend or foe,
   I am well pleas'd the Destinies did make
   Thee the good instrument of my content.
   Happie deceits, fortunate trecheries,   80
   And if you please merrie with us to be,
   Come then and take part of our joyes with us.
Cor. I have sufficient mirth, you pardon me,
   And that my heart is heald of her disease.
Mir. And I (Corisca) pardon all thy harmes   85
   Save this delaying of my sweet content.
Cor. You and your mirth I to the Gods commend.
Cho. Sh. *Come, holy* Himeneus, *come this even*
   According to our vowes, and to our songs,
   Dresse thou these Lovers as them best belongs.   90
   Both t'one and t'other of the seed of heaven,
   Knit thou the fatall knot this blessed eaven.

Act V Scene 10

MIRTILLO. AMARILLIS. CHORUS OF SHEPHEARDS.

Mir. I am so tyed to paine, that in the midst
   Of all my joyes I needs must languish still:
   Is't not inough this ceremonious pompe
   Doth hold us thus, but that Corisca must
   Come in to hinder us?

Am.   Th'art too quick, my deare.   5
Mir. O my sweet treasure, I am not secure,
     Yet do I quake for feare of leesing thee.
     This seemes a dreame, and still I am afraid
     My sleep should breake, and thou, my soule, shouldst flye away.
     In better proofe my sences would I steepe,   10
     That this sweet sight is not a dreaming sleepe.
Cho. Sh. Come, holy Himeneus, *come this even*
     According to our vowes, and to our songs
     Dresse thou these Lovers as them best belongs.
     Both t'one and t'other of the seed of heaven,   15
     Knit thou the fatall knot this blessed eaven.

CHORUS

O happie two,
That plaints have sow'd and reapéd smyles;
In many bitter grievous foyles
Have you imbellish'd your desires,
Henceforth prepare your amorous fires,   5
And bolden up your tender sprights,
Unto your true sincere delights.
You cannot have a sounder joy,
There is no ill can you annoy.
This is true joy, true pleasure, and true mirth,   10
T'which vertue got, in patience giveth birth.

FINIS

Notes to the *Pastor Fido*

I.i

4 *swaine ... troupe*: Shepherd follower of Diana.

9 *valure*: Valor, in contrast to IV.iii.44; *Ital.* "valor."

12 *Erimanthus*: A mountain in Arcadia, the haunt of the ravaging boar (slain by Hercules as one of his twelve labors).

13 *prevent*: Anticipate (freq.).

59 *prov'dst*: Tried (freq.).

71 *ought*: Anything; variant of *aught*.

81 *plaine*: Bemoan (freq.).

106–7 *that same star ... puissant son*: Venus and Cupid.

118–19 *lowe ... lowes*: Cf. Shakespeare, *Much Ado* V.iv.48: "Bull Jove, sir, had an amiable low"; the use of the same word in different grammatical senses is a popular rhetorical technique (polyptoton).

133 *dishumaning*: (Obs.); this example anticipates the first instance cited in the *OED* by more than fifty years.

141–44 *Omphale ... rocke*: One of the later labors of Hercules was to serve the queen of Lydia as a female slave.

144 *spindell*: A rod used in spinning.
    rocke: Distaff.

147 *lappe*: Bosom (freq.).

152 *generous*: Noble (arch.).

178 *Megér and Ptisifo*: Two of the avenging deities usually grouped among the Eumenides. The translator here substitutes Megaera for the third (Alecto) named in Guarini and uses (P)tisifo (Tisiphone) for metrical reasons.

I.ii

1 *bitter name*: As if *Amarillis* was derived from the Latin *amara*: bitter.

8 *learnéd*: Taught.

25 *nighing*: Approaching.

62 *happy paine ... fortunate distresse*: Paradoxical terms, much favored as a rhetorical technique (oxymoron).

137 *attending*: Awaiting, *OED, v.* III.13.

151 *spright*: Contraction of *spirit*.

177 *degree*: Descent, *OED, sb.* 3.

184 *contaminate*: Defiled (arch.).

201 *mischiefe*: Distress, *OED, sb.* 1.

I.iii

2 *fonder*: More foolish.

38 *thoughts ... think*: Another instance of polyptoton: cf. I.i.118–19.

78 *friends*: Lovers, *OED, sb.* 4 (obs.).

85ff. Here, and in her advice to Amarillis, Corisca echoes precepts in bk. 3 of Ovid's *Art of Love*.

92 *still*: Ever; the adverb (*OED* 7b) is frequent.
93 *store*: Abundance.
105 *No*: . . . leave: This accords with the Italian "No, ché l'odio non vuol."
108 *bewray*: Reveal, again at V.vii.50.

I.iv

34 *by your leave*: With your permission, used as an apology.
49 *Ladon*: A tributary of the river Alpheus (line 76).
81 *raught*: Reached (arch.).
112 *wot*: Know (arch.).
123 *Titan*: The sun god Phoebus Apollo; cf. V.iii.2.
135 *leesing*: Losing, from the *v. leese*, now arch. (freq).
138 *meet*: Proper.
141 *Go'w*: Let us go (*English Dialect Dictionary*, edited by J. Wright, Oxford Univ. Press, 1923) (freq.).

I.v

6 *kind*: Nature.
17 *largely*: Extensively (adv. modifying the verb).
20 *Hircane*: A Parthian area associated with the mountains of the Caucasus.
36 *barke*: Outside, *OED, sb.*^{1}, 5 (fig.).
44 *Pencill*: Brush.

Chorus

15 *starres Titanian*: *Ital.* "titanie stelle."
58 *justles*: Jostles, the common form in the seventeenth and eighteenth centuries.

II.i

8 *suffer*: Allow, *OED, v.* II.13.
13 *yealow*: *Ital.* "bionda chioma e colorita alquanto."
31 *head*: Beginning.
49 *Pisa and Eglidis*: Pisa, a city on the river Alpheus, which ran through the Elian plain in the northwest area of the Peloponnesus; the genitive form *E(g)lidis* apparently used for metrical reasons: *Ital.* "Elide" as in line 67.
77 *Megara*: A town in Sicily, also called Hybla, noted for its honey. In Shakespeare's *Julius Caesar*, Antony's eloquence is said to "rob the Hybla bees / And leave them honeyless" (V.i.34–35).
88 *to earnest*: To use in earnest, *OED, v.*^{1} (obs.); the first instance cited is this translation.
98–99 *who sweetly . . . staind*: This follows the ellipsis of the original: "i suoi begli occhi / dolcemente chinando, / di modesto rossor tutta se tinse."
107 *Megarence*: Maidens of Megara.
115 *Cypris canes*: Sugar canes.
125 *waxéd*: Became.
128 *eake*: Also.
132 *close*: Hidden; *Ital.* "ascoso."
145 *gentle*: Noble; *Ital.* "gentil."
147 *heavenly dog*: Sirius in the constellation *Canus major*, the cause of extreme heat and drought.
149 *vanquisht . . . in victory*: Another instance of paradoxical terms, as in I.ii.62.
161 *Tantalus*: For various crimes, his punishment in the underworld was to be

perpetually tantalized, e.g., reaching for grapes he could not grasp or standing in water that he could not drink.

173 *habitacle*: Habitation (obs.).
181 *prooved*: Turned out to be, *OED, v.* II.8.
185 *the bull . . . Capricorne*: I.e., from about 22 April until 22 December.
198 *quit*: Requite, *OED, v.* II.10 (obs.).

II.ii

23 *thicke*: Thicket, *OED, sb.* B.II (now rare).
39 *Or . . . or*: Either . . . or (freq.).
50 *loose*: Lose, a spelling variant; cf. II.v.108 for the reverse instance.
84 *Cyprian dame*: Venus, born from the foam of the sea, went ashore at Cyprus, whence her name.
89 *shelfe*: Rock; also figurative. *OED* cites a 1574 instance: "There is in love . . . infinite shelves, measurable sloughes, dangerous rockes."
137 *strait*: Immediately, spelling variant of "straight."

II.iii

9 *Do*: Variant of doe.
25 *lap . . . rest*: A *topos*; cf. Marlowe's *Hero and Leander* I.43–44: "[Cupid] laid his childish head upon her breast / And with still panting rockt, there took his rest."
27 *tew*: Gear (obs.); *Ital.* "l'armi."

II.v

18 *scarcely knees*: An awkward inversion.
22 *this riches*: Used in concord with a plural treated as a singular, though in this period "this" was also a form of "these," *OED* II, f.
23 *nere*: (Obs.), variant of ne'er, never.
30 *amaine*: With vehemence.
39 *discovers*: Reveals.
41 *troth*: Truth.
86 *honestie*: Chastity (freq.), as in *Aminta* I.i.105.
90 *divide me*: Separate myself.
108 *lose*: Loose; spelling variant.
115 *cannot*: Know not; *OED* cites a 1550 sermon by Hugh Latimer, "All that can it not may learne."
155 *let me alone*: Leave it to me, a common idiom; see, e.g., *Twelfth Night* III.iv.96, 183.
166 *by her words*: By means of her words.
   will she or nill she: Willy-nilly.
167 *bowels*: Center.

II.vi

53 *wont'st*: Commonly used with an auxiliary, but see the *Aminta* I.ii.109.
71 *Carogne*: Carrion; *Ital.* carogna.
74 *beslavered*: Covered with saliva.
75 *cave*: Grave; i.e., his body (metonymy); cf. Shakespeare, *Venus and Adonis*, line 757, "What is thy body but a swallowing grave?" *Ital.* "caverna."
79 *silly*: Defenseless.
81 *quick*: Alive.

83 *pay ... home*: Revenge myself fully, a frequent idiom; cf. Shakespeares's *I Henry IV* I.iii.289, for example.
87 *Go too*: A common expression of protest or incredulity, as here.
107 *Megeraes ... haires*: One of the avenging deities (see I.i.178), often portrayed with snakes in their hair.
113 *as vile*: I.e., as famous before.

Chorus

2 *teene*: Sorrow.
17 *tire*: Raiment; cf. Shakespeare's sonnet 53.8, "And you in Grecian tires are painted new."
20 *fond will*: Foolish desire.
28–47 *It is a pretie thing to kiss* ... : The soul-kiss *topos* was extremely popular in the period, and Guarini's version was much admired. A well-known example in English occurs in Marlowe's *Dr. Faustus* (c. 1592, pub. 1604): "Sweet *Hellen*, make me immortall with a kisse: / Her lips sucke forth my soule, see where it flies" (V.i.1770–71, edited by F. Bowers [1973], vol. 2, Cambridge Univ. Press).
38 *curious*: Delicate.
43 *entergreet*: Meet together; in the sixteenth and seventeenth centuries, *enter / inter* were frequently prefixed to English words, as in line 45.
44 *sowly*: Solely, spelling variant.
   sprightfull: Full of spirit.
45 *enter-speak*: Speak together, see n. to line 43.
   sowne: Sound, *OED*, *sb*. 3. The form with the excrescent *d* became established in the sixteenth century.

III.i

3 *turne*: Return, *OED*, *v.* IV.21(obs.; freq.).
6 *treasures lorn*: Lost treasures.
11 *worser*: A double comparative was common in both the sixteenth and seventeenth centuries.
16 *use*: Custom.

III.ii

14 *load-starre*: The polestar; variant of lodestar.
23 *Argos eies*: One hundred eyes were scattered over the body of Argus in order that he might guard Io from the wiles of Zeus; after his death his eyes were used to decorate the tail of the peacock.
49 *traine*: Deceive, *OED*, V.ii.4 (figurative, the most frequent early sense, now archaic).
68 *bat*: Hit, *OED*, *sb*. III.14.
77 *pinions*: Feathers.

III.iii

9 *great*: Tall.
14 *Put to*: Use, *OED*, *v.* IV.51b.
16 *Let me alone*: Leave it to me, as in II.v.155, but in contrast to its literal sense in lines 21, 22, and 25.
24 *treachours*: Tricksters (obs.).
38 *respective*: Respectful, *OED*, *a.* 2 and 3 (obs.).
44 *cast ... in my teeth*: Upbraid, *OED*, *v.* XII.65.

59 *attend*: Expect, *OED, v.* III.

73 *cumber*: Trouble, embarrassment, *OED, sb.* 2 (obs.).

75 *Speake small*: Speak little; Ital. "di poco," though in English the idiom means to speak in a piping voice, as in Shakespeare's *Midsummer Night's Dream* , I.ii.50 and *Coriolanus*, III.ii.113–14.

98 *seate*: Foundation; *Ital.* "le sue sedi."

114–15 *my loves Hesperus . . . ev'ning starre*: Hesperus is the evening star so that the translator seems tautological, though Phosphor, the morning star, was sometimes conflated with Hesperus; *Ital.* "l'alba . . . l'espero."

161–63 *Thracian Orfeus . . . Bacchus dames*: Having twice lost his beloved Eurydice to the underworld, Orpheus disdained the women of Thrace who then tore him to pieces during a Bacchic celebration and threw his head into the river Hebrus, where it continued to call out the name of Eurydice.

III.iv

16 *repugneth*: Opposeth.

III.v

13 *Cicute*: Hemlock, used as a poison.
   Aconite: Monkshead, also poisonous.

25 *let*: Hindrance.

32 *nice*: Reserved; cf. the *Aminta* II.ii.77.

34 *practisers*: Schemers, *OED, sb.* 2; *Ital.* "le poche pratique."

39 *closely*: Secretly.

57 *vilder*: More vile, common from c. 1580 to 1650.

59 *Know me thy selfe*: Sc. "as" following "me," an awkward ellipsis and inversion.
   it: That knowledge.

97 *shadow hedge*: *Ital.* "una siepe ombrosa"; the *OED* cites this attributive instance of the translation.

124 *Prevent*: Anticipate, as at I.i.13.

134 *me*: To me (dative).
    betime: In good time.

139 *slacke*: Let slip, *OED, v.* 1b (obs.).

142 *good passe*: Good completion; the *OED, sb.*², 11.5, cites a sermon of Calvin's, "God will bring all to good passe."

III.vi

4 *my love*: I.e., Amarillis.

6 *greedie will*: Desire; *Ital.* "fiera voglia."

21 *indurate*: Hardened.

26–27 *Beare . . . brood*: An alleged practice frequently alluded to in the period; see Pliny, *Natural History* 8.54.126.

33 *inveterate*: Obstinate.

47 *his kind*: Its proper nature.

56 *respect*: Relationship, *OED, sb.* II.8 (obs.).

89 *despight*: Ill-will.

101 *moodes*: Modes.

123–124: Cf. Corisca's invitational approach here with her soliloquy at I.iii.65ff.

135 *trace:* Track; the two words were practically interchangeable in this period.

III.vii

13 *Queene ... triple sky*: I.e., the third sphere of the seven planets; triple: third (obs.).

III.viii

34 *unvengéd*: Unrevenged.

III.ix

1 *beleeve Corisca*: The Satyr here thinks Mirtillo has an assignation with her despite her betrothal to Coridon.
2 *Ericina*: Venus; the name derives from a mountain in Sicily sacred to her.
5 *knottes more stranged*: ? Altered, *OED, v.* 2 (obs.); *Ital.* "piu tenaci nodi."
11 *overstanding*: Overhanging; *Ital.* "soprastante."
18 *leese*: Lose, as at I.iv.135.
24 *Pan Liceus ... a lover once*: The patron deity of shepherds, depicted with the horns and hoofs of a goat, his attributive name derives from a mountain in Arcadia, one of his favored haunts; despite his unprepossessing appearance, he had a number of love affairs.

Chorus

24 *stupendious*: The accepted form until the late seventeenth century.
31 *push ... down*: Reduce (in comparison).
32 *Ciclop-like*: Like the Cyclops, a race of monsters each having only one eye; in literary terms the most noted was Polyphemus; cf. *Aminta* II.i.35–42.
43 *tempesteous*: Spelling variant.

IV.i

8 *Conny*: Rabbit.
22 *newes*: New things, *OED, sb.* 1 (obs.; rare); *Ital.* "novità."

IV.ii

2 *rusty*: Antiquated, *OED, a.* 6.
31 *mought*: Might (obs. past tense, but extensively used in the literature of the sixteenth and seventeenth centuries).
36 *Elicet*: A mountain in the Erymanthian chain; cf. I.i.12.
37 *lawnd*: Wooded area.
45 *Cade*: Lamb, *OED, sb.*².
46 *cast*: Determined, *OED, vb.* 44 (obs.).
63 *Lupus*: Literally, wolf (*Ital.* "lupino"), characterized by his "servile" dress.
73 *Toyles*: Snares.
89–90 *excuse/Excuse*: Spare, a novel use, but see *OED, v.* I.4.
105 *taints*: Touches, strikes, *OED, v.* II.5 (obs.).
109 *Phoebes*: Diana's.
125 *wis*: Iwis, certainly; cf. Shakespeare's *Taming of the Shrew* I.i.62 and *Richard III* I.iii.102, for the shortened form.

IV.iii

11 *foomen*: Foemen, variant spelling.
44 *valure*: Worthiness (obs.); *Ital.* "virtute."
78 *fact*: Deed; also in the sense of "crime," the commonest sense in the sixteenth and seventeenth centuries, *OED, sb.* I.c.

109 *Provoking*: Urging, *OED, v.* II.4 (now arch.).

IV.v

5 *captivate*: Made captive.
27 *remorse*: Compunction; *Ital.* "un giusto sentimento interno."
41 *close*: Secret; cf. II.i.132.
91 *fond*: Foolish, as at I.iii.2.
150 *stonied sprights*: Benumbed spirits.

IV.vi

1-2 *child of great Alcides race . . . deface*: Descendant of Hercules, one of whose twelve labors included the slaying of the Erymanthean boar, a task here accomplished by Silvio; cf. I.i.12.
6 *trophee of our Demi-god*: Memorial of our god-like rescuer.

IV.vii

18 *disadventure*: Mishap.
25 *attir'd*: Dressed (freq.).

IV.viii

12 *daughter of the sea*: Venus.
13 *treacherous monster*: I.e., the sea; cf. II.ii.84 and n.
33 *fantastive Love*: Capricious Cupid; the common form was "fantastic," this apparently a coinage; *Ital.* "vana fantasima d'Amore."
35 *wreckling*: Puny (now dial.).
38 *Eccho*: The daughter of Earth and Air; she loved Narcissus, who spurned her with the result that she pined away, only her voice remaining. The device of repeating a word or its parts goes back to the *Greek Anthology*, but it was particularly favored during the Renaissance, and especially for pastoral poetry.
37-39 *I* and *y* are frequently interchanged in Renaissance orthography.
42 *her that for* Adonis: Venus's love for the beautiful youth who was enamored of hunting is well known from Shakespeare's erotic account in *Venus and Adonis* (1593).
44 *Concubine of Mars*: Venus again. Her husband Vulcan prepared a net to entrap her with the god of war so that their affair might become an object of ridicule to the other gods.
46 *O fine*: An exclamation, often used ironically as here.
56 *straight . . . straight*: Strict . . . immediately. In Italian the pun is with "alloggi . . . Oggi."
64 *incounter*: Meet (as in battle); *Ital.* "faran guerra."
68 *loden*: Oppressed, *OED, v.* 6 (fig.).

IV.ix

6 *hardst*: Heardst.
54 *companions*: Partners, *OED, sb.* 2 (obs.); *Ital.* "compagni."
56 *wont t' endure*: *Sc.* being silent.
118 *doome*: Judgment, as in *Aminta* I.ii.200.
130 *defende*: Protect.
152 *rushing*: Flowing.
155 *a head*: *Sc.* of a boar.
156 *pricke*: Pain.

Chorus

11 *over-haile*: Oppress, *OED, v.* 6.
28 *Carrolles*: Ring dances.
   sharpe Madrigales: Shrill ditties, associated with pastoral poetry in the Renaissance, as in Marlowe's "Passionate Shepherd to His Love": "By shallow rivers to whose falls / Melodious birds sing madrigals."
32 *Himen*: God of marriage.
36 *Wily-craft*: Apparently a coinage. Such combined forms were common in the period, as "wily-beguily."
44 *likelihoodes*: Probabilities, *OED, sub.* 3 (obs.).

V.i

9 *Adamant*: Loadstone (obs.).
25 *Elidis*: Elis, as at II.i.49.
48 *Aegon*: A common pastoral name, as in Virgil's Eclogue 3.2 and Theocritus, Idyll 4.26.
63 *buy*: Here, obtain; *Ital.* "acquista fei."
86 *Coosenage*: Cheating.
110 *Meonian trumpet of Achilles fame*: Homer, called thus from his purported birthplace; the *Iliad* stresses the exploits of Achilles in the Trojan War.
115 *Pernassus*: The mountain sacred to the Muses and Apollo, the god of poetry.
121 *Harbour house*: Lodging.

V.ii

7 *ill-cund*: Ill-conned, i.e., badly interpreted; *Ital.* "mali intesi oracoli."
36 *in the while*: In the meantime.
54-55 *Amintas love betrayed ... miserie*: See V.ii.118-19.
60 *Plutoes ... kingdome*: The Underworld.
80 *longes to*: Belongs to (aphetic).
116 *misteriall*: Mysterious.
120 *sacred Pompe*: Ceremonial procession.

V.iii

2 *sacred Titan*: Phoebe (Diana, as in IV.ii.109), the moon goddess; like Phoebus (the sun god), the two names reflect their quality of brightness.
24 *gentle*: Noble, as at II.i.145.
44 *containe*: Keep from, *OED, v.* 14.
51 *straight*: Immediately, as at IV.viii.56.

V.iv

14 *holocaust*: Sacrificial offering.
36 *maze*: Bewilderment, *OED, sb.* 3 (obs.).
45 *lets*: Hinders.
50 *insolent*: Contemptuous person (*OED, sb.* B), in contrast to its adjectival use at V.v.8.
52 *Patch*: Generic term for a fool; cf. Shakespeare's *Comedy of Errors* 3.i.32: "Mome, malt-horse, capon, coxcomb, idiot, patch"; Ital. "insolente e pazzo vecchio."
74 earst: Before.

V.v

11 *waigned*: ? Conveyed, *OED, s.v.* wain 2 (obs.); *Ital.* "non fu mai."
42 *convincéd*: Confuted; *Ital.* "convinto."
43 *convin'st*: Convinced; Renaissance, but not modern, English allows for this play on words.
44 *contraries*: Contradicts (obs.).
54 *Bedlam man*: Lunatic; a term derived from the Hospital of St. Mary of Bethlehem in London which was used for those thought to be deranged. The Italian is less forceful, "uomo importuno."
72 *hole*: Hiding place; *Ital.* "cespuglio."
89 *nill*: Will not (arch.).
97 *soone*: Straightway (an early usage).
105 *Let me alone*: Leave it to me, as at II.v.155.
147 *resteth*: Remaineth.
165 *My sleepe foretold*: Recounted at I.iv.76ff.

V.vi

15 *Linceus eyes*: These were so sharpsighted as to be able to see through the earth.
34 *conceive*: Comprehend, *OED, v.* III.12 (obs.).
35 *wretch*: Applicable both to the speaker and to Tirenio.
61 *O heavenly sonne*: Sun; perhaps the translator's conscious conflation; *Ital.* "o sommo Sole"; cf. the *Aminta*, Chorus IV.9.
68 *expect*: Await.
70 *turne into thy self*: Consider, *OED, v.* III.8; English usage postdates this translation; *Ital.* "torna in te stesso."
79 *auntient fault* . . . : The account of this "dolefull tragedy" is given at I.ii.88ff.
87 *fatal voice*: I.e., of the Fates.
120 *reteinéd*: Restrained, *OED, vb.* I (obs.); *Ital.* "ritenuta."

V.vii

8 *stepdame*: Used here for mother-in-law; in the Renaissance the two terms were interchangeable; see *OED, sub.* mother-in-law 2.
36 *mought*: Might, as at IV.ii.31.
50 *bewray'd*: Revealed, as at I.iii.108.
54 *vervine seed*: Variant of vervain, a plant valued for its medicinal qualities.
55 *Centaures blood*: Juice of the centaury plant, the properties of which were said to have been discovered by Chiron the centaur.
56 *Vertue*: Power.
64 *muscolous*: The muscular part, not in the *OED*. The translator apparently coined the adjective from Italian "muscolo."

V.viii

49 *reverence*: Sc. pays his respects; *Ital.* "ognun la riverisce, ognum l'abbraccia."
56 *neighbor-obsequies*: Nearby funeral rites; the adjectival use of "neighbor" is common c. 1580–1700; *OED, sb.* 4.
62 *prevents*: Anticipates, as at III.v.124.
71 *stained*: Eclipsed.
74 *sanguine*: Here, blushing; derived from the predominance of the sanguine humor (or complexion) that determined an amorous and cheerful nature; *Ital.* "beltà sanguigna."

V.ix

1 *Himeneus*: God of marriage, as at Chorus IV.32, often represented wearing a saffron gown and carrying a nuptial torch.
5 *fatall*: I.e., dependent on the Fates; cf. V.vi.87.
10 *will*: Desire, as at III.vi.6.
51 *impetrate*: Entreat.
80 *Happie deceits . . . treacheries*: Oxymorons again.

Chorus

3 *foyle*: Repulses, a noun, *OED*, *sb.*² 2 (arch.).

The Queenes Arcadia

The Queenes Arcadia

THE NAMES OF THE ACTORS

Melibaeus.　⎫
Ergastus.　⎭　two ancient Arcadians.
Colax, a corrupted traveller.
Techne, a subtle wench of Corinth.
Amyntas.　⎫
Carinus.　⎭　the lovers of Cloris.
Cloris.
Palaemon.　⎫
Silvia.　⎭　jealous lovers.
Mirtillus.
Dorinda.
Amarillis, in love with Carinus.
Daphne, abused by Colax.
Alcon, a Quacksalver.
Lincus, a Petyfogger.
Montanus, the father of Amyntas.
Acrysius, the father of Cloris.
Pistophoenax, a disguiser of Religion.

Actus primi. Scena 1.

ERGASTUS. MELIBAEUS.

Erg. How is it, Melibaeus, that we finde
  Our Countrey, faire Arcadia, so much changd
  From what it was; that was, thou knowst, of late,
  The gentle region of plaine honestie,
  The modest seat of undisguiséd trueth,   5
  Inhabited with simple innocence:
  And now, I know not how, as if it were
  Unhallowed, and divested of that grace,
  Hath put off that faire nature which it had,
  And growes like ruder countries, or more bad.   10
Mel. Indeed, Ergastus, I have never knowne
  So universall a distemperature,
  In all parts of the body of our state,
  As now there is; nor ever have we heard
  So much complaining of disloyaltie,   15
  Amongst our younger Nimphes, nor ever found
  Our heardsmen so deluded in their loves,
  As if there were no faith on either side.
  We never had in any age before
  So many spotlesse Nimphes, so much distaind   20
  With black report, and wrongfull infamie,
  That few escape the tongue of malice free.
Erg. And me thinkes, too, our very ayre is changd,
  Our holesome climate grown more maladive,
  The fogges, and the Syrene offends us more   25
  (Or we made thinke so), then they did before.
  The windes of Autumne now are said to bring
  More noysomnesse then those do of the Spring:
  And all of us feele new infirmities;
  New Fevers, new Catarres oppresse our powers,   30
  The milke wherewith we cur'd all maladies
  Hath either lost the nature, or we ours.
Mel. And we that never were accustoméd
  To quarrel for our bounds, how do we see
  Montanus and Acrysius interstrive   35
  How farre their severall Sheep-walkes should extend,
  And cannot be agreed, do what we can:
  As if some underworking hand strake fire
  To th'apt inkindling tinder of debate,

And fostred their contention and their hate.   40
Erg. And me thinkes, too, the beautie of our Nimphes
  Is not the same as it was wont to be.
  That Rosie hew, the glory of the Cheeke,
  Is either stolne, or else they have forgot
  To blush with shame, or to be pale with feare: 45
  Or else their shame doth make them alwayes blush,
  For alwayes doth their beauties beare one hew,
  And either Nature's false, or that untrue.
Mel. Besides their various habits grow so strange,
  As that, although their faces certaine are,   50
  Their bodies are uncertaine every day,
  And alwayes diffring from themselves so far,
  As if they scorn'd to be the same they are.
    And all of us are so transformd that we
  Discerne not an Arcadian by th'attyre.   55
  Our ancient Pastorall habits are dispisd,
  And all is strange—hearts, clothes, and all disguisd.
Erg. Indeed unto our griefe we may perceive
  The whole complection of Arcadia chang'd,
  Yet cannot finde th'occasion of this change: 60
  But let us with more wary eye observe
  Whence the contagion of these customes rise,
  That have infected thus our honest plaines,
  With cunning discorde, idle vanitie,
  Deceiptfull wrong, and causelesse infamie;   65
  That by th'assistance of our graver Swaines,
  We now at first may labour to prevent
  The further course of mischiefes, and restore
  Our late cleane woods to what they were before.
Mel. Content, Ergastus, and even here will be   70
  A place convenient for so fit a worke:
  For here our Nimphes and heardsmen on this Greene,
  Do usually resort, and in this Grove
  We may observe them best, and be unseene.

Scen. 2

COLAX. TECHNE.

Col. Come, my deare Techne, thou and I must plotte
  More cunning projects yet, more strange designes

Amongst these simple grosse Arcadians here,
That know no other world but their owne plaines,
Nor yet can apprehend the subtile traines   5
We lay, to mock their rurall ignorance.
But see, here comes two of their amorous Swaines
In hote contention; let us close convay
Our selves, here underneath this coverture,
And over-heare their passionate discourse.   10
Tech. Colax, this place well such a purpose fits;
Let us sit close, and faith, it shall goe hard
Unless we make some profit by their wits.

CARINUS. AMYNTAS.

Car. Now, fond Amyntas, how cam'st thou possest
With such a vaine presumption, as thou art,   15
To thinke that Cloris should affect thee best,
When all Arcadia knowes I have her heart?
Am. And how, Carinus, canst thou be so mad
T'imagine Cloris can, or doth, love thee,
When by so many signes as I have had,   20
I finde her whole affection bent to me?
Car. What are those signes by which you come to cast,
And calculate the fortune of your hopes?
Am. More certaine signes then thou canst ever shew.
Car. But they are more then signes that I can shew.   25
Am. Why, let each then produce the best he can,
To prove which may be thought the likeliest man.
Car. Content, Amyntas, and do thou begin.
Am. And I am well contented to begin.
First, if by chance, whilst she at Barley-breake   30
With other Nimphes, do but perceive me come,
Streight lookes her cheeke with such a Rosie red,
As gives the setting Sunne unto the West
When morrow tempests are prefiguréd.
Car. Even so that hew prognosticates her wrath,   35
Which brings to thee the stormie winds of sighes.
Am. And if I finde her with her fellow Nimphes
Gathering of flowers by some sweete Rivers side,
At my approach she straight way stands upright,
Forgets her worke, and downe lets slide her lap,   40
And out fall all her flowers upon the ground.
Car. So doth the sillie sheepe forget to feed,

When it perceives the greedy Wolfe at hand.
Am. And if she meete but with my dog, she takes
   And strokes him on the head, playes with his eares,   45
   Spits in his mouth, and claps him on the back,
   And says, come, come, Melampus, go with me.
Car. She may love what is thine, but yet hate thee.
Am. Whilst at a Chrystall spring the other day,
   She washt her lovely face, and seeing me come,   50
   She takes up water with her daintie hand,
   And with a downe-cast looke besprinckles me.
Car. That shews that she would gladly quench in thee
   The fire of love, or else like love doth beare
   As did the *Delian* Goddesse when she cast   55
   Disdainefull water on Acteons face.
Am. As Silvia one day sate with her alone,
   Binding of certaine choice selected hearbes
   To her leaft arme, against bewitching spels,
   (And I at th'instant comming) she perceiv'd   60
   Her pulse with farre more violence to beat
   (As sh'after told me) then it did before.
Car. The like is felt when natures enemy,
   The hatefull feaver, doth surprise our powers.
Am. And even but yester night, she going before   65
   With other maides, and seeing me following her,
   Lets fall this daintie Nosegay, having first
   Bestow'd a kisse thereon, to th'end I might
   Receive it so, and with it do the like.
Car. Poore withred favours, they might teach thee know   70
   That she esteemes thee, and thy love as light
   As those dead flowers she wore but for a show
   The day before, and cast away at night.
Am. Now, friend Carinus, thou that mutterest so
   At these plaine speaking figures of her love,   75
   Tell by what signes thou doest her favours prove?
Car. Now, silly man, doest thou imagine me
   So fond to blab the favours of my love?
Am. Was't not a pact agreed twixt thee and me?
Car. A pact to make thee tell thy secrecie.   80
Am. And hast thou then betrayd my easie trust,
   And dallyed with my open simplenesse?
Car. And fitly art thou serv'd, that so wilt vaunt
   The imagin'd favours of a gentle Nimphe;

And this is that which makes us feele that dearth   85
Of grace, t'have kindnesse at so hie a rate.
This makes them wary how they do bestow
The least regarde of common courtesie,
When such as you, poore, credulous, devout,
And humble soules, make all things miracles   90
Your faith conceives, and vainely doe convert
All shadowes to the figure of your hopes.

Am. Carinus, now thou doest me double wrong,
First to deride my easie confidence,
And then t'obrayd my trust, as if my tongue   95
Had here prophan'd faire Cloris excellence
In telling of her mercies, or had sin'd
In uttring th'honour of a modest grace
Bestowing comfort in so just a case.

Car. Why, man, thou hast no way deserv'd her love.   100

Am. Desert I cannot urge, but faith I can,
If that may have reward, then happy man.

Car. But you know how I sav'd her from the hands
Of that rude Satyre, who had else undone
Her honour utterly; and therefore ought   105
My love of due raigne Soveraigne in her thought.

Am. But how that free and unsubduéd heart,
Infranchisd by the Charter of her eyes,
Will beare the imposition of a due
I doe not see, since love knew never Lord   110
That could command the region of our will.
And therefore urge thy due; I for my part
Must plead compassion and a faithfull heart.

Car. Plead thou thy faith, whilst I will get thy love,
For you kinde soules do seldome gracefull prove.   115

Am. The more unkinde they, who should better way
Our honest vowes, and love for love repay;
But oft they beare the penance of their will,
And for the wrong they doe, they speed as ill.

Scen. 3

COLAX. TECHNE.

Col. Alas, poore fooles, how hotely they contend
  Who shall possesse a prey that's yet ungot.
  But, Techne, I must by thy help forestall
  The mart of both their hopes, and whilst they shall
  Pursue the Aire, I must surprise their game. 5
  And fitly now, thou maist occasion take
  By these advantages discovered here,
  T'impresse in Cloris tender heart that touch
  Of deepe dislike of both their vanteries,
  As may convert her wholy unto me. 10
Tec. Why, will you then Dorindas love forsake,
  For whom you travayled so, and made me take
  Such labour to intice her to your love?
Col. Tush, Techne, we desire not what we have
  But what we would; our longings never stay 15
  With our attainings, but they goe beyond.
Tec. And why? Dorinda is as fayre as shee.
Col. That I confesse, but yet that payes not mee,
  For Cloris is another, and tis that,
  And onely that which, Techne, I desire. 20
  Some thing there is peculiar, and alone
  To every beawtie, that doth give an edge
  To our desires, and more we still conceive
  In that we have not then in that we have.
  And I have heard abrode, where best experience 25
  And witt is learnd, that all the fairest choyce
  Of women in the world serve but to make
  One perfect beautie, whereof each bringes part.
  One hath a pleasing smile, and nothing els;
  Another but some sillie Mole to grace 30
  Th' area of a disproportion'd face;
  Another pleases not but when shee speakes,
  And some in silence onely graceful are:
  Some till they laugh, we see, seeme to be fayre,
  Some have their bodies good, their gestures ill, 35
  Some please in Motion, some in sitting still,
  Some are thought lovely, that have nothing faire,
  Some again fayre that nothing lovely are.
  So that we see how beauty doth consist

Of divers peeces, and yet all attract   40
And therefore unto al my love aspires;
As beauty varies, so doth my desires.
Tec. Ah, but yet, Colax, doe not so much wrong
  Unto a Nimph, now when thou hast subdude
  And wonne her heart, and knowst she holds thee deare. 45
Col. Tush, wrong is as men thinke it, and I see
  It keepes the world the best in exercise
  That els would languish, and have nought to do.
  Discord in parts makes harmon' in the whole;
  And some must laugh, whilst othersome condole. 50
  And so it be not of the side we are,
  Let others beare it; what need we to care?
  And now Dorinda something hath to doe,
  Now she may sit, and thinke, and vexe and plott
  For ease, and joying of her full delight 55
  Would but have dulld her spirits, and marrd her quite.
Tec. Alas, yet I must pittie her, poore soule,
  In this distresse, I being one my selfe
  Of that frayle corporation, and do know
  That she will take it verie grevously. 60
  And yet, in troth, sh'is servd but well inow,
  That would neglect Mirtillus honest love,
  And trust strange protestations, and new othes;
  Be wonne with garded words, and gawdie clothes.
Col. Well, well, Dorinda shall not waile alone; 65
  She shal have others to consort her mone:
  For since my last returne from Telos Court
  I have made twenty of their coyest Nimphes
  Turne lovers, with a few protesting words
  And some choyce complementall perjuries; 70
  I made Palaemon, to suspect the faith
  Of his chast Silvia, and chast Silvia his;
  In hope thereby to worke her love to me.
  I wrought coy Daphne to infringe her vow
  Made to Menalcas; and I told her how 75
  Those fetters which so heavily were layde
  Upon our free affections onely were
  But customary bandes, not naturall.
  And I thinke, Techne, thou hast done thy parte
  Here, in this gentle region of kind heartes, 80
  Since thou cam'st hither, for I see thou thriv'st.

Tec. In deede whilst I in Corinth did remaine,
    I hardly could procure the meanes to live,
    There were so many of my trade that sold
    Complexions, dressings, tiffanies and tyres,   85
    Devisors of new fashions and strange wiers,
    Bedbrokers, night wormes, and Compositors;
    That though I knew these arts as well as they
    Yet being so many we could get smale pay.
    Here, who but Techne now is all in all?   90
    Techne is sent for, Techne onely shewes
    New strange devises to the choycest Nimphes:
    And I thinke Techne teaches them those trickes,
    As they wil not forget againe in haste.
    I have so opened their unapt conceipts   95
    Unto that understanding of themselves,
    As they will shew in time they were wel taught,
    If they observe my rules, and hide a fault.
Col. Ah well done, Techne. Thus must thou and I
    Trade for our profit with their ignorance,   100
    And take our time, and they must have their chaunce.
    But pray thee, Techne, do not thou forget
    To lay a traine for Cloris. So adieu.
Tec. Colax, I will not, and the rather too,
    For that I beare a little leaning love   105
    To sweete Amintas; for mee thinkes he seemes
    The loveliest Shepheard all Arcadia yeeldes,
    And I would gladly intercept his love.

Scena 4.

MELIBAEUS. ERGASTUS.

Mel. So this is well; here's one discovery made;
    Here are the heads of that distemperature,
    From whence these strange debaushments of our nimphs
    And vile deluding of our Shepheards Springs:
    Here is a monster that hath made his lustes   5
    As wide as is his will, and leaft his will
    Without all bounds, and cares not whom he wrongs,
    So that he may his owne desires fulfill,
    And being all foule himselfe would make all ill.
    This is that Colax that from forraine lands   10

Hath brought home that infection which undoes
His countrie goodnesse, and impoysons all.
His being abroad would marre us quite at home:
Tis strange to see, that by his going out,
He hath out-gone that native honestie   15
Which here the breeding of his countrey gave.
For here I doe remember him a childe,
The sonne of Nicoginus of the Hill,
A man though low in fortune, yet in minde
High set, a man still practising   20
T'advance his forward sonne beyond the traine
Of our Arcadian breed, and still me thought
I saw a disposition in the youth,
Bent to a selfe conceipted surlinesse,
With an insinuating impudence.   25

Erg. A man the fitter made for Courts abroad,
Where I would God he had remainéd still,
With those loose-living wanton Sybarites,
Where luxurie hath made her outmost proofe.
From whence I heare he comes, and hither brings   30
Their shames to brand us with the like reproach.
    And for this other viper which you saw,
I doe remember how she came of late
For succour to these parts, and sought to teach
Our younger maides to dresse, and trie out Flaxe,   35
And use the Distaffe, and to make a hem,
And such like skill, being skill inough for them;
But since I see she hath presum'd to deale
In points of other science, different farre
From that plaine Arte of honest huswiferie,   40
And as it seemes hath often made repaire
Unto the neighbour Citties round about,
From whom she hath these strange disguises got
T'abuse our Nimphes, and as it seemes desires
To sute their mindes as light as their attires;   45
But we shall soone prevent this growing plague
Of pride and folly, now that she discry
The true symptoma of this maladie;
And by this overture thus made, we trust
We shortly shall discover all the rest.   50

Actus II. Scen. 1

SILVIA. CLORIS.

Sil. O Cloris, here have thou and I full oft
  Sate and bene mery in this shadie Grove.
  Here have we sung full many a Rundelay,
  Told Riddles, and made Nosegayes, laught at love,
  And other passions, whilst my selfe was free   5
  From that intollerable miserie,
  Whereto affection now invassels me.
  Now, Cloris, I shall never more take joy
  To see, or to be seene, with mortall eye;
  Now sorrow must be all my companie.   10
Clo. Why, Silvia, whence should all this griefe arise?
Sil. I am undone, Cloris, let that suffice.
Clo. Tell me, sweete Silvia, how comes that to passe?
Sil. O Cloris, if thou be, as once I was,
  Free from that miserable plague of love,   15
  Keepe thee so still; let my affliction warne
  Thy youth, that never man have power to move
  Thy heart to liking, for beleeve me this,
  They are the most unfaithfull impious race
  Of creatures on the earth; never beleeve   20
  Their protestations, nor their vowes, nor teares:
  All is deceipt; none meanes the thing he sweares.
  Trust a mans faith? Nay rather will I goe
  And give my selfe a prey to Savage beasts;
  For all they seeke, and all they labour for,   25
  Is but t'undoe us; and when that is done,
  They goe and triumph on the spoile the'have wonne.
  Trust men, or take compassion when they grieve,
  O Cloris, tis to chearish and relieve
  The frozen Snake, which with our heat once warmd   30
  Will sting us to the heart in recompence,
  And O no marvaile tho the Satyre shund
  To live with man, when he perceiv'd he could
  With one and the same breath blow heat and cold.
  Who would have ever thought Palaemons othes   35
  Would have prov'd false? Who would have judgd the face
  That promisd so much faith and honestie,
  Had bene the visor but of treacherie?
Clo. Is't possible Palaemon should b'untrue?

Sil. 'Tis possible; Palaemon is untrue.   40
Clo. If it be so, deare Silvia, I thinke then
  That thou saist truth: there is no trust in men.
  For I protest I never saw a face
  That promisd better of a heart then his,
  And if he faile, whose faith then constant is?   45
Sil. O Cloris, if thou didst but know how long,
  And with what earnest suite, he sought my love,
  What vowes he usd, what othes, what teares among,
  What shewes he made his constancie to proove,
  You would admire; and then againe to see   50
  How I, although I lov'd him with my heart,
  Stood out, and would by no meanes urgèd be
  To shew the least affection of my part.
  For I had heard, that which (O now too well)
  I finde, that men were cunning, and would not   55
  Regard the thing that easily was got.
Clo. Silvia, indeed and I have heard so too.
Sil. And therefore I would trie him, and not seeme
  His vowes, nor protestations to esteeme.
  At length one day, here in this selfe-same place,   60
  (Which I shall ever, and good cause I have
  To thinke on whilst I live) walking with me,
  After he had urgd me most earnestly:
  O Silvia, said he, since nor othe, nor vow,
  Nor teares, nor prayers, have the power to move,   65
  Nor all that I can doe can make thee know
  How true a heart I offer to thy love;
  I must trie some way else to shew the same,
  And make thy undiscerning wilfull youth
  Know, though too late (perhaps unto thy shame)   70
  Thy wayward error, and my constant truth:
  When thou maist sigh, and say in griefe of minde,
  Palaemon lov'd, and Silvia was unkinde.
  With that, wringing my hand, he turnes away,
  And though his teares would hardly let him looke,   75
  Yet such a looke did through his teares make way,
  As shew'd how sad a farewell there he tooke.
  And up towards yonder craggie Rock he goes,
  His armes incross'd, his head downe on one side,
  With such a mournfull pace, as shewd his woes   80
  Way'd heavier then his passions could abide.

Faine would I have recald him backe, but shame
And modestie could not bring forth his name;
And faine would I have followed, yet me thought
It did not fit the honour of a maide   85
To follow one; yet still I sent from me,
T'attend his going, feare, and a carefull eye.
   At length when he was gotten to the top,
I might perceive how with unfolded armes,
And lookes bent up to heaven, he stands and turnes   90
His wofull face unto the other side,
Whereas that hidious fearefull downfall is:
And seem'd as if he would have throwne him off;
And as I thought, was now upon the point,
When my affrighted powers could hold no more,   95
But pittie breaking all those bands of shame
That held me back, I shrikd, and ran, God knowes,
With all the speed my feeble feete could make,
And clammering up at length (with much adoo)
Breathlesse, I got, and tooke him by the hand,   100
And glad I had his hand, and was not come
Too late to have it, and I puld him back:
But could not speake one word; no more did he.
Sense seem'd to faile in him, and breath in me.
And on before I went, and lead him on,   105
And down conducted him into this plaine,
And yonder loe, under that fatall tree,
Looke, Cloris, there, even in that very place,
We sate us downe, my arme about his neck,
Which, *Jove* thou know'st, held never man before.   110
There onely did my teares conferre with his,
Words we had none; it was inough to thinke;
For passion was too busie now within,
And had no time to come abroad in speach.
And though I would have spoken, yet me thought   115
I should not, but my silence told him this,
That tolde too much, that all I was was his.
Clo. Well, Silvia, I have heard so sad a tale,
  As that I grieve to be a woman borne,
  And that by nature we must be exposd   120
  Unto the mercie of unconstant men.
  But what saide then Palaemon in the ende?
Sil. Oh what he said, and what deepe vowes he made

When joy and griefe had let his senses loose;
Witnes, O gentle tree under whose shade   125
We sate the while, witnes, if ever mayde
Had more assurances by othes of man.
And well may you beare witnes of this deede,
For in a thousand of your barkes he hath
Incarv'd my name, and underwrote his vowes,   130
Which will remaine so long as you beare bowes.
But, Cloris, learne this lesson now of mee;
Take heed of pittie; pittie was the cause
Of my confusion; pittie hath undone
Thousands of gentle natures in our sexe;   135
For pittie is sworne servant unto love:
And this be sure, where ever it begin
To make the way, it lets your maister in.
Clo. But what assurance have you of his fraud?
It may be you suspect him without cause.   140
Sil. Ah, Cloris, Cloris, would I had no cause!
He who beheld him wrong mee in these woods,
And heard him courting Nisa, and protest
As deepe to her, as he had done to me,
Told me of all his wicked treachery.   145
Clo. Pray, who was that? Tell me, good Silvia, tell.
Sil. Why it was Colax, one I know full well
Would not report untruthes to gaine the world,
A man of vertue, and of worthy partes.
He told me all, and more then I will shew,   150
I would I knew not halfe of that I know.
    Ah, had he none but Nisa, that base trull,
The scorne and jest of all Arcadia now
To serve his lusts, and falsifie his vow!
Ah, had it yet bene any els, the touch   155
Of my disgrace had never bin so much;
But to be leaft for such a one as she,
The stale of all, what will folke thinke of me?
Cloris, in troth, it makes me so much loath
My selfe, loath these woods, and even hate the day,   160
As I must hide my griefes out of the way.
I will be gone, Cloris, I leave thee here;
I cannot stay, and prethee, Cloris, yet
Pitty thy poore companion Silvias care,
And let her fortune make thee to beware.   165

Clo. Silvia, adieu, the Gods relieve thy woes,
  Since men thus faile, and love no pittie showes.

Scen. 2.

CLORIS. TECHNE.

Clo. Love? Nay, I'me taught from loving whilst I live,
  Silvia, thy counsell hath lockt up my heart
  So fast from love, as let them sigh, and grieve,
  And pine and waile who will, I for my part
  Will pittie none of all this race of men.   5
  I see what showes so ever they pretend,
  Their love is never deadly; none of these
  That languish thus have dide of this disease
  That ever I could heare; I see all do
  Recover soone, that happen thereinto.   10
  And if they did not, there were no great hurt;
  They may indure; they are of stronger powers;
  Better their hearts should ake, then they breake ours.
    Well, had I not bene thus forewarnd to day,
  Out of all question, I had shortly falne   15
  Into the melting humour of compassion too;
  That tender pittie that betrayes us thus.
  For something I began to feele, me thought,
  To moove within me, when as I beheld
  Amyntas walke so sadly, and so pale;   20
  And ever where I went, still in my way,
  His lookes bent all to me, his care of mee,
  Which well I saw, but would not seeme to see.
  But now he hath his arrent, let him go,
  Pittie shall never cure that heart of his   25
  T'undoe mine owne; the griefe is best where tis.
Tec. What, Cloris, al alone, now fie for shame,
  How ill doth this become so faire a face,
  And that fresh youth to be without your love?
Clo. Love, Techne? I have here as many loves   30
  As I intende to have, whilst I have breath.
Tec. Nay, that you have not, never hault with mee,
  For I know two at least possessors be
  Of your kind favours, as themselves doe boste.
Clo. Boste of my favours, no man rightly can;   35

And otherwise, let them say what they can.
Tec. No, Cloris, did not you the other night
   A gallant nosegay to Amyntas give?
Clo. I never gave him nosegay in my life.
Tec. Then trust me, Cloris, he doth wrong you much,   40
   For he produc'd it there in open sight,
   And vaunted to Carinus that you first
   Did kisse the same, then gave it unto him;
   And tolde, too, how farre gone you were in love,
   What passion you would use when he was by,   45
   How you would jest with him, and wantonly
   Cast water in his face; cal his dogge yours,
   And shew him your affections by your eye.
   And then Carinus on the other side
                  He vaunts that, since he had redeeméd you   50
   Out of the satyres hands, he could commaund
   Your love and all, that you were onely his.
   This and much more, I heard them, I protest,
   Give out of you; how truly you know best.
Clo. Techne, their idle talke shall not vexe me;   55
   I know the ground I stand on, and how free
   My heart and I injoye our liberty;
   And if Amyntas hath interpreated
   My lookes according to his owne conceipt,
   He hath mistooke the text, and he shall finde   60
   Great difference twixt his comment, and my minde.
   And for his Nosegay, it shall make me take
   More care hereafter how I scatter flowers:
   Let him preserve it well, and let him make
   Much of his gaines, he gets no more of ours.   65
   But thus had I bene serv'd, had I reveald
   The least regarde of common courtesie
   To such as these: but I doe thanke the Gods
   I have reserv'd me from that vanitie:
   For ever I suspected this to be   70
   The vaine of men, and this now settles me.
   And for Carinus, let him vaunt what good
   He did for me, he can but have againe
   My hearty thankes, the paiment for his paine;
   And that he shall, and ought in woman-hood.   75
   And as for love, let him go looke on her
   That sits and grieves and languishes for him,

Poore Amarillis, who affects him deare,
And sought his love with many an wofull teare.
And well deserves a better man then he,   80
Though he be rich Lupinus sonne, and stands
Much on his wealth, and his abilitie,
She'is wittie, faire, and full of modestie.
And were she of my minde, she rather would
Pull out her eyes then that she would be seene,   85
To offer up so deare a sacrifice
To his wilde youth, that scornes her in that wise.
Tec. Cloris, in troth, I like thy judgement well,
In not affecting of these home-bred Swaines,
That know not how to manage true delight,   90
Can neither hide their love, nor shew it right.
Who would be troubled with grosse ignorance,
That understands not truely how to love?
No, Cloris, if thou didst but know how well
Thou art esteemd of one that knowes indeed   95
How to observe thy worth, and his owne wayes,
How to give true delight, how to proceed
With secrecie and witte in all assayes,
Perhaps you might thinke one day of the man.
Clo. What, is this creature then you praise a man?   100
Tec. A man? Yes, Cloris, what should he be else?
Clo. Nought else; it is enough he be a man.
Tec. Yea and so rare a man as ever yet
Arcadia bred, that may be provd she bred
A person of so admirable parts;   105
A man that knowes the world, hath seene abrod,
Brings those perfections that do truly move,
A gallant spirit, an understanding love.
O if you did but know how sweete it were
To come unto the bed of worthinesse,   110
Of knowledge, of conceipt, where strange delights
With strange discourses still shall intertaine
Your pleaséd thoughts with fresh variety.
Ah, you would loath to have your youth confin'de,
For ever more betweene th'unskilfull armes   115
Of one of these rude unconceiving Swaines,
Who would but seeme a trunke without a minde;
As one that never saw but these poore plaines,
Knowes but to keepe his sheepe, and set his folde,

Pipe on an Oaten Reede some Rundelayes,   120
And daunce a Morrice on the holydayes.
And so should you be always sweetly sped
With ignorance, and two fooles in a bed.
But with this other gallant spirit you should
Be sure to overpasse that tediousnesse,   125
And that society which cloyes this life,
With such a variable cheerefulnesse,
As you will blesse the time t'have bene his wife.
Clo. What, hath this man you thus commend a name?
Tec. A name? Why yes, no man but hath a name.   130
His name is Colax, and is one I sweare
Doth honour even the ground whereon you tread,
And oft, and many, many times, God knowes,
Hath he with tender passion talkt of you;
And said, Well, there is one within these woods   135
(Meaning by you) that yet of all the Nimphes
Mine eyes have ere seene upon the earth,
In all perfections doth exceed them all.
For all the beauties in that glorious Court
Of Telos, where I liv'd, nor all the Starres   140
Of Grece beside, could sparkle in my heart
The fire of any heat but onely she.
Then would he stay, and sigh; and then againe:
Ah, what great pittie such a creature should
Be tide unto a clogge of ignorance,   145
Whose body doth deserve to be imbrac'd,
By the most mighty Monarch upon earth.
Ah, that she knew her worth, and how unfit
That private woods should hide that face, that wit.
    Thus hath he often said, and this I say,   150
Observe him when you will, you shall not see
From his hye forehead to his slender foote,
A man in all parts better made then he.
Clo. Techne, me thinkes, the praises that you give
Shewes your owne love; and if he be that man   155
You say, 'twere good you kept him for your selfe.
Tec. I must not love impossibilities;
Cloris, he were a most fit man for you.
Clo. For me? Alas, Techne, you move too late.
Tec. Why, have you past your promise t'any yet?   160
Clo. Yes sure, my promise is already past.

Tec. And if it be, I trust you are so wise
  T'unpasse the same againe for your owne good.
Clo. No, that I may not when it is once past.
Tec. No, Cloris, I presume that wit of yours   165
  That is so piersive can conceive how that
  Our promise must not prejudice our good:
  And that it is no reason that the tongue,
  Tye the whole body to eternall wrong.
Clo. The Tongue is but the Agent of the heart,   170
  And onely as commissioner allowd
  By reason, and the will, for the whole state,
  Which warrants all it shall negotiate.
Tec. But prithee, tell me to what rusticke Swaine
  You pass'd your word to cast away your selfe?   175
Clo. No, I have past my word to save my selfe
  From the deceiptfull, impious perjuries
  Of treacherous men, and vowd unto my heart,
  Untill I see more faith then yet I see,
  None of them all shall triumph over me.   180
Tec. Nay then, and be no otherwise, tis well;
  We shall have other time to talke of this,
  But, Cloris, I have fitted you, in faith,
  I have here brought the most conceipted tyre,
  The rarest dressing ever Nimph put on,   185
  Worth ten of that you weare; that, now me thinkes,
  Doth not become you, and besides, tis stale.
Clo. Stale, why? I have not worne it scarce a moneth.
Tec. A moneth? Why you must change them twise a day:
  Hold hither, Cloris, this was not well laid.   190
  Here is a fault; you have not mixt it well
  To make it take, or els it is your haste
  To come abroad so soone into the Ayre.
  But I must teach you to amend these faults,
  And ere I shall have done with you, I thinke,   195
  I shall make some of these inamored youthes
  To hang themselves, or else runne madde for love.
  But goe, let's trie this dressing I have brought.

Scen. 3.

PALAEMON. MIRTILLUS.

Pal. Mirtillus, did Dorinda ever vow,
  Or make thee any promise to be thine?

Mir. Palaemon, no, she never made me vow,
   But I did ever hope she would be mine,
   For that I had delivered up my youth, 5
   My heart, my all, a tribute to her eyes,
   And had secur'd her of my constant truth
   Under so many faithfull specialties,
   As that although she did not graunt againe,
   With any shew the acquittance of my love, 10
   Yet did she ever seeme to intertaine
   My affections, and my services t'approove.
   Till now of late, I know not by what meane,
   (Ill fare that meane) she grew to that dispight,
   As she not onely clowds her favours cleane. 15
   But also scorn'd to have me in her sight;
   That now I am not for her love thus mov'd,
   But onely that she will not be belov'd.
Pal. If this be all th'occasion of thy griefe,
   Mirtillus, thou arte then in better case 20
   Then I suppos'd, and therefore cheere thy heart,
   And good cause too, being in the state thou art,
   For if thou didst but heare the historie
   Of my distresse, and what part I have shar'd
   Of sad affliction, thou wilt then soone see 25
   There is no miserie unlesse compar'd.
   For all Arcadia, all these hills, and plaines,
   These holts, and woods and every Christall spring,
   Can testifie my teares, and tell my flames,
   And with how cleene a heart, how cleere a faith 30
   Palaemon lovèd Silvia, and how long.
   And when consum'd with griefe, and dri'd with care,
   Even at the poynt to sacrifice my life
   Unto her cruelty, then lo she yeelds,
   And was content for ever to be mine: 35
   And gave m'assurance underneath her hand,
   Sign'd with a faithfull vow, as I conceiv'd,
   And witnesséd with many a lovely kisse,
   That I thought sure I had attain'd my blisse.
   And yet (aye me) I gote not what I got, 40
   Silvia I have, and yet I have her not.
Mir. How may that be, Palaemon, pray thee tell?
Pal. O know, Mirtillus, that I rather could
   Runne to some hollow cave, and burst and die

In darknes, and in horror, then unfold 45
Her shamefull staine, and mine own infamie.
But yet it will abrode, her impudence
Will be the trumpet of her owne disgrace,
And fill the wide and open mouth of fame
So full, as all the world shall know the same. 50
Mir. Why, what is Silvia false, or is she gone?
Pal. Silvia is false and I am quite undone.
Mir. Ah, out alas, who ever would have thought
That modest looke, so innocent a face,
So chast a blush, that shamefast countenance, 55
Could ever have told how to wantonise?
Ah, what shal we poore lovers hope for now
Who must to win, consume, and having wonne
With hard and much adoe, must be undone?
Pal. Ah, but Mirtillus, if thou didst know who 60
Is now the man her choyce hath lighted on,
How wouldst thou wonder? For that passes all,
That I abhorre to tell, yet tell I shall;
For all that would will shortly know't too well:
It is base Thyrsis, that wild hare-braine youth 65
Whom every milkmaid in Arcadia skornes:
Thyrsis is now the man with whom she walkes
Alone, in thickets, and in groves remote.
Thyrsis is all in all, and none but he;
With him she dallies under every tree. 70
Trust women? Ah, Mirtillus, rather trust
The Summer windes, th'Oceans constancie,
For all their substance is but levitie.
Light are their waving vailes, light their attires,
Light are their heads, and lighter their desires: 75
Let them lay on what coverture they will
Upon themselves of modestie and shame,
They cannot hide the woman with the same.
Trust women? Ah, Mirtillus, rather trust
The false devouring Crocodiles of Nile; 80
For all they worke is but deceipt and guile:
What have they but is faind? Their haire is faind,
Their beauty fain'd, their stature fain'd, their pace,
Their jesture, motion, and their grace is fain'd:
And if that all be fain'd without, what then 85
Shall we suppose can be sincere within?

For if they do but weepe, or sing, or smile,
Smiles, teares, and tunes are ingins to beguile.
And all they are, and all they have of grace,
Consists but in the out-side of a face. 90
O love and beautie, how are you ordaind
Like unto fire, whose flames farre of delight,
But if you be imbrac'd, consume us quight?
Why cannot we make at a lower rate
A purchase of you, but that we must give 95
The treasure of our hearts, and yet not have
What we have bought so dearely for all that?
O Silvia, if thou needs wouldst have bene gone,
Thou shouldst have taken all away of thee;
And nothing leaft to have remain'd with me. 100
Thou shouldst have carryed hence the portraiture
Which thou hast left behinde within my heart,
Set in the table-frame of memory,
That puts me still in minde of what thou wert,
Whilst thou were honest, and thy thoughts were pure; 105
So that I might not thus in every place,
Where I shall set my carefull foote, conferre
With it of thee, and evermore be told,
That here sate Silvia underneath this tree,
And here she walkt, and len't upon mine arme; 110
There gathred flowers, and brought them unto me;
Here by the murmour of this rusling spring,
She sweetly lay, and in my bosome slept;
Here first she shew'd me comforts when I pin'de,
As if in every place her foote had stept, 115
It had leaft Silvia in a print behind.
But yet, O these were Silvias images,
Then whilst her heart held faire, and she was chaste;
Now is her face all sullied with her facts;
And why are not those former prints defac'd? 120
Why should she hold still in the forme she was,
Being now deform'd, and not the same she was?
O that I could, Mirtillus, lock her out
Of my remembrance, that I might no more
Have Silvia here, when she will not be here. 125
Mir. But, good Palaemon, tell what proofes hast thou
Of her disloyalty, that makes thee show
These heavie passions, and to grieve so much?

Pal. Mirtillus, proofes that are, alas, too plaine;
    For Colax, one thou know'st can well observe   130
    And judge of love, a man both staid and wise,
    A gentle heardsman, out of love, and care
    He had of me, came and reported all;
    And how he saw them divers times alone,
    Imbracing each other in the woods.   135
    Besides she hath of late with sullaine lookes,
    That shew'd disliking, shund my company,
    Kept her aloofe; and now I thinke to day
    Is gone to hide her quite out of the way.
      But, Silvia, though thou goe and hide thy face,   140
    Thou canst not hide thy shame, and thy disgrace;
    No secret thicket, grove, not yet close grott,
    Can cover shame, and that immodest blot.
    Ah, didst thou lend thy hand in kinde remorse
    To save me from one death, to give m'a worse?   145
    Had it not yet bene better I had dy'de
    By thy unspotted honest cruelty,
    Then now by thy disgracéd infamie?
    That so I might have carried to my grave
    The image of chaste Silvia in my heart,   150
    And not have had these notions to ingrave
    A stainéd Silvia there, as not thou art?
    Ah yes, it had bene better farre, I prove,
    T'have perisht for thy love, then with thy love.
Mir. Ah, good Palaemon, cease these sad complaints,   155
    And moderate thy passions; thou shalt see
    She may returne, and these reports be found
    But idle fictions on uncertaine ground.
Pal. Mirtillus, I perceive my tedious tale
    Begins to be distastefull to thine eare;   160
    And therefore will I to some desart vale,
    To some close Grove to waile, where none shall heare
    But beasts, and trees, whose sense I shall not tyre
    With length of mone; for length is my desire.
    And therefore, gentle Shepheard, now adieu,   165
    And trust not women, for they are untrue.
Mir. Adue, Palaemon, and thy sad distresse,
    Shall make me wey Dorindas losse the lesse:
    For if I should be hers, and she prove so,
    Better to be mine owne and let her go.   170

Scena 4.

ERGASTUS. MELIBAEUS.

Erg. Now, Melibaeus, who would have supposd,
    That had not seene these impious passages,
    That ever monstrous wretch could have exposd
    Two honest hearts to these extremities,
    T'attaine his wicked ends? By having wrought   5
    First in, unto their easie confidence
    A way, by an opinion to be thought,
    Honest, discreet, of great experience.
       Whereby we see open-fac't villany
    Without a maske, no mischiefe could have done;   10
    It was the coverture of honestie
    That laid the snare, whereby they were undone.
    And that's the ingine that confounds us all;
    That makes the breach whereby the world is sackt,
    And made a prey to cunning, when we fall   15
    Into the hands of wise dishonestie:
    When as our weake credulitie is rackt
    By that opinion of sufficiencie,
    To all the inconveniences that guile,
    And impious craft can practise to beguile.   20
       And note but how these cankers alwayes seaze
    The choyest fruites with their infections,
      How they are still ordainéd to disease,
    The natures of the best complections.
Mel. Tis true. And what an instrument hath he there got,   25
    To be the Agent of his villany?
    How truely she negotiats, and doth plot,
    To undermine fraile imbecillitie.
    How strong these spirits combine them in a knot
    To circumvent plaine open honesty?   30
       And what a creature there is to converse
    With feeble maides, whose weaknesse soone is led
    With toyes, and new disguises, to reverse
    The course wherein by custome they were bred?
    And then what fitnesse, too, her trade affordes   35
    To trafficke with the secrets of their heart,
    And cheapen their affections with faire words,
    Which women straight to women will impart?
    And then to see how soone example will

Disperse it selfe, being met with our desire?   40
How soone it will inkindle others ill,
Like Naptha that takes fire by sight of fire?
So that unlesse we runne with all the speed
We can, to quench this new arising flame
Of vanitie, and lust, it will proceed   45
T'undoe us, ere we shall perceive the same:
How farre already is the mischiefe runne
Before we scarse perceiv'd it was begun?

Actus III. Scen. 1.

ALCON. LINCUS.

Alc. What, my friend Lincus, now in troth well met.
Lin. Well met, good Alcon, this falls happilie
　That we two thus incounter all alone,
　Who had not any conference scarse this moneth.
Alc. In troth I longd to heare how you proceed   5
　In your new practise here among these swaines;
　For you and I must grace each others Arte;
　Though you knew me, when I in Patras dwelt
　And waited on a poore Phisitions man,
　And I knew you a Pronotories boy,   10
　That wrote Indentures at the Towne-house dore;
　Yet are you here now a great man of law,
　And I a grave Phisition full of skill,
　And here we two are held the onely men.
　But how thrive you in your new practise now?   15
Lin. Alcon, in troth, not any thing to speake,
　For these poore people of Arcadia here
　Are so contented each man with his owne,
　As they desire no more, nor will be drawne
　To any contestation; nor indeed   20
　Is there yet any frame composd, whereby
　Contention may proceede in practicke forme,
　For if they had this forme once to contend,
　Then would they brawle and wrangle without end.
　For then might they be taught, and councell'd how   25
　To litigate perpetually you know;
　And so might I be sure to doe some good.

But having here no matter where upon
To furnish reall actions, as els where;
No tenures, but a customarie hold   30
Of what they have from their progenitors
Common, without individuitie;
No purchasings, no contracts, no comerse,
No politique commands, no services
No general Assemblies but to feast,   35
And to delight themselves with fresh pastimes;
How can I hope that ever I shall thrive
Here where no wrangling discontentments strive?
Alc. Ist possible that a societie
   Can with so little noyse and sweat subsist?   40
Lin. It seems it may, before men have transform'd
   Their state of nature in so many shapes
   Of their owne managements, and are cast out
   Into confusion, by their knowledges.
   And either I must packe me hence, or els   45
   Must labour wholy to dissolve the frame
   And composition of their strange built state,
   Which now I seeke to doe, by drawing them
   To appr'hend of these proprieties
   Of *mine and thine*, and teach them to incroch   50
   And get them states apart, and private shares.
   And this I have already set a worke
   If it will take, for I have met with two
   The aptest spirits the countrey yelds, I know,
   Montanus and Acrisius, who are both   55
   Old, and both cholericke, and both perverse,
   And both inclinable to Avarice;
   And if there quarrell hold, as tis begun,
   I do not doubt but all the rest will on.
   And if the worst should fall, if I could gaine   60
   The reputation but to arbitrate,
   And sway their strifes, I would get well by that.
Alc. Tis marvayle that their long and easie peace
   That fosters plentie and gives nought to doe,
   Should not with them beget contention too,   65
   As well as other where we see it doth.
Lin. This peace of theirs is not like others peace,
   Where craft layes trapps t'inrich it selfe with wiles,
   And men make prey of men, and rise by spoyles.

This rather seemes a quiet then a peace.   70
For this poore corner of Arcadia here,
This little angle of the world you see,
Which hath shut out of doore all th'earth beside
And are barrd up with mountaine, and with rocks,
Hath had no intertrading with the reste   75
Of men, nor yet will have, but here alone,
Quite out of fortunes way, and underneath
Ambition, or desire, that waies them not,
They live as if still in the golden age,
When as the world was in his pupillage.   80
    But for myne owne parte, Alcon, I protest
I envie them that they thus make themselves,
An everlasting holyday of rest,
Whilst others worke, and I doe thinke it fit
Bcing in the world, they should be of the world;   85
And if that other states should doe this too
As God forbid, what should we Lawyers doe?
But I hope shortly yet we shall have here
As many of us as are other where:
And we shall sweate, and chafe, and talke as loud,   90
Brawle our selves hoarse, as well as they shall doe
At Patras, Sparta, Corinth, or at Thebes,
And be as arrogant and even as proud;
And then 'twill be a world, and not before.
But how dost thou with thy profession frame?   95
Alc. No man can wish a better place then this
To practise in my arte, for here they will
Be sicke for companie, they are so kinde.
I have now twenty patients at this time,
That know not what they aile; no more doe I: 100
And they have physicke all accordingly.
First Phillis got running at Barly-breake
A little cold, which I with certaine druggs
I ministred was thought to remedie;
Doris saw that how Phillis physicke wrought   105
(For Phillis had told her she never tooke
So delicate a thing in all her life
That more reviv'd her heart, and clear'd her blood);
Doris would needes be sicke too, and take some.
Melina seeing that, she would the like,   110
And so she had the very same receipt,

For to say troth, I have no more but that,
And one poore pill I use for greater cures.
But this is onely sweet and delicate,
Fit for young women, and is like th'hearbe John,   115
Doth neither good nor hurte, but that's all one.
For if they but conceive it doth, it doth;
And it is that Physitians hold the chiefe
In all their cures, *conceipt and strong beleefe:*
Besids I am a straunger come from far   120
Which doth adde much unto opinion too.
For who not but th'Arabian or the Jewe
In foreign lands are held the onely men,
Although their knowledge be no more then mine.
Lin. 'Tis true, friend Alcon, he that hath once gote   125
Th'Elixir of opinion hath got all,
And h'is th'man that turnes his brasse to gold.
Alc. Then can I talke of Gallen, Averois,
Hippocrates, Rasis, and Avicen,
And bookes I never read, and use strange speach   130
Of Symptoms, Crisis, and the Critique dayes;
Of Trochises, Opiats, Apophlegmatismes,
Eclegmats, Embrochs, Lixives, Cataplasmes,
With all the hideous termes Arte can devise
T'amuse weake and admiring ignorance.   135
Lin. And that is right my tricke; I over-whelme
My practise too, with darknesse and strange words,
With Paragraphs, Condictions, Codicilles,
Acceptilations, Actions rescissorie,
Noxall, and Hypothecall, and involve   140
Domestic matter in a forraine phrase.
Alc. Then am I as abstruse and mysticall
In Caracter, and giving my receipt,
Observing still th'odd number in my pills,
And certaine houres to gather and compound   145
My simples, and make all t'attend the Moone.
Then do I shew what rare ingredients
I use for some great cures, when need requires:
The liver of a Wolfe, the Lions gall,
The leaft side of a Mole, the Foxes heart,   150
The right foote of a Tortuse, Dragons bloud;
And such strange savage stuffe, as even the names
Are physicke of them selves to move a man.

And all the drugs I use must come from farre,
Beyond the Ocean, and the Sunne at least,   155
Or else it hath no vertue Phisicall;
These home-bred simples doe no good at all.
Lin. No, no, it must be forraine stuffe, God wot,
Or something else that is not to be got.
Alc. But now in faith I have found out a trick   160
That will perpetually so feede their rheumes,
And intertaine their idle weaknesses,
As nothing in the world could doe the like,
For lately being at Corinth, 'twas my chance
T'incounter with a Sea-man, new ariv'd   165
Of Alexandria, who from India came,
And brought a certaine hearbe wrapt up in rowles,
From th'Island of Nicosia, where it growes:
Infus'd, I thinke, in some pestiferous juyce,
(Produc'd in that contagious burning clime,   170
Contrarious to our nature, and our spirits)
Or else steep'd in the fuming sap, it selfe
Doth yeeld, 't'inforce th'infecting power thereof;
And this in powder made, and fir'd, he suckes
Out of a little hollow instrument   175
Of calcinated clay the smoake thereof,
Which either he convayes out of his nose,
Or downe into his stomack with a whiffe.
And this, he said, a wondrous vertue had
To purge the head and cure the great Catarre,   180
And to drie up all other meaner rheumes,
Which when I saw, I streight way thought how well
This new fantasticall devise would please
The foolish people here growne humerous.
And up I tooke all this commoditie,   185
And here have taught them how to use the same.
Lin. And it is easie to bring in the use
Of any thing, though never so absurd,
When nations are prepar'd to all abuse,
And th'humour of corruption once is stird.   190
Alc. Tis true, and now to see with what a strange
And gluttenous desire to exhaust the same,
How infinite, and how insatiably,
They doe devour th'intoxicating fume,
You would admire; as if their spirits thereby   195

Were taken, and inchanted, or transformd
By some infuséd philter in the drug.
  For whereas heretofore they wonted were
At all their meetings, and their faestivalls,
To passe the time in telling wittie tales, 200
In questions, riddles, and in purposes,
Now do they nothing else, but sit and suck,
And spit, and slaver all the time they sit.
That I go by and laugh unto my selfe,
And thinke that this will one day make some worke 205
For me or others; but I feare it will
B'another age will finde the hurt of this.
But sure the time's to come, when they looke backe
On this, will wonder with themselves to thinke
That men of sense could ever be so mad, 210
To suck so grosse a vapour that consumes
Their spirits, spends nature, dries up memorie,
Corrupts the blood, and is a vanitie.
Lin. But Alcon, peace, here comes a patient, peace.
Alc. Lincus, there doth indeed; therefore away. 215
Leave me alone, for I must now resume
My surly, grave, and Doctorall aspéct.
This wench I know; tis Daphne who hath wrongd
Her love Menalcas, and plaid fast and loose
With Colax, who reveald the whole to me. 220

Scena 2.

DAPHNE. ALCON.

Dap. Good Doctor Alcon, I am come to crave
Your counsaile, to advise me for my health,
For I suppose, in troth, I am not well;
Me thinkes I should be sicke, yet cannot tell:
Some thing there is amisse that troubles me, 5
For which I would take Phisicke willingly.
Alc. Welcome, faire nimph, come let me try you pulse.
I cannot blame you t'hold you selfe not well.
Some thing amisse, quoth you; here's all amisse.
Th'whole Fabrick of your selfe distempred is; 10
The Systole and Dyastole of your pulse,
Do shew your passions most hystericall.

It seems you have not very carefull bene,
T'observe the prophilactick regiment
Of your owne body, so that we must now   15
Descend unto the Therapeuticall;
That so we may prevent the syndrome
Of Symtomes, and may afterwards apply
Some analepticall Elexipharmacum,
That may be proper for your maladie.   20
It seemes, faire Nimph, you dreame much in the night.
Dap. Doctor, I doe indeed.
Alc.   I know you doe;
   Y'are troubled much with thought.
Dap. I am indeed.
Alc.   I know you are.
   You have great heavinesse about your heart.   25
Dap. Now truly so I have.
Alc.   I know you have.
   You wake oft in the night.
Dap.   In troth I doe.
Alc. All this I know you doe;
   And this unless by phisicke you prevent,
   Thinke whereto it may bring you in the end.   30
   And therfore you must first evacuate
   All those Colaxicall hote humours which
   Disturbe your heart, and then refrigerate
   Your bloud by some Menalchian Cordials,
   Which you must take and you shall streight finde ease: 35
   And in the morning I will visit you.
Dap. I pray, Sir, let me take of that you gave
   To Phillis th'other day; for that, she said,
   Did comfort wondrously, and cheere her heart.
Alc. Faire Nimph, you must, if you wil use my arte,   40
   Let me alone, to give what I thinke good;
   I knew what fitted Phillis maladie,
   And so, I thinke, I know what will serve you.   *Exit.*

DAPHNE *sola.*

O what a wondrous skilfull man is this?
Why he knowes all? O God, who ever thought   45
Any man living could have told so right
A womans griefe in all points as he hath?

Why this is strange that by my very pulse
He should know all I ayle, as well as I.
Beside I feare he sees too much in me,   50
More then I would that any man should see.
Me thought (although I could not well conceive
His words, he spake so learnéd and so strang)
He said I had misruld my bodie much,
As if he meant that in some wanton sorte   55
I had abus'd my bodie with some man.
O how should he know that? What is my pulse
Become th'intelligencer of my shame?
Or are my lookes the index of my heart?
Sure, so he said, and me thought, too, he nam'd   60
Menalcas, or els something very like;
And likewise nam'd that cunning trecherous wretch
That hath undone me, Colax, that vile devill,
Who is indeed the cause of all my griefe,
For which I now seeke physicke, but O what   65
Can phisicke doe to cure that hideous wound
My lusts have given my Conscience? Which I see
Is that which onely is diseas'd within,
And not my body now; that's it doth so
Disquiet all the lodging of my spirits,   70
As keeps me waking; that is it presents
Those ougly formes of terror that affright
My broken sleepes; that layes upon my heart
This heavy loade that weighes it downe with griefe;
And no disease beside, for which there is   75
No cure I see at all, nor no redresse.
    Didst thou alledge, vile man, to my weake youth,
How that those vowes I made unto my love
Were bands of custome, and could not lay on
Those manacles on nature, which should keepe   80
Her freedome prisoner by our dome of breath?
O impious wretch, now nature gives the lie
To thy foule heart and telles my grievéd soule,
I have done wrong to falsifie that vow
I first to my deare love Menalcas made.   85
And sayes th'assurance and the faith is given
By band on earth, the same is seald in heaven.
    And therefore how Menalcas, can these eyes
That now abhorre to looke upon my selfe,

Dare ever view that wrongéd face of thine,   90
Who hast relide on this false heart of mine?

Scen. 3.

COLAX. TECHNE.

Col. Ist possible, sweet Techne, what you say,
  That Cloris is so wittie, and so coy?
Tec. 'Tis as I tell you, Colax, sh'is as coy
  And hath as shrewd a spirit, as quicke conceipt,
  As ever wench I brook'd in all my life.   5
Col. Then there's some glory in attaining her;
  Here now I shall be sure t'have someting yet
  Besides dull beautie; I shall lie with wit.
  For these faire creatures have such feeble spirits,
  And are so languishing, as gives no edge   10
  To appetite, and love, but stuffes delight.
Tec. Well, if you get her, then you shall be sure
  To have your wish; and yet perhaps that store
  You finde in her may check your longing more
  Then all their wants whom you have tride before.   15
Col. How, if I get her? What, do you suppose
  I shall not get her? That were very strange.
Tec. Yes, sir, she may be got, but yet I know
  Sh'will put you to the tryall of your wit.
Col. Let me alone; could I find season fit   20
  To talke with her in private, she were mine.
Tec. That season may you now have very well.
  For, Colax, she hath promisd faithfully
  This evening late to meete me at the cave
  Of *Erycina*, underneath the hill,   25
  Where I must fit her with a new attyre
  Where with sh's far in love, and th'other day
  Thinking to try it at her fathers house,
  (Whether I went with her to deale for you)
  The old Acrisius was himselfe at home,   30
  Which did inforce us to deferre our worke
  Untill this evening, that we might alone
  There out of sight, more closely do the same:
  Where while she stayes (for I will make her stay
  For me a while) you at your pleasure may   35
  Have th'opportunitie which you desire.

Col. O Techne, thou hast blest me; if I now
  On this advantage conquere not her minde,
  Let me be loathéd of all womenkind.
  And presently will I goe sute my selfe   40
  As bravely as I can, go set my lookes,
  Arme my discourse, frame speaches passionate,
  And action both, fit for so great a worke.
  Techne, a thousand thankes, and so adieu.   *Exit.*
Tec. Well, Colax, she may yet deceive thy hopes,   45
  And I perswade my selfe she is as like
  As any subtile wench was ever borne
  To give as wise a man as you the scorne:
  But see, where one, whose faith hath better right
  Unto her love then you, comes here forlorne   50
  Like fortunes out-cast, full of heavines.
  Ah, poore Amintas, would thou knewst how much
  Thou art esteemd, although not where thou wouldst,
  Yet where thou shouldst have love in that degree,
  As never living man had like to thee.   55
  Ah, see how I who setts for others love,
  Am tooke my selfe, and intricated here
  With one that hath his heart another where!
  But I will labour to divert the streame
  Of his affections, and to turne his thoughts   60
  From that coye Cloris, to the libertie
  Of his owne heart, with hope to make him mine.

Scen. 4.

TECHNE. AMYNTAS.

Tec. Now fie, Amyntas, why should you thus grieve
  For a most foolish wayward girle that scornes
  Your honest love, and laughes at all you doe;
  For shame, Amyntas, let her go as sh'is.
  You see her vaine, and how perversly set;   5
  Tis fond to follow what we cannot get.
Am. O Techne, Techne, though I never get,
  Yet will I ever follow whilst I breath,
  And if I perish by the way, yet shall
  My death be pleasing that for her I die.   10
  And one day she may hap to come that way,

(And be it O her way) where I shall lye,
And with her proud disdainefull foote she may
Tread on my tombe, and say, loe where he lyes,
The triumph and the conquest of mine eyes.   15
And though I loose my selfe, and loose my teares,
It shall be glory yet that I was hers.
What have I done of late should make her thus
My presence with that strange disdaine to flie,
As if she did abhorre my company?   20
Cloris, God knowes, thou hast no cause therefore,
Unlesse it be for loving more and more.
Why, thou were wont to lend me yet an eare,
And though thou wouldst not helpe, yet wouldst thou heare.
Tec. Perhaps she thinkes thy heat wilbe allayd,   25
   The fire being gone, and therefore doth she well
   Not to be seene there where she will not aide.
Am. Alas, she knowes no hand but hers can quench
   That heat in mee, and therefore doth she wrong
   To fyre my heart, and then to runne away;   30
   And if she would not ayde, yet might she ease
   My carefull soule, if she would but stand by
   And only looke upon me while I die.
Tec. Well, well, Amintas, little dost thou know
   With whom that cunning wanton sortes her selfe,   35
   Whil'st thus thou mourn'st, and with what seacret wiles
   She workes, to meete her lover in the woodes;
   With whom in groves and caves she dallying sitts,
   And mockes thy passions and thy dolefull fitts.
Am. No, Techne, no, I know that cannot bee,   40
   And therefore doe not wrong her modestie;
   For Cloris loves no man, and that's some ease
   Unto my griefe, and gives a hope that yet
   If ever soft affection touch her heart,
   She will looke backe, and thinke on my desert.   45
Tec. If that be all, that hope is at an end,
   For if thou wilt this evening but attend
   And walke down under *Ericinas* grove,
   And place thy selfe in some close secret bush,
   Right opposite unto the holow cave   50
   That looks into the vallye, thou shalt see
   That honestie and that great modestie.
Am. If I see Cloris there, I know I shall

See nothing els with her but modestie.
Tec. Yes, something els will grieve your heart to see: 55
    But you must be content, and thinke your selfe
    Are not the first that thus have bene deceivd,
    With fayre appearing out-sides, and mistooke
    A wanton heart, by a chaste seeming looke.
    But I conjure you by the love you beare   60
    Unto those eyes which make you (as you are
    Th'example of compassion to the world)
    Sit close and be not seene in any case.
Am. Well, Techne, if I shall see Cloris there
    It is enough; then thither will I goe   65
    Who will go any where to looke on her.
    And, Cloris, know, I do not goe to see
    Any thing else of thee, but onely thee.
Tec. Well, goe and thinke yet of her honest care,
    Who gives thee note of such a shamefull deede;   70
    And judge, Amyntas, when thou shalt be free,
    Who more deserves thy love, or I or she.

Scen. 5.

MELIBAEUS. ERGASTUS.

Mel. Now what infernal projects are here laid,
    T'afflict an honest heart, t'expose a maide,
    Unto the danger of a lone assault,
    To make her to offend without her fault.
Erg. And see what other new appearing spirits   5
    Would raise the tempests of disturbances
    Upon our rest, and labour to bring in
    All the whole Ocean of unquietnesse
    To overwhelme the poore peace we live in?
    How one would faine instruct, and teach us how   10
    To cut our throates with forme, and to contend
    With artificiall knowledge, to undoo
    Each other, and to brabble without end.
    As if that nature had not tooke more care
    For us, then we for our owne selves can take,   15
    And makes us better lawes then those we make.
    And as if all that science ought could give
    Unto our blisse, but onely shewes us how

The better to contend, but not to live.
And evermore we see how vice doth grow 20
With knowledge, and brings forth a more increase,
When skilfull men begin, how good men cease.
And therefore how much better doe we live,
With quiet ignorance, then we should doe
With turbulent and ever-working skill, 25
Which makes us not to live, but labour still.

Mel. And see that other vaine fantastick spirit,
Who would corrupt our bodies too likewise,
As this our mindes, and make our health to be
As troublesome as sicknesse, to devise 30
That no part of us ever should be free;
Both forraging on our credulitie,
Take still th'advantage of our weakenesses;
Both cloath their frivolous uncertainties
In strange attyres to make it seene the lesse. 35

Actus 4. Scen. 1

TECHNE. AMYNTAS.

Tec. Amyntas must come back, I know, this way,
And here it will be best for me to stay;
And here indeed he comes, poore man, I see
All quite dismaide: and now this makes for me.
Come, who tels troth, Amyntas, who deceives 5
Your expectation now, Cloris, or I?

Am. Peace, Techne, peace, and do not interrupt
The griefe that hath no leasure to attend
Ought but it selfe, and hath shut up with it
All other sense in private close within, 10
From doing any thing but onely thinke.

Tec. Thinke? Whereon should you think? Y'have thought ynow
And too too much, on such a one as shee,
Whom now you see y'have tride her honestie:
And let her goe, proud girle, accordingly. 15
There's none of these young wanton things that know
How t'use a man, or how to make their choyse,
Or answere mens affections as they ought;
And if y'will thinke, thinke sh'is not worth a thought.

Am. Good Techne, leave mee, for thy speach and sight 20

Beare both that disproportion to my griefe,
As that they trouble trouble, and confound
Confusion in my sorrowes, which doth loath
That sound of wordes that answeres not the tone
Of my dispayres in accents of like mone.   25
And now hath sorrow no worse plague I see
Then free and unpartaking companie,
Who are not in the fashion of our woes,
And whose affection do not looke likwise
Of that complection as our miseries.   30
And therefore, pray thee, leave me, or else leave
To speake, or if thou speake, let it not be
To me, or else let me, not answere thee.
Tec. Wel, I say nothing; you know what y'have seene.
Am. Tis true, I doe confesse that I have seene   35
The worst the world can shew me, and the worst
That can be ever seene with mortall eye.
I have beheld the whole of all where in
My heart had any interest in this life;
To be disrent and torne from of my hopes,   40
That nothing now is leaft why I should live:
That ostage I had given the world, which was
The hope of her that held me to hold truce
With it, and with this life is gone; and now
Well may I breake with them, and breake I will   45
And rend that pact of nature, and dissolve
That league of bloud that ties me to my selfe.
For, Cloris, now hath thy immodestie
Infranchiz'd me, and made me free to die:
Which otherwise I could not, least it might   50
Have bene some staine and some disgrace to thee.
    Ah, was it not ynow for this poore heart
T'indure the burthen of her proud disdayne,
That weigh'd it to the earth, but that it must
Be crusht thus with th'oppression of her stayne?   55
The first wound yet though it were huge and wide,
Yet was it cleanely made, it festred not;
But this, now given, comes by a poysoned shott
Against all lawes of honor that are pure,
And rankles deadly, is without all cure.   60
    Ah, how she blusht when as she issued forth
With her inamor'd mate out of the cave!

And well then might she blush at such a deed,
And with how wild a looke she casts about
Her fearefull eyes! As if her loathsome sinne   65
Now comming thus into the open sight,
With terror did her guiltines affright;
And up she treades the hill with such a pace,
As if shee gladly would have out gone shame,
Which yet for all her hasting after came.   70
    And at their comming forth, me thought I heard
The villayne use my name, and she returne
The same againe in very earnest sorte,
Which could be for no good, I know, to mee,
But onely that perhaps it pleas'd her then   75
To cast me up by this way of her mouth
From of her heart, least it might stuffe the same.
    But, Cloris, know thou shalt not need to feare,
I never more shall interrupt thy joyes
With my complayntes, nor more observe thy waies;   80
And O I would thy heart could be as free
From sinne and shame, as thou shalt be from mee.
    I could (and I have reason so to do)
Revenge my wrong upon that wicked wretch,
Who hath surpris'd my love, and robb'd thy shame,   85
And make his bloud th'oblation of my wrath
Even at thy feete, that thou mightst see the same
To expiate, for this injustice donne,
But that the fact examind would display
Thy infamie abroad unto the world   90
Which I had rather die then once bewray.
And, Techne, pray-thee, tell her thus from me,
But yet, ah tell it softly in her eare,
And be thou sure no living creature heare,
That her immodestie hath lost this day   95
Two the most honest guardians of her good
She had in life, her honour, and my bloud.
Tec. Now I may speake; I trust you speake to me.
Am. No, not yet, Techne, pray-thee stay a while;
    And tell her, too, though she spares not her shame,   100
My death shall shew that I respect her fame.
Tec. Then now I may.
Am.   O Techne, no, not yet.
    And bid her not forget Amyntas faith,

Though she despiséd him; and one day yet
She may be toucht with griefe, and that ere long,   105
To thinke on her dishonour, and his wrong.
Now, Techne, I have done, and so farewell.
Tec. But stay, Amyntas, now must I begin.
Am. I cannot stay, Techne; let goe your hold;
  It is in vaine, I say; I must be gone.   110
Tec. Now, deare Amyntas, heare me but one word.
  Ah, he is gone; and in that furie gone
  As sure he will in this extremitie
  Of his dispaire do violence to himselfe;
  And therefore now what helpe shall I devise   115
  To stay his ruine? Sure there is no meanes
  But to call Cloris, and perswade with her
  To follow him, and to prevent his death;
  For though this practice was for mine owne good,
  Yet my deceipts use not to stretch to bloud.   120
  But now I know not where I should finde out
  That cruell maide; but I must cast about.

Scen. 2

AMARILLIS. DORINDA.

Ama. Dorinda, you are yet in happie case,
  You are belov'd, you need not to complaine;
  'Tis I have reason onely to bewaile
  My fortunes, who am cast upon disdaine,
  And on his rockie heart that wrackes my youth   5
  With stormes of sorowes, and contemnes my truth;
  'Tis I that am shut out from all delight
  This world can yeeld a maide, that am remov'd
  From th'onely joy on earth, to be belov'd:
  Cruel Carinus scornes this faith of mine,   10
  And lets poore Amarillis grieve and pine.
Do. Tis true, indeed, you say I am belov'd,
  Sweete Amarillis, and perhaps much more
  Then I would be: plentie doth make me poore;
  For now my heart, as if devided stands   15
  Betwixt two passions, love and pitty both,
  That draw it either way with that maine force
  As that I know not which to yeeld unto.

And then feare in the midst holds m'in suspence,
Least I lose both by mine improvidence.   20
Ama. How may that be, Dorinda? You know this,
You can enjoy but one, and one there is
Ought to possesse your heart, and love alone;
Who hunts two Hares at one time catches none.
Do. I must tell you, deare friend, the whole discourse,   25
From whom I cannot any thing conceale;
Arcadia knowes, and every Shepheard knowes
How much Mirtillus hath deserv'd of me,
And how long time his wofull sute hath laine,
Depending on the mercie of mine eyes;   30
For whom I doe confesse, pittie hath bene
Th'Atturnie evermore that stands and pleades
Before my heart the justice of his cause,
And sayes he ought have love, by loves owne lawes.
But now the maister sov'raigne Lord of hearts,   35
That great commander, and that tyrant love,
Who must have all according to his will,
Whom pittie onely Ushers, goes before,
As lightning doth the thunder, he sayes, no,
And will that Colax onely have my heart,   40
That gallant heardsman, full of skill and arte,
And all experience of loves mysteries;
To whom, I must confesse me, to have given
The earnest of my love; but since that time
I never saw the man, which makes me much   45
To wonder that his dealings should be such:
For either love hath, in respect that I
Despiséd have the true and honest faith
Of one that lov'd me with sinceritie,
Made me the spoile of falshood and contempt,   50
Or else perhaps the same is done to trie
My resolution, and my constancie.
    But yet I feare the worst, and feare I may,
Least he now having got the victorie,
Cares for no more: and seeing he knowes my love   55
Turnes towards him, he turnes his backe to me.
So that I know not what were best resolve,
Either to stand unto the doubtfull faith
Of one that hath so dangerously begun,
Or else returne t'accept Mirtillus love,   60

Who will perhaps when mine begins have done:
So that inwrapt in this distracted toyle
I vexe, and know not what to do the while.
And therefore, Amarillis, I thinke sure
(Se'ing now how others love in me hath prov'd)   65
You are most happy not to be belov'd.

Scen. 3.

CLORIS. AMARILLIS. DORINDA.

Clo. Now here betweene you two kind loving soules,
  I know there can be no talke but of love;
  Love must be all the scope of your discourse.
  Alas, poore hearts, I wonder how you can
  In this deceiptfull world thinke of a man.   5
  For they doe nothing but make fooles of you,
  And laugh when they have done, and proove untrue.
Ama. Well, Cloris, well; rejoyce that you are free;
  You may be toucht one day as well we.
Clo. Indeed and I had like to this last night,   10
  Had I not lookt with such an angry eye,
  And frownd so sowre, that I made love afeard.
  There was a fellow needs forsooth would have
  My heart from me whether I would or not,
  And had as great advantage one could have;   15
  I tell you that he had me in a Cave.
Do. What in a Cave? Cloris, how came you there?
Clo. Truly, Dorinda, I will tell you how:
  By no arte magique, but a plaine devise
  Of Techne, who would trie her wit on me,   20
  For she had promisd me, to meete me there
  At such an houre, and thither bring with her
  A new strange dressing she had made for me,
  Which there, close out of sight, I should trie on:
  Thither went I, poore foole, at th'houre decreed,   25
  And there, expecting Technes company,
  In rushes fleering Colax after me,
  Whom sure she sent of purpose to the place.
  And there with his affected apish grace
  And strainéd speach, offring to seaze on me,   30
  Out rusht I from him, as indeed amaz'd

At his so sodaine and unexpected sight.
And after followes hee, vowes, sweares, protests
By all the gods, he never lov'd before
Any one living in the world but me;   35
And for me onely would he spend his life.
Do. Alas, and what am I fogotten then?
Why these were even the words he spake to mee.
Clo. And then inveighes against Amintas love,
Vants his owne partes, and his great knowledges,   40
And all so idle as, in troth, me thought,
I never heard a man more vainely talke,
For so much as I heard; for up the hill
I went with such a pace, and never staide
To give regard to any thing he said: 45
As at the last I scarse had leaft him breath
Sufficient to forsweare himselfe with all.
Do. Ah, what hath then my silly ignorance done
To be deceivd and mockt by such a one?
Clo. And when I had recoverd up the hill,   50
I fayrely ran away and leaft my man
In middst of his conjuring perjuries;
All emptie to returne with mightie losse
Of breath and labour, having cast away
Much foolish paines in tricking up him selfe   55
For this exployte, and goes without his game,
Which he in hope devourd before he came;
And I, too, mist my dressing by this meanes.
   But I admire how any Woman can
Be so unwise to like of such a man,   60
For I protest I see nought else but froth,
And shallow impudence, affected grace,
And some few idle practisd complement:
And all the thing he is, he is without,
For affection strives but to appeare,   65
And never is of substance nor Sincere.
And yet this dare of falshood hath beguild
A thousand foolish wenches in his dayes.
Do. The more wretch he, and more hard hap was theirs.
Clo. Why do you sigh, Dorinda? Are you toucht   70
With any of these passages of mine?
Do. Noe truly, not of yours, but I have cause
In my particular that makes me sigh.

Clo. Well, well, come on, to put us from this talke,
   Let us devise some sporte to passe the time. 75
Ama. Faith, I have no great list to any sporte.
Do. Nor I, in troth, 'tis farthest from my minde.
Clo. Then let us tell old tales, repeat our dreames,
   Or any thing, rather then thinke of love.
Ama. And now you speake of dreames, in troth last night 80
   I was much troubled with a feareful dreame.
Do. And truly, Amarillis, so was I.
Clo. And now I do remember, too, I had
   A foolish idle dreame, and this it was:
     Me thought the fayrest of Montanus lambs, 85
   And one he lov'd the best of all his flocke
   Was singled out, and chac'd b'a cruell curre,
   And in his hote pursuit makes towards me,
   (Me thought) for succour, and about mee ran,
   As if it begd my ayde to save his life, 90
   Which I long time deferrd, and still lookt on,
   And would not rescue it, untill at length
   I saw it even quite wourried out of breath,
   And panting at my feete, and could no more:
   And then, me thought, I tooke it up from death 95
   And cherist it with mee, and brought it back
   Home to Montanus, who was glad to see
   The poore recoverd creature thus restor'd;
   And I my selfe was greatly please'd, me thought,
   That by my hand so good a deede was wrought; 100
   And, Amarillis, now tell us your dreame.
Ama. Me thought as I in Eremanthus walkt,
   A feareful woolfe rusht forth from out a brake,
   And towards me makes with open hideous jawes.
   From whom I ranne with all the speed I could, 105
   T'escape my danger, and t'overtake
   One whom I saw before, that might lend ayde
   To me distrest; but he, me thought, did runne
   As fast from me, as I did from the beast.
   I cride to him (but all in vaine) to stay; 110
   The more I cride, the more he ranne away;
   And after I, and after me the wolfe
   So long, as I began to faint in minde,
   Seeing my despaire before, my death behinde.
   Yet ranne I still, and loe, me thought, at length 115

A little he began to slack his pace;
Which I perceiving, put to all my strength
And ranne as if desire had wingd my heeles;
And in the end, me thought, recov'red him.
But never woman felt more joy it seem'd   120
To overtake a man, then I did him,
By whom I scapte the danger I was in;
That when I wak'd, as presently I wak'd,
Toucht with that sodaine joy, which my poore heart,
God knowes, had not bene usd unto of late,   125
I found my selfe all in a moist faint sweate,
Which that affrighting horrour did beget,
And though I were deliv'red of my feare,
And felt this joy, yet did the trembling last
Upon my heart, when now the feare was past.   130
Clo. This, Amarillis, may your good portend,
  That yet you shall have comfort in the end.
Ama. God grant I may, it is the thing I want.
Clo. And now, Dorinda, tell us what you dreamt.
Do. I dreamt that having gone to gather flowers,   135
  And weary of my worke, reposing me
  Upon a banke neere to a Rivers side,
  A subtile Serpent lurking in the grasse,
  Came secretly, and seizd on my left breast,
  Which, though I saw, I had no power to stirre,   140
  But lay me still, till he had eate a way
  Into my bosome, whence he tooke my heart,
  And in his mouth carrying the same away,
  Returnes, me thought, againe, from whence he came,
  Which I perceiving presently arose,   145
  And after it most wofully I went,
  To see if I could finde my heart againe:
  And up and downe I sought, but all in vaine.
Clo. In troth, 'tis no good lucke to dreame of Snakes;
  One shall be sure t'heare anger after it.   150
Do. And so it may be I have done to day.
Clo. Indeed, and I have heard it never failes.

Scen. 4

TECHNE. CLORIS. AMARILLIS. DORINDA.

Tec. Come, you are talking here in jollitie,
  Whilst I have sought you, Cloris, all about:
  Come, come, good Cloris, quickly come away.
Clo. What is the newes? What have we now to doo?
  Have you another Cave to send me too?   5
Tec. Ah, talke no more of that but come away,
  As ever you will save the wofull life
  Of a distresséd man that dyes for you.
Clo. Why, what doth Colax whom you sent to me
  Into the Cave, faint now with his repulse?   10
Tec. I sent him not; you would so wisely goe,
  In open sight, as men might see you goe,
  And trace you thither all the way you went.
  But come, ah, 'tis not he; it is the man
  You ought to save: Amyntas is the man   15
  Your cruelty and rigour hath undone:
  O quickly come, or it will be too late;
  For 'twas his chance, and most unluckely,
  To see both you and Colax, as you came
  Out of the Cave, and he thinkes verily   20
  You are possest by him, which so confounds
  His spirits, and sinckes his heart, that sure h'is runne
  T'undoe himselfe; and O I feare 'tis done.
Clo. If it be done, my help will come too late;
  And I may stay, and save that labour here.   25
Ama. Ah, Cloris, haste away if this be so,
  And doe not, if thou hast a heart of flesh,
  And of a woman, stay and trifle time;
  Goe runne, and save thine owne, for if he die,
  'Tis thine that dyes, his blood is shed for thee,   30
  And what a horrour this will ever be
  Hereafter to thy guiltie conscience, when
  Yeares shall have taught thee wit, and thou shalt finde
  This deed instampt in bloudy Characters,
  Within the blacke recordes of thine owne thoughts,   35
  Which never will be raz'd whilst thou hast breath,
  Nor yet will be forgotten by thy death.
  Besides, wide Fame will Trumpet forth thy wrong,
  And thou shalt be with all posteritie,

Amongst th'examples held of crueltie,   40
And have this savage deed of thine be made
A sullein subject for a Tragedie,
Intitled *Cloris*; that thereby thy name
May serve to be an everlasting shame;
And therefore go prevent so foule a staine.   45
Do. Ah goe, goe, Cloris, haste away with speed.
Clo. Why whether should I goe? I know not where
To finde him now, and if he doe this deed,
It is his eror, and no fault of mine.
Yet pray thee, Techne, which way went the man?   50
Tec. Come, Cloris, I will shew which way he went,
In most strange furie, and most desperate speed,
Still crying, Cloris, hast thou done this deed?
Clo. Why had not you staid, and perswaded him?
Tec. I could not stay him by no meanes I usd,   55
Though all the meanes I could devise I usd.
Clo. Well, I will goe, poore man, to seeke him out,
Though I can do him else no other good.
I know indeed he hath deserv'd my love,
And if I would like any, should be him,   60
So that I thought he would be true to me.
But thus my dreame may now chance come to passe,
And I may happen to bring home indeed
Montanus sonne, Amyntas, that deere Lambe
He loves so well, and by my gracious deed   65
He may escape the danger he was in,
Which if I doe, and thereby doe inthrall
My selfe, to free anothers misery,
Then will I sit and sigh, and talke of love
As well as you, and have your company.   70
For something I do feele begin to move,
And yet I hope 'tis nothing else but feare;
Yet what know I? That feare may hap be love.
Well, Techne, come, I would not have him yet
To perish, poore Amyntas, in this fit.
                          Exeunt [Techne and Cloris]   75
Ama. Well, Cloris, yet he may, for ought I see
Before you come, unlesse you make more haste.
Ah, cruell maide, she little knowes the griefe
Of such a heart that's desperate of reliefe,
Nor understands she her owne happinesse,   80

To have so true a lover as he is.
And yet I see sh'is toucht, if not too late,
For I perceiv'd her colour come and goe;
And though in pride she would have hid her woe,
Yet I saw sorrow looke out at her eyes.   85
And poore Amyntas, if thou now be gone,
Thou hast (like to the Bee that stinging dyes,
And in anothers wound leaft his owne life),
Transpiercéd by thy death that marble heart,
Which, living, thou couldst touch by no desert.   90
And if thou shalt escape, thou hast surviv'd
Her crueltie, which now repents her wrong,
And thou shalt by her favours be reviv'd,
After the affliction thou hast suffred long,
Which makes me thinke that time, and patience may   95
Intenerat at length the hardest heart,
And that I may yet after all my woe,
Live t'overtake Carinus mercie too.

Do. And here this sad distresse of such a true
And constant lover, overcome with griefe,   100
Presents unto my guilty memorie
The wrongs Mirtillus hath indur'd of me.
And O I would I knew now how he doth:
I feare he is not well; I saw him not
Scarse these three dayes; I mervaile where he is,   105
And yet what need I mervaile, who have thus
Chac'd him from me with frownes and usage vile,
And fondly leaft the substance of his faith
To catch the shadow of deceipt and guile?
  Was Colax he I thought the onely man,   110
And is he now prov'd to be such a one?
O that I ever lent an easie eare,
Unto so false a wretches flatteries,
Whose very name I now abhorre to heare;
And loath my selfe, for being so unwise.   115
What shall I doe, sweet Amarillis, now?
Which way shall I betake me to recover
The losse of shame, and losse of such a lover?

Ama. Indeed, Dorinda, you have done him wrong,
But your repentance, and compassion now   120
May make amends, and you must learne to do
As I long time have done, indure and hope,

And on that turne of Fortunes Scene depend,
When all extremities must mend, or end.

Scen. 5.

MELIBAEUS. ERGASTUS.

Mel. Well, come Ergastus, we have seene ynow,
And it is more then time that we prepare
Against this Hydra of confusion now,
Which still presents new hideous heads of feare:
And every houre we see begets new broiles,   5
And intricates our youth in desperate toyles.
    And therefore let th'advantage of this day,
Which is the great and generall hunting day
In Eremanthus, serve for this good deed:
And when we meete (as all of us shall meete   10
Here in this place anone, as is decreed)
We will advise our Shepheards to intermit
That worke, and fall to this imports us more;
To chase out these wild mischiefs that doe lurke,
And worse infest then th'Eremanthian Boare,   15
Or all Beasts else, which onely spoile our fields,
Whilst these which are of more prodigious kindes,
Bend all their forces to destroy our mindes.
Erg. And this occasion will be very fit
Now to be tooke, for one day lost may lose   20
More by example then we shall regret
In thousands, for when men shall once disclose
The way of ill that lay unknowne before,
Scarce all our paines will ever stop it more.
Man is a creature of a wilfull head,   25
And hardly 'is driven but easily is lead.

Actus 5. Scen. 1.

AMARILLIS. CARINUS.

Ama. Ah, gentle Lelaps, prety loving dogge,
Where hast thou leaft thy maister? Where is hee,
That great commander over thee and mee?
Thou wert not wont be far off from his feete,

And O no more would I, were he so pleasd;   5
But would as well as thou goe follow him,
Through brakes and thickets, over cliffes and rockes
So long as I had life to follow him,
Would he but looke upon me with that eye
Of favour, as h'is us'd to looke on thee.   10
Thou canst be clapt and strookt with that faire hande
That thrustes away my heart, and beates it backe
From following him, which yet it ever will;
And though he fly mee, yet I must after still.
But here he comes; me thought he was not farre.   15
Car. What meane you, Amarillis, in this sorte
    By taking up my dogge to marre my sporte?
Ama. My deare Carinus, thou dost much mistake,
    I do not marre thy sport; tis thou marrst mine,
    And killst my joyes with that hard heart of thine.   20
    Thy dogge perhaps by some instinct doth know
    How that I am his maisters creature too,
    And kindely comes himselfe and fawnes on me
    To shew what you in nature ought to doe.
Car. Fie, Amarillis, you that know my minde   25
    Should not, me thinkes, thus ever trouble me.
Ama. What, is it troublesome to be belov'd?
    How is it then, Carinus, to be loath'd?
    If I had done like Cloris, skorned your sute,
    And spourn'd your passions, in disdainefull sorte,   30
    I had bene woo'd and sought, and highly prizd,
    But having n'other arte to win thy love,
    Save by discovering mine, I am despisd
    As if you would not have the thing you sought,
    Unles you knew it were not to be gote.   35
    And now because I lie here at thy feete,
    The humble booty of thy conquering eies,
    And lay my heart all open in thy sight,
    And tell thee I am thine, and tell thee right;
    And doe not sute my lookes, nor cloth my words   40
    In other colours then my thoughts do weare,
    But doe thee right in all, thou skornest me
    As if thou didst not love sinceritie;
    Never did Crystall more apparantly
    Present the colour it contayn'd with in   45
    Then have these eyes, these teares, this tongue of mine,

Bewreyd my heart, and told how much I'm thine.
Car. Tis true I know you have too much bewrayd,
   And more then fitts the honour of a mayde.
Ama. O if that nature hath not arm'd my breast 50
   With that strong temper of resisting proofe,
   But that by treason of my weake complection, I
   Am made thus easy to the violent shott
   Of passion, and th'affection, I should not,
   Me thinkes; yet you out of your strenth and power, 55
   Should not disdayne that weakenes, but should thinke
   It rather is your vertue, as indeed
   It is, that makes me thus against my kinde,
   T'unlock my thoughts, and to let out my minde,
   When I should rather die and burst with love, 60
   Then once to let my tongue to say, I love.
   And if your worthy partes be of that power
   To vanquish nature, and I must be wonne,
   Do not disdayne the worke when you have don;
   For in contemning me you do dispise 65
   That power of yours which makes me to be thus.
Car. Now what adoe is here with idle talke?
   And to no purpose; for you know I have
   Ingagd long since my heart, my love and all
   To Cloris, who must have the same and shall. 70
Ama. Why there is no such odds twixt her and me;
   I am a Nimph, tis knowne as well as shee.
   There is no other difference betwixt us twaine
   But that I love, and she doth thee disdaine.
   No other reason can induce thy minde, 75
   But onely that which should divert thy minde.
   I will attend thy flockes better than she,
   And dresse thy Bower more sweete, more daintily,
   And cheerish thee with Salets, and with Fruites,
   And all fresh dainties as the season sutes; 80
   I have more skill in hearbes then she, by farre,
   I know which nourish, which restoring are:
   And I will finde Dictamnus for thy Goates,
   And seeke out Clover for thy little Lambes,
   And Tetrifoll to cheerish up their Dammes. 85
   And this I know, I have a better voyce
   Then she, though she perhaps may have more arte,
   But, which is best, I have the faithfulst heart.

Besides Amyntas hath her love, I know,
And she begins to manifest it now.   90
Car. Amyntas have her love? That were most strange,
  When he hath gotten that, you shall have mine.
Ama. O deere Carinus, let me rest upon
  That blessed word of thine, and I have done.

Scen. 2

MIRTILLUS. CARINUS. AMARILLIS.

Mir. Well met, Carinus, I can tell you newes,
  Your rivall, poore Amyntas, hath undone
  And spoild himselfe, and lyes in that weake case,
  As we thinke never more to see his face.
Car. Mirtillus, I am sorry t'heare so much: 5
  Although Amyntas be competitor
  In th'Empire of her heart, wherein my life
  Hath chiefest claime, I doe not wish his death:
  But by what chance, Mirtillus, pray thee tell.
Mir. I will, Carinus, though I grieve to tell.   10
  As Titerus, Menalcas, and my selfe
  Were placing of our toyles (against anon
  That we shall hunt) below within the straight
  Twixt Eremanthus, and Lycaeus mount,
  We might perceive under a ragged cliffe,   15
  In that most uncouth desart, all alone,
  Distrest Amyntas lying on the ground,
  With his sad face turn'd close unto the rock,
  As if he loathd to see more of the world,
  Then that poore space, which was twixt him and it: 20
  His right hand stretcht along upon his side,
  His leaft he makes the pillor to support
  His carefull head; his Pipe he had hung up
  Upon a Beach tree by, where he likewise
  Had plac'd his Sheephooke and his Knife, wherewith   25
  He had incarv'd an wofull Elegie,
  To shew th'occasion of his miserie.
  His dogge Melampus sitting by his side,
  As if he were partaker of his woe:
  By which we knew t'was he, and to him went,   30
  And after we had call'd and shooke him up,

And found him not to answere, nor to stirre,
And yet his eyes abroad, his body warme;
We took him up, and held him from the ground,
But could not make him stand by any meanes;   35
And sincking downe againe, we searcht to see
If he had any wound, or blow, or wrinch;
But none could finde: at last by chance we spide
A little horne which he had flung aside,
Wherby we gest he had some poyson tooke.   40
And thereupon we sent out presently
To fetch Urania, whose great skill in hearbes
Is such, as if there any meanes will be,
As I feare none will be, her onely arte
Must serve to bring him to himselfe againe.   45
Car. Indeed Urania hath bene knowne t'have done
    Most desperate cures, and peradventure may
    Restore him yet; and I doe wish she may.
Mir. But having there us'd all the helpe we could,
    And all in vaine, and standing by with griefe,   50
    (As we might well, to see so sad a sight,
    And such an worthy Shepheard in that plight)
    We might perceive come running downe the hill,
    Cloris and Techne, with what speed they could;
    But Cloris had got ground, and was before,   55
    And made more haste, as it concernd her more.
    And neerer as she came, she faster went,
    As if she did desire to have bene there
    Before her feete, too slow for her swift feare.
    And comming to the place, she sodainely   60
    Stopt, startes, and shrikt, and having made such haste
    T'have something done, now could she nothing doe.
    Perhaps our presence might perplexe her too,
    As being asham'd that any eye should see
    The new appearing of her naked heart,   65
    That never yet before was seene till now.
Car. And 'tis ill hap for me it was seene now.
Mir. For we perceiv'd how *Love* and *Modestie,*
    With sev'rall Ensignes, strove within her cheekes
    Which should be Lord that day, and chargéd hard   70
    Upon each other, with their fresh supplies
    Of different colours, that still came and went,
    And much disturb'd her; but at length dissolv'd

Into affection; downe she casts her selfe
Upon his senselesse body, where she saw   75
The mercie she had brought was come too late:
And to him calles, O deare Amyntas, speake
Looke on me, sweete Amyntas, it is I
That calles thee, I it is that holds thee here,
Within those armes thou hast esteem'd so deare.   80
    And though that love were yet so young in her
As that it knew not how to speake, or what,
And that she never had that passion prov'd,
Being first a lover ere she knew she lov'd;
Yet what she could not utter, she supplide   85
With her poore busie hands that rubb'd his face,
Chafd his pale temples, wrung his fingers ends,
Held up his head, and puld him by the hands,
And never leaft her worke, nor ever ceast.
Ama. Alas, the least of this regarde before,   90
    Might have holpe all, then when 'twas in her power
T'have saved his heart, and to revive his minde.
Now for all this, her mercie is unkinde;
The good that's out of season is not good.
There is no difference now twixt cruelty,   95
And the compassion that's not understood.
Mir. But yet at length, as if those daintie hands,
    Had had a power to have awakened death,
We might perceive him move his heavie eyes,
Which had stood fixt, all the whole time before,   100
And fastens them directly upon her.
Which when she saw, it strooke her with that force,
As that it pierc'd through all the spirits she had,
Made all the powers and parts of her shrinke up,
With that convulsion of remorse and griefe,   105
As out she shrik'd, O deere, O my deere heart;
Then shrinkes againe, and then againe cryes out.
For now that looke of his did shake her more
Then death or any thing had done before;
That looke did read t'her new conceiving heart,   110
All the whole tragicke Lecture of his love,
All his sad suffrings; all his griefes and feare,
And now in th'end what he had done for her.
And with that powerfull force of moving too,
As all a world of words could never doe.   115

Ah, what a silly messenger is Speach
To be imploi'd in that great Embassie
Of our affections, in respect of th'eye?
Ah, 'tis the silent rhetoricke of a looke
That workes the league betwixt the states of hearts;   120
Not words I see, nor knowledge of the booke,
Nor incantations made by hidden artes,
For now this looke so melts her into teares,
As that she powr'd them downe like thunder droppes;
Or else did Nautre, taking pittie now   125
Of her distresse, imploy them in that store
To serve as vailes, and to be interposde
Betwixt her griefe and her, t'impeach her sight,
From that full view of sorrow thus disclosde.
    And now with this came in Urania there,   130
With other women, to imploy their best
To save his life, if b'any meanes they can.
And so we came our way, being sent for now
About some conference for our hunting sportes,
And with us Techne comes, who is supposde,   135
T'have beene a speciall cause of much of this.
Car. Alas, this sad reporte doth grieve me much,
   And I did never thinke that Cloris had
   So deerely lov'd him as I finde she doth;
   For by this act of hers I plainely see,   140
   There will be never any hope for me.
Ama. There may for me, if now, Carinus, thou
   Wilt stand but to thy word, as thou hast said.
Mir. Ah, would to God Dorinda had bene there,
   T'have seene but Cloris acte this wofull part;   145
   It may be, it might have deterr'd her heart
   From cruelty so long as she had liv'd.
Ama. And I am glad Carinus hath but heard
   So much this day, for he may hap thereby
   To have some feeling of my miserie;   150
   But for Dorinda, never doubt at all,
   She is more yours, Mirtillus, then you thinke.
Mir. Ah, Amarillis, I would that were true.
   But loe, where come our chiefest heardsmen now
   Of all Arcadia, we shall know more newes.   155

Scen. 3.

MELIBAEUS, ERGASTUS, MONTANUS, ACRYSIUS, with other
ARCADIANS, bringing with them ALCON, LINCUS, COLAX,
TECHNE.

Mel. You gentle Shepheards and inhabitors
  Of these remote, and solitarie parts
  Of Mountaynous Arcadia, shut up here
  Within these Rockes, these unfrequented Clifts,
  The walles and Bulwarkes of our libertie,   5
  From out the noise of tumult, and the throng
  Of sweating toyle, ratling concurrencie,
  And have continued still the same and one
  In all successions from antiquitie;
  Whilst all the states on earth besides have made   10
  A thousand revolutions, and have rowld
  From change to change, and never yet found rest
  Nor ever bettered their estates by change.
  You I invoke this day in generall,
  To doe a worke that now concernes us all: 15
  Least that we leave not to posteritie
  Th'Arcadia that we found continued thus
  By our forefathers care who leaft it us.
    For none of you I know, whose judgements grave
  Can ought discerne, but sees how much we are   20
  Transformd of late, and changd from what we were;
  And what distempers dayly doe arise
  Amongst our people, never felt before;
  At which I know you mervaile, as indeed
  You well may marvaile whence they should proceed;   25
  And so did good Ergastus here, and I,
  Untill we set our selves more warily
  To search it out, which by good hap we have,
  And found the Authors of this wickednesse.
  Which Divels attyr'd here in the shape of men,   30
  We have produc'd before you to the end
  You may take speedy order to suppresse
  Our growing follies, and their impiousnesse.
Erg. Indeed, these odious wretches which you see,
  Are they who have brought in upon our rest   35
  These new and unknowne mischiefes of debate,
  Of wanton pride, of scandulous reportes,

Of vile deluding chaste and honest loves,
Of undeserv'd suspitious desperate griefes,
And all the sadnesse we have seene of late.   40
　　And first this man, this Lincus here you see,
Montanus you, and you Acrysius know,
With what deceipt, and with what cunning arte,
He intertaind your strifes, abusd you both,
By first perswading you that you had right   45
In your demandes, and then the right was yours;
And would have made as many rightes as men
Had meanes, or power, or will to purchase them;
Could he have once attain'd to his desires.
Mon. We doe confesse our errour, that we were   50
Too easily perswaded by his craft
To wrangle for imagin'd titles, which
We here renounce, and quit for evermore.
Acry. And we desire the memory thereof
May dye with us, that it be never knowne   55
Our feeble age hath such example showne.
Erg. And now this other strange impostor here,
This Alcon, who like Lincus hath put on,
The habite too of emptie gravitie,
To catch opinion, and conceipt withall,   60
Seekes how to set us all at variance here
With nature, as this other with our selves;
And would confound her, working with his arte;
And labours how to make our mindes first sick
Before our bodies, and perswade our health   65
It is not well; that he may have thereby
Both it and sicknesse ever under cure.
And forraine druggs bringes to distemper's here
And make us like the wanton world abroad,
Reckning us barbarous, but if this their skil   70
Doth civilize, let us be barbarous stil.
Mel. But here are two the most pernitious spirits
The world, I thinke, did ever yet produce:
Colax and Techne, two such instrumentes
Of Wantonnesse, of Lust and treacherie,   75
As are of power t'entice and to debaush
The universall state of honesty.
And to approve the horrible effect
Of both their impious subtle practises

(Besides this last exploit they wrought upon   80
Amyntas who, poore youth, lyes now ful weake
Under Uranias cure, whose skill we heare
Hath yet recald him to himselfe againe).
Here loe come divers others who can shew
What mischiefe graceles craft can doe.   85

Scen. 4.

PALAEMON. MIRTILLUS. CARINUS. SILVIA. DORINDA. AMARILLIS.
DAPHNE. CLORIS. AMYNTAS. [ALCON. LINCUS. COLAX. TECHNE.
PISTOPHOENAX. and ARCADIANS.]

Erg. Come, good Palaemon, and good Silvia come,
  You have indur'd too much, and too too long.
Sil. Ah why, Ergastus, doe you set our names
  So nere together, when our hearts so far
  Are distant from each other as they are?   5
  Indeed, whilst we were one as once we were,
  And as we ought to be, were faith observd,
  Palaemon should not have bene nam'd without
  A Silvia, nor yet Silvia without him.
  But now we may, Ergastus; we are two.   10
Pal. Silvia, there in the greater wrong you doe.
Sil. Palaemon, nay the greater wrong you doe.
Erg. Alas, we know well where the wrong doth lie.
Sil. I know you doe, and all the world may know.
Pal. Silvia, you see your fault cannot be hid.   15
Sil. It is no fault of mine, Palaemon, that
  Your shame doth come to be revealéd here;
  I never told it; you your selfe have not
  Conceald your worke so closely as you should.
Pal. But there stands one can tel what you have bin.   20
Sil. Nay, there he stands can tel what you have bin;
  And sure is now in publicke here producd
  To testifie your shame, but not set on
  By me, I doe protest, who rather would
  Have dide alone in secret with my griefe   25
  Then had your infamie discovered here,
  Wherein my shame must have so great a share.
Pal. I have not sought to manifest your shame,
  Which, Silvia, rather then have done I would

Have beene content t'indure the worst of deathes,   30
  I having such an intrest in the same.
Col. No, Silvia, no Palaemon, I stand here
  Not t'accuse you, but t'accuse my selfe
  Of wrong; you both, God knowes, are cleare;
  I have abusd your apt credulitie,   35
  With false reportes of things that never were:
  And therefore here crave pardon for the same.
Pal. Why, Colax, did not Silvia intertaine
  The love of Thyrsis then as you told me?
Col. Palaemon, no; she never intertaind   40
  His love, nor wrongd you as I ever knew.
Sil. But, Colax, you saw how Palaemon did
  With Nisa falsifie his vow to me.
Col. Silvia, by heaven and earth I sweare, not I,
  But onely faind it out of subtiltie;   45
  For some ungodly ends I had decreed.
Pal. O let not this be made some cunning baite
  To take my griefes with false beleefe, for I
  Had rather live with sorrow then deceipt,
  And still b'undone, then to have such relief.   50
Sil. Ah, let not this devise be wrought to guilde
  My bitternesse, to make me swallow't now
  That I might be another time beguilde
  With confidence, and not trust what I know.
Pal. Ah, Silvia now, how were I cleer'd of griefe,   55
  Had I the power to unbeleeve beliefe.
  But ah, my heart hath dwelt so long in house
  With that first tale, as this which is come new
  Cannot be put in trust with my desire
  So soone; besides 'tis too good to be true.   60
Sil. Could I, Palaemon, but unthinke the thought
  Of th'ill first heard, and that it were not so,
  How blest were I? But loe, I see how doubt
  Comes in farre easier then it can get out.
  And in these miseries of jealousie,   65
  Our eare hath greater credit then our eye.
Mel. Stand not confus'd, deare lovers, any more,
  For this is now the certaine truth you heare,
  And this vile wretch hath done you both this wrong.
Pal. Ist possible, and is this true you say,   70
  And do I live, and doe I see the day?

Ah then come, Silvia, for I finde this wound
That pierc'd into the center of my heart,
Hath let in love farre deeper then it was.
Sil. If this be so, why then Palaemon know 75
I likewise feele the love that was before
Most in my heart is now become farre more:
And now O pardon me, you worthy race
Of men, if I in passion uttred ought
In prejudice of your most noble sexe; 80
And thinke it was m'agrievéd errour spake
It knew not what, transported so, not I.
Pal. And pardon me, you glorious company,
You starres of women, if m'inragéd heat
Have ought profan'de your reverent dignitie, 85
And thou, bright *Pallas*, sov'raigne of all Nimphes,
The royall Mistresse of our Pastorall Muse,
And thou *Diana*, honour of the woodes
To whom I vow my songes, and vow my selfe,
Forgive me mine offence, and be you pleasd 90
T'accept of my repentance now therefore,
And grace me still, and I desire no more.
Sil. And now I would that Cloris knew this much,
That so she might be undeceivéd too,
Whom I have made beleeve so ill of men: 95
But loe, see where she comes, and as it seemes
Brings her beliefe already in her hand,
Prevents my act, and is confirmd before.
Looke Cloris, looke, my feares have idle beene;
Palaemon Loves me; there is trust in men. 100
Clo. And Silvia, I must now beleeve so too,
Or else, god help, I know not what to doe.
Pal. Looke here, Mirtillus, looke; what I told you
Is now prov'd false, and women they are true.
Mir. So I perceive, Palaemon, and it seemes 105
But vaine conceipt that other wise esteemes.
Mon. Alas, here comes my deare restoréd sonne,
My lovely child Amyntas here is come.
Acry. And here is Cloris my deare daughter come,
And lookes as if she were affrighted still, 110
Poore soule, with feare, and with her sodaine griefe.
Clo. Lo here, Montanus, I have brought you home
Although with much adoe, your sonne againe,

And sorry am with all my heart that I,
Have bene the cause he hath indur'd so much.   115
Mon. And I restore him backe againe to you
    Deare Cloris, and doe wish you to forget
    Your sorowes past, and pray the Gods you may
    From henceforth lead your life with happie joy.
Acry. Doe, Cloris, take him, and I wish as much.   120
Erg. Well then, to make our joyfull festivals
    The more complet, Dorinda, we intreat
    You also to accept Mirtillus love,
    Who we are sure hath well deservéd yours.
Do. Although this be uppon short warning, yet   125
    For that I have bene sommonéd before
    By mine owne heart and his deserts to me
    To yeeld to such a motion, I am now
    Content t'accept his love, and wilbe his.
Mir. Dorinda, then I likewise have my blisse,   130
    And reckon all the sufferings I have past
    Worthy of thee to have this joy at last.
Mel. And you, Carinus, looke on that good Nimph
    Whose eye is still on you, as if she thought
    Her suffrings, too, deservd some time of joy,   135
    And now expects her turne, hath brought her lap
    For comfort too whilst fortune deales good hap.
    And therefore let her have it now, poore soule,
    For she is worthy to possesse your love.
Car. I know she is, and she shall have my love,   140
    Though Colax had perswaded me before
    Never t'accept or to beleeve the love
    Of any Nimph, and oft to me hath sworne
    How he had tryde them all, and that none were
    As men beguild by shewes suppos'd they were;   145
    But now I doe perceive his treachery,
    And that they have both love and constancie.
Ama. O deare Carinus, blest be this good houre,
    That I have liv'd to over take at last
    That heart of thine which fled from me so fast.   150
Erg. And Daphne, too, me thinkes your heavy lookes
    Shew how that something is amisse with you.
Dap. Nothing amisse with me, but that of late
    I took a fall, which somewhat grieves me yet.
Erg. That must advise you, Daphne, from henceforth   155

To looke more warily unto your feete;
Which if you doe, no doubt all will be well.
Mel. Then thus we see the sadnesse of this day
   Is ended with the evening of our joy:
   And now, you impious spirits, who thus have raisd   160
   The hideous tempest of these miseries,
   And thus abusd our simple innocence;
   We charge you all here presently t'avoyd
   From out our confines, under paine to be
   Cast downe and dasht in peeces from these rockes,   165
   And t'have your odious carkases devour'd
   By beasts, being worse yourselves then beasts to men.
Col. Well then, come Techne, for I see we two
   Must even be forst to make a marriage too.
   And goe to Corinth, or some Citie neere,   170
   And by our practise get our living there,
   Which both together joynd, perhaps we may:
   And this is now the worst of miseries
   Could come unto me, and yet worthily,
   For having thus abusd so many Nimphs,   175
   And wrong'd the honour most unreverently
   Of women, in that sort as I have done,
   That now I am forst to undergoe therefore,
   The worst of Plagues: To marry with a W[hore].
Alc. But Lincus, let not this discourage us,   180
   That this poore people jealous of their rest,
   Exile us thus, for we no doubt shall finde
   Nations enough that will most ready be
   To entertaine our skill, and cherish us.
   And worthier people too, of subtler spirits,   185
   Then these unfashion'd and uncomb'd rude swaines.
Lin. Yea and those Nations are farre sooner drawne
   T'all frivolous distractions then are these;
   For oft we see, the grosse doe manage things,
   Farre better then the subtle; cunning brings   190
   Confusion sooner then doth ignorance.
Alc. Yea, and I doubt not whilst there shall be found
   Fantasticke puling wenches in the world,
   But I shall florish, and live jollily,
   For such as I by women must begin   195
   To gaine a name, and reputation winne:
   Which, when we have attaind to, you know then

How easily the women draw on men.
Lin. Nor do I doubt but I shall likewise live,
    And thrive, where ever I shall plant my selfe;   200
    For I have all those helps my skill requires,
    A wrangling nature, a contesting grace,
    A Clamorous voyce, and an audacious face.
    And I can cite the law t'oppugne the law,
    And make the glosse to overthrow the text;   205
    I can alledge and vouch authoritie
    T'imbroyle th'intent, and sense of equitie.
    Besides, by having been a Notarie
    And us'd to frame litigious instruments
    And leave advantages for subtilty   210
    And strife to worke on, I can so devise
    That there shalbe no writing made so sure
    But it shall yeeld occasion to contest
    At any time when men shall thinke it best.
    Nor be thou checkt with this, Pistophoenax,   215
    That at thy first appearing thou art thus
    Discov'red here; thou shall along with us,
    And take thy fortune too, as well as we.
Pist. Tush, Lincus, this cannot discourage me,
    For we that trafficke with credulitie,   220
    And with opinion, still shall cherisht bee;
    But here your errour was to enter first
    And be before me, for you should have let
    Me made the way, that I might have dislinkt
    That chaine of Zeale that holds in amitie,   225
    And calld up doubt in their establisht rites;
    Which would have made you such an easy way,
    As that you might have brought in what you would,
    Upon their shaken and discattered mindes,
    For our profession any thing refutes,   230
    And all's unsetled whereas faith disputes.
Mel. Now what a muttring keepe you there; away,
    Begone I say, and best too whilst you may.
      And since we have redeem'd our selves so well
    Out of the hands of mischiefe, let us all   235
    Exile with them their ill example too,
    Which never more remaynes, as it begun,
    But is a wicked sire t' a far worse sonne,
    And stayes not till it makes us slaves unto

That universall Tyran of the earth   240
Custome, who takes from us our priviledge
To be our selves, reades that great charter too
Of nature, and would likewise cancell man:
And so inchaynes our judgments and discourse
Unto the present usances, that we   245
Must all our senses thereunto refer.
Be as we finde our selves not as we are,
As if we had no other touch of truth
And reason then the nations of the times
And place wherein we live, and being our selves   250
Corrupted, and abastardizéd thus,
Thinke all lookes ill that does not looke like us.
And therefore let us recollect our selves
Dispers'd into these strange confuséd ills,
And be againe Arcadians as we were   255
In manners, and in habits as we were.
   And so solemnize this our happie day
   Of restauration, with other feasts of joy.

FINIS

Notes to the *Queenes Arcadia*

I.i

24 *maladive*: Affected with sickness.

25 *Syrene*: Not identified, though the reading appears in all editions; perhaps intended for "Sciron," a northwest or, sometimes, a southwest wind, or "Sirocco," a sultry southeast wind.

I.ii

55–56 *Delian goddess ... Acteons face*: Seen bathing with her nymphs on Mt. Citheron by the hunter Acteon, Diana turned him into a stag who was devoured by his own hounds.

95 *obrayd*: Corrupt form of "upbraid."

I.iii

9 *vanteries*: Vauntings; obsolete form of "vauntery."

30 *silly*: Insignificant, *OED, a*. 2.

66 *consort*: Harmonize, *OED, v*. III.

85 *tiffanies*: Transparent silks.
   tyres: Headdresses.

87 *night wormes*: Prostitutes, *OED, sb*. IV.14.
   Compositors: Compounders (in a negative sense).

103 *traine*: Trap, *OED, sb.*² (obs.).

I.iv

3 *debaushments*: Seductions; Daniel's is the earliest example cited in the *OED*. The spelling follows the French pronunciation.

6 *will ... will*: Desire.

29 *outmost*: Utmost, the common form between 1575 and 1675.
   proof: Test.

39 *science*: Knowledge.

48 *symptoma*: A late Latin form.

II.i

7 *invassels*: Envassals: Daniel's is the earliest example cited in the *OED*.

133–38 A stock *topos*; cf. *Aminta* IV.i.126–34.

II.ii

7–8 *none ... have died ... I could heare*: Cf. *Aminta* III.i.130–32 and Shakespeare's *As You Like It* 4.i.106–8.

24 *arrent*: Mission, sixteenth-century form of errand, *OED, v*. 2.

32 *hault*: Play false.

50–51: See I.ii.103–5.

111 *conceipt*: Apprehension, *OED, sb*. I.2.

166 *piersive*: Penetrating.

184 *conceipted*: Ingenious, *OED, sb.* III.8.
187 *stale*: Out of date (fig.).
190 *well laid*: Well trimmed (obs.).
191 *mixt*: Blended.
192 *To make it take*: To ... please, *OED, sb.*[4] and *v.* 10 (to charm).

II.iii

56 *wantonize*: To play the wanton; cf. Daniel's earlier usage, "For sweetly it fits the fayre to wantonize," *Complaint of Rosamond* (1592), line 364 (in *Poems and a Defence of Ryme*, edited by A. C. Sprague [Harvard Univ. Press, Cambridge, 1930]).
92 *of*: Variant of "off."
103 *table-forme*: Tablet, *OED, sv. sb.* 2b (obs.).
119 *facts*: Deeds; cf. *Pastor Fido* IV.iii.78 and n.

II.iv

24 *complections*: Constitutions; used in reference to the balance or superiority of one of the four humours, as at *Aminta* II.i.39; used again at V.i.52 below.

III.i

10 *Pronotories boy*: Apprentice to a pronotary or court recorder (obs.).
20 *contestation*: Controversy, *OED,* II.4.5.
95 *how ... frame*: Get on with, *OED, v.* 2 (obs.).
102 *Barly-breake*: A country game, described by Sidney in Lamon's song at the end of the *Old Arcadia*; it appears at line 208ff. (p. 247 in *The Poems*, edited by William A. Ringler, Jr., [Clarendon Press, 1962].).
111 *receipt*: Prescription (now rare).
115 *hearbe John*: St. John's wort, used proverbially for something inert or indifferent; cf. M. P. Tilley, J7.
116 *that's all one*: proverbial for "no matter." Cf. Shakespeare's *Twelfth Night* (ed. E. S. Donno, Cambridge Univ. Press, 1985), V.i.181, 351, and 384.
128–29 *Averois*: Averroes, a twelfth-century Spanish-Arabian physician.
    Rasis and Avicen: Rhazes and Avicenna, ninth and thirteenth-century physicians.
131 *Critique days*: The crisis of a disease.
132–33 *Trochises*: Lozenges.
    Apophlegmatismes: Purging agents.
    Eclegmats: Semi-fluid medicines.
    Embrochs: Rubbing elements.
    Lixives: Solutions of alkaline salts.
    Cataplasmes: Poultices.
134 *Arte*: Learning.
138–40 *Paragraphs*: Articles of legal documents.
    Condictions: Formal claims of restitution of money that has never been paid (Roman law).
    Acceptilations: importing remissions of debt from the creditor (Roman law).
    Actions recissorie: Revocation of legal actions.
    Noxall: Actions for damage by a person or his animal.
    Hypotheticall: Improper pledge of a thing not delivered but only covenanted.
167–213 This long description of the use of tobacco, though set forth in the words of the quack doctor, was clearly intended to please King James, whose own *Counter-blast to Tobacco* was published in 1604.

167-68 *roules / From ... Nicosia*: The reference to Cyprus perhaps suggested by the reference to sugar canes in the *Pastor Fido*, II.i.115.
171 *Contrarious*: Repugnant (now rare).
184 *humerous*: Capricious.
185 *commodity*: Supply.

III.ii

19 *analepticall Elexipharmacum*: Restorative.

III.iii

11 *stuffes delight*: Satiates; Daniel uses the same expression in describing his negative response in the *Defence of Ryme* (1603), to the "continuall cadences" of couplets (Sprague, 155).
20 *Let me alone*: Leave it to me, a frequent idiom in the period; cf. *Pastor Fido* II.v.155; III.iii.16; and *Twelfth Night* (ed. E. S. Donno) II.iii.114; III.iv.84, 95, 153.
25 *Erycina*: I.e., Venus, as in *Pastor Fido* III.ix.2.
57 *intricated*: Entangled, as again at IV.v.6.

III.iv

8 *breath*: Breathe, used interchangeably in this period, as in Shakespeare's *Love's Labor's Lost* V.ii.722.

IV.i

4 *this makes for me*: Serves my turn.
86 *oblation*: Victim; Daniel's *Cleopatra* (1594), IV.996 (in Grosart, 3.67).
120 *use not to*: Customarily did not.

IV.ii

14 *plentie ... poore*: From Ovid's *Metamorphoses* 3.466, so frequently cited as to be included in Tilley's *Dictionary of the Proverbs in England*, P427.
24 *Who hunts ... none*: Proverbial, Tilley H163.

IV.iv

96 *Intenerat*: Mollify.

IV.v

12 *intermit*: Suspend.
15 *infest*: Molest, *OED, v.*² (now rare).

V.i

23 *kindely*: Punning on "naturally" and "with kindness."
83 *Dictamnus*: Dittany.
85 *Tetrifoll*: Laburnum.

V.ii

33 *eyes abroad*: Fixed; cf. V.ii.99–100 below.
94 *The good ... good*: Proverbial, Tilley S190.
119 *silent rhetoricke*: Daniel's favorite oxymoron; see *The Complaint of Rosamond*, line 121; cf. also "Dombe eloquence," line 122. [Sir] John Davies in his epigram

"In Dacum" (#45) mocks Daniel for his use of the term "silent eloquence" (though it may be noted that Sidney in his *Astrophel and Stella* [#61] had also used the phrase "dombe eloquence").

V.iv

98 *Prevents*: Anticipates.
136 *lap*: Bosom, as in *Aminta* II.ii.40 and *Pastor Fido* I.i.147.

Appendix 1
Collation of Texts

The *Aminta*

The single edition of the *Aminta* was quite well printed; of the nine press variants noted in the four copies collated, only three are substantive—two omissions of a word required for the meter and one misreading. Though they might not have escaped the attention of an alert printing-house proofreader, one other which corrects the elision (piety' of *to* pi'ety of) suggests the translator's involvement, as would be likely for a first edition in any case.

In addition to these corrections, there are a dozen listed in the errata at the end of the Prologue (A2ᵛ) which have been silently corrected in this text.

The *Pastor Fido*

The readings of the two editions—1602 and 1633—are indicated by the last two digits of the publication date given on the title pages. The death of the translator during the process of publication (see Introduction, p. xxi) may account for the errors in 1602. Misprints are ignored except for that in I.ii.118 which is included to illustrate the difficulty to the printer in deciphering secretary hand.

I. i.title *IL PASTOR*] *33*; *PASTOR 02*
    Dra. Pers. 6 *the high*] *33*; *high 02*
    i.64   I'm] *33*; It am *02*
    ii.118   inevitable] *33*; menitable *02*
    ii.148   stands] *33*; stand *02*
    iv.24   like] *02*; love *33*

II. i.12   merry-countnaun'st] *02*; merry countenanc'd
    i.55   great'st] *33*; greatest *02*
    i.106   place] *33*; plate *02*
    i.115   canes] *This edn*; caues *02, 33*
    i.128   eake] *33*; *om. 02*
    ii.11   th' happy *33*; th' appie *02*
    v.7   spots *02*; sports *33*
    v.99   rather have *02*; rather had *33*
Chorus 44   sowly *02*; slowly *33*

III. ii.23   *Argus*] *33*; *Arons 02*

ii.39 you ... you] *33;* you ... *02*
iii.61 do] *33;* to do *02*
iii.95 them] *02;* not *33*

III. iii.176 beest] *33;* art beest *02*
iii.185 will what hee] *33;* will he what he *02*
viii.17 pleasures] *02;* pleasure *33*
Chorus 59 for] *02; Om. 33*

IV. i.33 *It may] This edn.;* T'may *02, 33*
ii.17 scare] *33;* scarre *02*
ii.109 Then] *33;* The *02*
v.12 *Montan'es] 02; Montanus 33*
v.42 wert] *33;* wer't *02*
Chorus 40 courtest] *33;* courrest *02*
50 deceives] *33;* deceive *02*

V. i.46 only should me] *02;* should me only *33*
ii.34 come] *02;* comes *33*
ii.67 draw] *33;* drave *02*
iii.34 so] *This edn.; not in 02, 33*
iv.19 th'ead] *02;* t'head *33*
iv.59 by] *33;* why *02*
v.90 speake] *02;* spoke *33*
v.112 which] *This edn.;* with *02, 33*
v.166 true] *33;* time *02*
v.208 *Montane] 02; Montanus 33*
vi SH *Tirenio] 33; Tireme 02*
vi.83 holy] *33;* only *02*
vi.113 begin] *33;* begun *02*
vii.64 muscolus] *This edn.;* musclouse *02, 33*
viii.36 SH *Er.] This edn.;* Erg. *33; om. 02*
x. *Dra. Pers.* *Shepherds] 33; Shepherd 02*

The Queenes Arcadia

Sigla here correspond to the last two digits of the year of publication; the orthography is that of the earliest edition cited, and misprints, unless they make a possible reading, are not recorded.

Dra. Pers. Pistophoenax] *6; om. 07–23*
I. i.16 our] *06, 07;* your *11, 23*
ii.27 made] *06, 07;* may *11, 23*
ii.31 do] *06, 07;* to *11, 23*
ii.76 signes] *06, 07, 11;* signe *23*
ii.79 pact] *06, 07;* pack *11, 23*

	ii.96	excellence] *06–11*; excellencie *23*
	iii.5	game] *07*; gaine *06, 11, 23*
	iii.23	still] *06, 07*; will *11, 23*
	iii.24	then] *06–11*; them *23*
	iii.55	joying] *06, 07*; joyning *11, 23*
	iii.82	did] *06, 07*; doe *11, 23*
	iii.87	Compositors] *06–11*; Impositors *23*
	iv.7	bounds] *06–11*; bonds *23*
	iv.11	which] *06–11*; that *23*
	iv.35	out] *06, 07*; our *11, 23*
II.	i.29	tis] *06–11*; *om. 23*
	i.65	power] *06–11*; powers *23*
	i.77	As] *06–11*; He *23*
	i.90	bent up] *06, 07*; up bent *11, 23*
	i.132	now] *06–11*; well *23*
	i.157	be] *06–11*; *om. 23*
II.	ii.1	from] *Grosart*; for *06–23*
	ii.61	comment] *06, 07*; commend *11, 23*
	ii.63	here] *06, 07*; *om. 11, 23*
	ii.133	many, many] *06*; many *07–23*
	ii.177	*om.* from *23*
	iii.8	faithfull] *06, 07*; *om. 11, 23*
	iii.112	murmour] *06–11*; murmurs *23*
	iii.119	facts] *07*; fact *06, 11, 23*
	iii.147	thy] *06–11*; the *23*
	iv.4	extremities] *06, 07*; extremitie *11, 23*
	iv.6	unto] *06, 07*; uhio *11*; *om. 23*
	iv.39	then] *06–11*; when *23*
III.	i.1	well met] *06, 07*; tell me *11, 23*
	i.18	so] *06, 07*; soone *11, 23*
	i.21	yet] *06–11*; *om. 23*
	i.38	Here ... strive] *07*; *om. 6, 11, 23*
	i.68	it selfe] *06, 07*; himselfe *11, 23*
	i.75	Hath] *06–11*; Have *23*
	i.80	his] *06, 07*; this *11, 23*
	i.86	states] *06–11*; starres *23*
	i.86	this] *06–11*; so *23*
	i.112	to say] *06, 07*; so sayth *11, 23*
	i.128	SH *Grosart*; *om. 6–23*
	i.130	bookes] *06, 07*; booket *11*; booke *23*
	i.138	Condictions] *06, 07*; Conditions *11, 23*
	i.144	still] *06, 07*; *om. 11, 23*
	i.147	what] *06, 07*; that *11*; the *23*

i.191   to] *This edn.*; th' *06–23*
i.212   spends] *06–11*; sends *23*
i.213   is] *Grosart*; in *06–23*
i.216   now] *06–11*; not *23*
i.216   surly] *06, 07*; surely *11, 23*
ii.32   humours] *Grosart*; humour *06–23*
ii.39   wondrously] *06–11*; wonderfully *23*
ii.43   serve] *06–11*; fit *23*
ii.44   skilfull] *06–11*; skill *23*
ii.72   ougly] *06–11*; onely *23*
ii.88   how] *06–11*; now *23*
iii.8   lie] *06–11*; lay *23*
iii.39   womenkind] *06, 07*; womankind *11, 23*
iv.36   what] *06, 07*; that *11, 23*
iv.36   wiles] *07–23*; willes *06*
iv.55   something] *07–23*; sometime *06*
iv.70   thee] *06, 07*; the *11, 23*
iv.70   deede] *07, 23*; dead *06, 11*
v.32   on] *06, 07*; *om. 11, 23*
v.35   seene] *06, 07*; seeme *11, 23*

IV. i.4   this makes for me] *07*; ile worke on him *06, 11, 23*
i.20   SH] *11, 23*; *om. 06, 07*
i.25   in accents] *06, 07*; in th' accents *11, 23*
i.54   that] *06–11*; *om. 23*
i.88   injustice] *06, 07*; unjustice *11, 23*
i.120   to] *06, 11, 23*; the *07*
ii.20   lose] *11, 23*; loath *06, 07*
ii.46   dealings] *06, 07*; dealing *11, 23*
iii.10   to] *23*; so *06–11*
iii.58   And] *06, 07*; I *11, 33*
iii.64   he is, he is without] *06, 07*; he is without he is *11, 23*
iii.66   nor] *06, 07*; not *11*; or *23*
iii.74   on] *06, 07*; one *11, 23*
iii.90   save] *06–11*; have *23*
iii.121   I did] *06, 07*; did I *11, 23*
iii.123   as ... wak'd] *06, 07*; as ... awak'd *11, 23*
iii.132   shall] *07–23*; may *06*
iii.139   left] *06, 07*; *om. 11, 23*
iv.26   this] *06, 07*; it *11, 23*
iv.37   thy] *06, 11*; the *07, 23*
iv.73   be] *06, 07*; to *11, 23*
iv.83   perceiv'd] *06, 07*; perceive *11, 23*
iv.89   thy] *06, 07*; the *11, 23*

V. i.26   thus] *23*; this *06–11*
   i.27   is it] *06, 07*; it is *11, 23*
   i.39   thee ... thee] *06–11*; thee ... the *23*
   i.80   as] *06–11*; that *23*
   ii.107   shrinke] *06–11*; shrikes *23*
   ii.112   All] *06–11*; And *23*
   ii.115   a] *06–11*, the *23*
   ii.118   affections] *06–11*; affection *23*
   iii.   *Dra. Pers. Pistophoenax*] *om. 07*
   iii.37   reportes] *06–11*; report *23*
   iii.70   to end of sc.] *rev. 07*
   iii.70–71 *also in 06, 11, 23*
   iii.72–77 *substantially in 06, 11, 23 after 69*
   iii.78–85] *07; 06, 11, 23 read:*

Erg. But, *Techne*, who is that standes there by you?
   What, is your companie increast of late?
Tec. Truely it is a very honest man,
   A friend of mine that comes to see me here.
Erg. He cannot then but be an honest man,
   If he be one of your acquaintance sure.
Mel. This man I found with them now since you went,
   Mayntayning hote dispute with *Titerus*
   About the rites and misteries of *Pan.*
Erg. H'is like to be of their associats then:
   Techne, what is this secret friend of yours?
Tec. For-sooth he is a very holy man.
Erg. A very holy man? What is his name?
Tec. Truly, his name, Sir, is *Pistophoenax.*
Erg. What, is he maskt, or is that face his owne?
Tec. He is not maskt; tis his complection sure.
Erg. *Techne,* we cannot credite thy report.
   Let one try whether it be so or not:
   O see, a most deforméd ougly face,
   Wherewith if openly he should appeare,
   He would deterre all men from comming nere.
   And therefore hath that cunning wretch put on
   This pleasing visor of apparencie
   T'intice and to delude the world withal;
   So that you see with what strange inginiers
   The project of our ruine is forecast.
   How they implanted have their battery here
   Against all the maine pillors of our state,
   Our Rites, our Customes, Nature, Honestie
   T'imbroyle, and to confound us utterly. *Followed by 70–71*

iii.70   this] *07*; thus *06, 11, 23*
iii.78   And ... effect] *07*; But now to shew ... effects *06, 11, 23*
iii.79   Of ... subtle] *07*; Of *Colax* and of *Technes* *06, 11, 23*
iii. After 83] *06, 11, 23 read*:

We have sent out abrode into the woods,
For *Silvia* and *Palaemon*, two chast soules
Whom they have torturd so with jealosie
Of each the other, as they made them run
A part, to languish severally alone;
And we have sent for divers others too,
Whose heartes have felt what impious craft can do.
And here they come, and now you shall know all.

V. iv.   *Dra. Pers.*[Colax. Alcon. Lincus. and Arcadians.] *om. 07,23*
      iv.1   SH] *06, 11*; *om. 07, 23*
      iv.50   b'undone] *06, 07*; t'be undone *11, 23*
      iv.70   you] *06, 11, 23*; I *07*
      iv.93   this] *06, 07*; thus *11, 23*
      iv.157   all will] *07*; but all will *06*; but all this will *11, 23*
      iv.163   presently] *06–11*; present *23*
      iv.233   too] *06, 07*; doe *11, 23*
      iv.235   hands] *06, 07*; bonds *11, 23*
      iv.254   ills] *Grosart*; ill *06–23*

Daniel's Version of the Chorus to Act I from the *Aminta*

A Pastoral

O Happie golden Age,
  Not for that Rivers ranne
  With streames of milke, and hunny dropt from trees,
  Not that the earth did gage
  Unto the husband-man   5
  Her voluntary frutes, free without fees:
  Not for no cold did freeze,
  Nor any cloud beguile,
  Th' eternall flowring Spring
  Wherein liv'd every thing,   10
  And whereon th' heavens perpetually did smile;
  Not for no ship had brought
  From forraine shores, or warres or wares ill sought
But onely for that name,
  That Idle name of winde: 15
  That Idoll of deceit, that empty sound
  Call'd HONOR, which became
  The tyran of the minde,
  And so torments our Nature without ground;
  Was not yet vainly found: 20
  Nor yet sad griefes imparts
  Amidst the sweet delights
  Of joyfull amorous wights.
  Nor were his hard lawes knowne to free-borne harts.
  But golden lawes like these   25
  Which nature wrote. *That's lawfull which doth please.*
Then amongst flowres and springs
  Making delightfull sport,
  Sate Lovers without conflict, without flame;
  And Nymphs and shepheards sings,   30
  Mixing in wanton sort
  Whisp'rings with Songs, then kisses with the same
  Which from affection came:
  The naked virgin then
  Her Roses fresh reveales,   35

Which now her vayle conceales:
The tender Apples in her bosome seene.
And oft in Rivers cleere
The Lovers with their Loves consorting were.
HONOR, thou first didst close   40
　　The spring of all delight:
Denying water to the amorous thirst
Thou taught'st faire eyes to lose
　　The glorie of their light,
Restrain'd from men, and on themselves reverst.   45
Thou in a lawne didst first
Those golden haires incase,
Late spred unto the winde;
Thou mad'st loose grace unkinde,
Gav'st bridles to their words, art to their pace.   50
O Honour it is thou
That mak'st that stealth, which love doth free allow.
It is thy worke that brings
　　Our griefes, and torments thus:
But thou fierce Lord of Nature and of Love,   55
The quallifier of Kings,
What doest thou here with us
That are below thy power, shut from above?
Goe and from us remove,
Trouble the mighties sleepe,   60
Let us neglected, base,
Live still without thy grace,
And th' use of th' ancient happie ages keepe:
Let's love: this life of ours
Can make no truce with time that all devours.   65

　　Let's love: the sun doth set, and rise againe,
　　But when as our short light
　　Comes once to set, it makes eternall night.
　　　　　　　　　　　　　　(1601)

N.B. Following Grosart, W. W. Greg in *Pastoral Poetry and Drama* (120) mistakenly accepts the 26-line "Ode" appearing at the end of *Delia* (1592) as Daniel's "rendering" of the Chorus to Act I of the *Aminta*. In fact, his translation of "O bella età de l'oro" first appeared in the *Works* (1601) with Daniel carefully following the form of the original—five strophes rhyming a b c a b c c d e e plus a 3-line conclusion.

Sir Kenelm Digby's Version of the homage to Arcadia from the *Pastor Fido*

Oh deare and blessed woods,
and you solitarie and silent horrors
true harbourers of rest and peace
how gladly I returne to you!
And if my starres had left unto my choice   5
the maner of my life, I would not change
your gentle shade for the Elisian fieldes,
the happie garden of the Demi-Gods:
For if the wisest erre not in their observations,
these transitorie goods are but vexations;   10
who most abound's with them he hath the lesse,
and is posses't more then he doth possesse:
Not richesse; but such snares as tye
their owners from their libertye.
What doth avayle to one the stile of beautie   15
                                modestie.
in freshest yeares; or fame of *honestie*;
a high descent and noble birth;
the graces both of heav'n and earth,
here large and fertile fieldes,
there meddowes, pastures, and a flocke that yieldes   20
a dayly harvest of encrease
if with all this their hart is not in peace?
Happy shepheardesse, whose clothes are but a white wastcoat,
and on her flanc a poore but cleanly petticoate;
rich onely of herselfe, and without theft   25
adorn'd alone with bounteous natures guift;
that in sweete poverty doth feel no neede,
nor yet the troubles which great treassures breede;
and onely so much is her store
as shee's not vex'd with the desire of more: 30
and shee with natures guiftes her guiftes doth cherish,
her milke with other milke doth nourish;
and with the honye of the painefull bee
seasons those sweetes that in her native be;
and of that spring which for her drinke shee takes,   35
a bath and looking glasse shee makes.
for her, the sky growe's clowdie but in vaine,
and armes it selfe with thunder or with raine,
for this her povertie doth nothing feare:
and onely one sweete pleasing care   40
doth harbour in her brest,
which is (whiles that her flocke doth graze or rest)
to feede with her faire eyes her loving swaine;
not such a one as starres or men ordaine,

but him of whom her love hath freely made   45
election, and they lying in the shade
of some greene mirtle grove they favour
do freely speake and court each other;
nor any flames of love shee feeles
that from his knowledge she conceales;   50
nor sooner shee discovers them but he
those flames doth feele as well as shee.
    Thus they a perfect happy life enjoy
    and know not what death meanes before they dye.

From Sir Kenelm Digby's papers, edited by Henry A. Bright, Roxburgh Club, 1877.

Three Renaissance Pastorals: Tasso—Guarini—Daniel makes essential texts for the study of pastoral drama available and demonstrates the generic and developmental links between Tasso, Guarini, and Daniel.

The two Italian pastorals stirred international interest for two centuries in both the original and translated versions. In England, the originals appeared together in one volume in 1591. By extolling a golden world freed from the allegiance to chastity or *onor,* Tasso's *Aminta* provided the paradigm for pastoral poetry. The presentation of simple characters in a simple plot, underscored by the ingenious and subtle handling of the verse, struck a surprisingly responsive chord among sophisticated readers. Following Tasso, Guarini's *Pastor Fido* introduced the new literary genre of tragicomedy.

The third work, *Queene's Arcadia* by Samuel Daniel, added a new dimension to the form. While combining aspects from his Italian predecessors, Daniel also introduced topical satire into the pastoral, and in so doing, became the first avowed writer of pastoral drama in England.

The introduction provides an account of the publishing venture that made the two Italian works available to English readers before translations were available. Each text is provided with linguistic and historical annotations.

Elizabeth Story Donno is a Senior Research Associate at the Huntington Library. She is the editor of *Sir John Harington's* Metamorphosis of Ajax (Columbia & Routledge Kegan Paul, 1962), *Elizabethan Minor Epics* (Columbia & Routledge Kegan Paul, 1963), *Complete Poetry of Andrew Marvell* (Penguin, 1972), *An Elizabethan in 1582: The Diary of Richard Madox* (Hakluyt Society, 1976), *Andrew Marvell* (Critical Heritage Series) (Routledge & Kegan Paul, 1978), and *Twelfth Night* (The New Cambridge Shakespeare, 1985).

mrts

medieval & renaissance texts & studies
is the publishing program of the
Center for Medieval and Early Renaissance Studies
at the State University of New York at Binghamton.

mrts emphasizes books that are needed —
texts, translations, and major research tools.

mrts aims to publish the highest quality scholarship
in attractive and durable format at modest cost.